RED ROSES OF SARAJEVO
Volim te Sarajevo

Sister book to Nurses in Battledress

SUNSHINE ON A RAINY DAY

In April 1994 I started off on a journey from Swansea railway station. This, however, was not going to be an ordinary journey; it was a trip to an adventure that I could never of imagined. Earlier in the year I managed to get an interview with the NAAFI and through that I secured a job with them. It was not going to be an easy task just to get up and go as I had friends and a home It had to be done though as it was a chance to improve my life if even for only a year.

My NAAFI job started at a place called Worthy Down, which is in Hampshire and the nearest city is Winchester. It was a rainy morning when I left Swansea, I had bought a copy of the Daily Telegraph before I got on the train, my main intention was to do the crossword but there was no way I was relaxed enough to read the paper let alone concentrate on a complicated puzzle, I ended up giving it to the guy sitting next to me. Of course, the night before I had a few beers as after all it was my last night, but I didn't want to drink too much as I knew I would suffer from it.

The journey to the south of England is always a pleasant one. After passing through the city of Bath then onto the beautiful rolling hills of Wiltshire with the mysterious barrows. There are also a few military camps on the way and the most notable being Warminster where the train goes through the middle of the camp. However, on this occasion the main thing on my mind was the anxieties of what lay ahead for me. Thoughts kept coming into my head like, what was at Worthy Down? Maybe an infantry regiment and how would they treat me? Maybe they wouldn't like me because I am Welsh and an ex Royal Regiment of Wales Infantry soldier. I had to change trains somewhere along the line I was told it was Cardiff, but I knew the connecting train also stopped at Newport which is a lot quieter with less fuss with the luggage, not that I had much at this time. I eventually reached Winchester and disembarked the train, my instructions were to get a taxi and tell the driver to take me to Worthy Down, that was exactly what I did. The driver told me that it was quite a distance, indeed he was right, having said that most military camps are out in the sticks.

Signs were popping up Worthy this and Worthy that and even a sign saying the Worthies, eventually there was the red sign saying Worthy Down – red signs are mostly military establishments- I told the driver that I needed to get to the NAAFI so he got off the main road and down an avenue, it was about a half mile when we got to a building with NAAFI written on it. Well, what could go wrong? It wasn't the massive building that I imagined it to be, more like the size of a house.

I got out of the taxi and approached the building, it was quiet, and there was an open door but not any sign of anyone. I thought to myself "hey I can live with this" I went back to the taxi and took out my luggage, paid the driver and all of a sudden, I was alone in the world. I went back into the NAAFI and called out again but still nothing, so I waited. Eventually a lady appeared, and she looked surprised to see me. I said, "hello I am Miles, and I am starting work here today" "well that's news to me" she replied. She picked up her phone and dialed a number then started talking to someone and after a short conversation she put the phone down. "You have come to the wrong NAAFI, you should of gone to the NAAFI on the camp, this is the family's shop". Well, it did strike me odd, that a NAAFI would be in the middle of a long road in a residential area.

The lady told me that someone would be here to pick me up, sure enough ten minutes later a car pulled up and another lady put her head out of the window and said "hello Miles" she told me to put my luggage in the back of the car and jump in. The lady told me that she was the assistant manager and her name was Marge, she drove for what must have been another half a mile until we reached something that now really did look like an Army camp, i.e. large fences and barbed wire on the top. She stopped off at a guard post where she told the guard that I was just starting at the NAAFI, he waved us on, we went through the gate and stopped at another guard post where I had to fill in a form, I was then given a temporary pass and was told that I had to stay on the camp and I would have to be escorted everywhere until I got my NAAFI id card. It was back in the car another hundred yards around a corner and finally arrived at the Junior Ranks Club. I had arrived at my destination.

We went into the building and into a large room, where Marge told me to leave my luggage as I was going to meet the manager, he was going to give me the rundown and tell me what was expected of me. Marge led me to the corridor where his office was, she told me to wait until I was called in. I sat outside the office for a while when Marge arrived accompanied by a young lady, she was also told to sit down. Of course we started talking, she explained to me that she had a long journey and was drunk. She had also arrived to work here at Worthy Down. Minutes later and the office door opened, and the manager came out and said "come in Miles" we, shook hands, he told me his name was Bryn. He started the meeting off by telling me that he kept a tight ship and that I would be on probation for six weeks. I would be starting work in the morning, I would have to be downstairs at 0700, and Marge would be there to meet me to show me around. There was to be no drinking whilst on duty and I would be doing split shifts to start with, first in the canteen then in the bar in the evening.

I couldn't help but notice that on his desk there was a model of an artillery gun, so I asked Bryn what it was about, he explained that he was an ex-warrant officer with the Royal Horse Artillery, and it was presented to him when he retired.

He told me that was all for now and to go back outside and wait for him as he was going to give me a quick tour of the canteen. He then took the young lady into the office. They were in there for ten minutes before they came out, she went off somewhere and that was the last I saw of her.

Bryn took me into the canteen area and told me that this is where I would be working in the morning. I was then led into the storeroom that was mainly stocked with chocolates sweets and cans of pop, from there it was into the main bar, which was quite large, looking from behind the bar there was a big hall with plenty of chairs and tables. Then at the back of the bar was another hatch looking into another smaller lounge, this was the permanent staff and Corporals bar, Bryn told me that this was strictly to be adhered to. Then it was into the cellar, which was very simple as they only sold John Smiths bitter Foster's lager and Guinness, Squaddies weren't too fussed about what they drank. We then arrived back at Bryn's office where Marge happened to be.

Bryn told her to take me to the accommodation to put my belongings in my room and then try to find some uniform that will fit me. In the corridor by the cellar were some stairs that led to our living quarters. There was a little room that contained all sorts of uniform mostly for females there wasn't much there for me, all I could find was a brown sleeveless jumper and a lemon fleece. I was told that I could wear my civilian clothes while the rest of my uniform was sent to me. She then showed me where my room was situated at the end of the corridor on the left so I dropped my luggage off; here Marge then said she would give me a tour of the living quarters. Just a few doors away on the left, the living room with a few settees and a TV. Further along there was the kitchen that had all the trimmings, a cooker microwave fridge and a freezer I was given a bit of a warning, Marge said to be careful what you take from the fridge, as I have seen people fight over a pint of milk before now. It was bright kitchen as it had a massive window with a view over the back of the camp and the trees beyond. We went back to the corridor; there were ladies and men's shower rooms and ablutions. Marge then said I was free to go; we will meet at 0700 in the morning downstairs.

Back in my new room I thought things hadn't been too bad, the room was a bit small with a single bed and a wardrobe, it was fine by me, as I didn't have many belongings. The best part was that I didn't have to share a room which I was told at one of the interviews was a possibility. What I did notice was that it was very quiet. I decided to have a shower, and it was great, powerful and hot. There was not much sign of any people around, I heard a bit of movement when I went into the kitchen, I looked out and I saw a ghost of someone who had disappeared into their room.

At eight o'clock I went downstairs to the bar I had about £10 to my name, it was sufficient though as it was only about a pound a pint then. I sat at the bar and started talking to the barmaid and I asked her what the place was like she said it was ok. I asked what Regiment was based here on the camp, she replied that there was no Regiment as it was a training camp and HQ of the Adjutant General Corps (AGC). Lately the army had made a great restructuring all the pay corps and admin corps had amalgamated into the AGC. It was a training camp for Clerks who had just finished basic and were now on their trade training. Another course would be for Junior ranks to gain more knowledge to help in their promotion. Next stage up from there was Corporals to get the necessary knowledge for them to get promoted to Senior ranks i.e. Sergeant. I of course asked her name at one point; she told me it was Janice.
There were also training facilities for SNCOs and officers, but this didn't involve us at the NAAFI.

I. This was really a relief to me as my anxieties were groundless. Most of the evening I was alone at the bar, only a few people were drinking, some came in for food and left. I said to the barmaid that I noted that it was quiet and she replied that there were not many courses on at the time.

Well, I had sufficient beer to calm me down and I was ready to face the morning.
It was my first day at work with the NAAFI. I went down the stairs that led to the facilities but there was no sign of Marge. I waited outside Bryn's office for ten minutes, and then an angry looking Marge approached me and said, "where have you been I told you to meet me in the kitchen." I really didn't recall anything of the sort.
The first job was to go into the lounge and collect all the glasses from the night before, the reason being the barperson that worked the previous evening would just pull down the shutters and then go and count their takings. I had to empty the ashtrays, clean the tables, restock the fridges and clean the bar and then of course do the same in the permanent staff bar. Later in the morning cleaners would arrive to vacuum etc.
When these tasks were finished, we went into the office where I had to fill in a form to apply for my NAAFI id card, have my photo taken and get measured up for my uniform. "Right then Miles we had better go upstairs and try to find you some more uniform."
Upstairs was massive, there was a function room, Marge said that we rarely used this room, it seemed like a ballroom that had seen better days. There were a few members of staff, but they didn't appear to have any interest in me. We went into another room that must have been a Theatre with massive curtains and a wooden floor in front of it. On the stage there was a tea chest with more uniform in it but nothing much for me except for a few old shirts "that will do until your new uniform arrives" said Marge, she then told me to put the things into my room then go back downstairs to see Bryn as he wanted me to work in the canteen.
I went to his office and knocked on his door, he then came out holding a till drawer and told me to follow him into the canteen. Bryn told me that there was a NAAFI break at 10.00 and it would be hectic as the troops had only 15 minutes. At 09.55 we started pouring cups of tea and at 10.00 the door opened, suddenly, the place was buzzing with troops who were wanting a cup of tea, a chocolate bar or a cake. At 10.15 the place was empty again, except for empty cups, half empty cups, sweet wrappers and sugar sachets on the tables and the floor.
So, then we started cleaning black bags for the rubbish, cups put into the dishwasher, replenish the chocolates and cakes on the shelves then lock the doors.
I was given the good news that we will be doing the same at 15.00. We had a bit of a break, during which Bryn explained how we went about getting our staff messing, basically our food to live on. We had an allowance of £15 a week to buy food. This didn't seem much to me, but it turned out quite sufficient. We could buy food from the NAAFI, but this was an expensive option. The idea was that we could go to a

supermarket, buy food and keep the receipt, then bring it back to Bryn, he would check it and if it was ok, he would reimburse you, provided that there were no items that attracted VAT i.e. crisps chocolate bars or cans of pop. It did seem to me that this system was open to abuse. What if some dishonest member of staff went to a supermarket to pick up receipts from the floor and claimed them.

There was some cleaning and work to do in the storeroom but by 12.00 the place would be locked up. I would have to be back downstairs by 14.45 so we could do a re-run of the mornings NAAFI break. It soon turned out to be the same chaos but this time I was working on the till and Bryn was serving, the good thing about this was at least I was getting to know the troops, they were fine, polite and friendly. After all the cleaning Bryn showed me how to refloat the till which basically left me with the £50 and what was left over was the takings. The good news was that tomorrow I was going to do it on my own.

When all things were done Bryn told me that I was going to be working at the bar in the evening and I would have to be on duty at 18.30. I could do a bit of chilling out, so I had a walk around outside of the club, one thing I did notice, a sign at the entrance with the name The Worthies club.

At 18.30 I went down to do my first bar shift with Janice, the girl I was talking to the previous night. It was a quiet evening with a steady flow of people, but it was notable that Janice was doing very little work and was sat down most of the time, a customer who was sat at the bar commented on this, Janice just said "I am supervising" with a smirk on her face. I did feel like saying that she couldn't supervise a party, I managed to keep my mouth shut, as I wanted Janice to show me how to refloat the bar at the end of the shift.

The morning soon came around I went downstairs and collected the glasses and the other chores. At 09.45 Bryn took the float out and put it in the till, He was going to help me this morning, but I was going to be on my own in the afternoon. Things were coming together, I was getting to know where things belonged and where to get supplies from. The mornings NAAFI break was ok, and Bryn was confident that I could cope on my on the next shift.

After clearing up I went back upstairs I saw some female members of staff, but they practically ignored me, one in particular, a red haired one who didn't crack a smile.

Soon enough I was back downstairs doing the afternoon NAAFI break. Troops poured in and I was doing ok but something went wrong, I knew that I had made a mistake, but I didn't know how to rectify it, what could I do but carry on, I didn't know what a void was then. After clearing up I checked the till and took it to Bryn's office I told him that I thought I made a mistake but wasn't sure.

The next morning before the NAAFI break Bryn said that the till was £5 down. "You can't count" that was the end of that and nothing more was said.

Days started passing by and I was getting into the routine. My NAAFI id card had arrived; I had a new uniform and no more mistakes on the till. However, the girls were still distancing themselves and it seemed to me that Hazel the unfriendly was the ringleader.

I had to work a month in advance so money was a bit tight, not to say the NAAFI would let you starve, far from it. Janice lent me a five quid to get by with, I bought a pack of cigs with it, she later told me off for that.

After about three weeks at Worthy Down I had a frightening experience. Early one morning I was awakened with a searing pain in my head it was so intense and more frightening I looked at my pillow and it was covered in blood, I was convinced it was a brain hemorrhage, and I was going to die. I went down to Bryns' office and waited for him to arrive for work. I was so glad to see him, I explained to him what had happened he said, "get some toilet paper and put it in your ear, and of course rip off a few sheets off first". Not a good idea really.

He told me that he would take me to Winchester Royal Infirmary. We got in his car, and he drove me to the hospital, there he dropped me off at A&E, "go in and tell them what had happened and get back to Worthy Down as soon as possible".

I went to the reception, and I told a Nurse what had happened, she told me a doctor would see me soon. I sat down waiting, then a doctor approached me, he told me to follow him to his surgery, where he could investigate the problem.

I sat down and he investigated my ear with his otoscope, I soon heard the diagnostic, he told me that I had a perforated eardrum, I had probably scratched it in my sleep. I, after all, was going to live.

Now my biggest problem is, how do I get back to Worthy Down? I didn't have enough money in my pocket to get a taxi, so I decided to walk to the bus station, how far that was I didn't know. There were pedestrian signs showing the way so I thought that it couldn't be far. I was walking along and some guy said to me "have you just come out of there" pointing to a building and laughing, I was perplexed but didn't think much more of it, I had enough on my mind than to worry about something trivial.

I eventually got to the bus station and asked a member of staff what bus I needed to get for Worthy Down. The person told me that I would have to get the bus for Kings Worthy, Worthy Down is the stop before, as it happened a bus was due to leave soon. I found the bay and got on the bus; it was nearly an hour's journey. Well, I managed to get back to the NAAFI. If I thought I was going to get a bit of sympathy I was sadly mistaken, all I got was dirty looks, I could see the disdain in Hazels eyes, I could see she made a snide remark, anyway I was told that I would be on bar duty that evening.

One of the girls had been a bit friendlier of late, Joanne a typical scouser.

I met her in the staff kitchen one morning and I asked her what the problem with the other girls was, she explained that my predecessor had worked for a few weeks, went home for a weekend but never came back leaving, the girls having to work his shifts. And more to the point he was Welsh and so naturally I was going to do the same. So that cleared that one up. I also mentioned to her what the bloke said to me near the hospital in Winchester, Joanne chuckled and said, "yes that was Winchester prison".

A few days later, a bit of good news, Hazel was gone, apparently, she was a well-known troublemaker. Suddenly, I was accepted into the gang.

A month had passed by, and I got paid, the money wasn't that great, but it was sufficient, and I had started putting weight back on.

Before I joined the NAAFI I had a bit of a drink problem, if all I had was a pound I would rather buy a pint of lager than a loaf of bread, for some people that is illogical. I remember one day I was walking in the street back home, I bumped into my dear Father, his face went white, he looked shocked, I realized I had a problem I was down to 9 stone.

When I went to sign on the dole I had to hitch a ride into Swansea, but I would have to walk back, I always hoped that I would find some money on the way but that never happened.

One thing I have to say about the NAAFI is that they always had bad press for their service; I was one of them once. The pay was not the highest but there were perks to the job and they employed a lot of people, indeed many made a career out of it and received a good pension. It seemed to me that the NAAFI were easy pickings and couldn't answer back. It was also a source where people could vent their anger for wrongdoings by the military.

In those days they were a massive company that employed tens of thousands of people. Every Military camp would probably have at least four establishments like a shop on camp, a family's shop, a post office and a Junior Ranks Club. They had a fleet of lorries, warehouses and a massive supply system. While travelling on a motorway there would be a good chance you would see a blue articulated lorry with their symbol N in a circle.

Meanwhile back at the bar I had got into a routine, and I managed to convince Marge that the beer lines needed cleaning every Friday morning. I had learned to do this in my previous job working in a busy pub. I really hadn't got over my drinking problem though. Each barrel of beer would need at least a pint of beer to be wasted pushing the beer line cleaner through, this was supposed to go down the drain, but I can assure you that it didn't.

As I was now an accepted member of staff I was allowed to go to Winchester on the weekends after work. We would end up in some disco, we had some good times. Interestingly there was an Indian restaurant called the Mahatma Ghandi, this would always remind me of my ex-landlord Pete, who was always shouting "Mahatma Ghandi". Before we went into Winchester we would have to 'cash up' in normal times this would take about 15 minutes but watching Janice cashing up in turbo mode was an amazing sight, I reckon she could do it in under 3 minutes. Locked up, lights out, doors locked in 6 minutes.

Everyone who joins NAAFI must do a basic hygiene course. Before I could work in the kitchen, I would have to get a certificate. It was arranged that a few others and I would do our course in an Army training depot called Flower Down, it was the training camp for the Light Infantry, about five miles from Worthy Down. A minibus came to pick us up to take us there. We met up with other NAAFI staff from nearby camps, mostly girls. It was a day's course with a break at 11 am. The course had plenty of humour and some serious stuff too. The instructor was talking about salmonella, especially regarding eggs and where the egg comes from, i.e. the chicken's bottom. Five years would pass before I ate another egg.

We had a mock exam late in the morning where a pass mark of 75% was acceptable, for some reason I struggled in this in this test and only just passed. After more intense training in the afternoon came the final test where you had to get 90% or fail, I am sure the rest of the class were expecting me to fail but I excelled and was one of the few to get 100%. There was a good reason why we all had to do the food hygiene course, we knew that things were going to get busier, Bryn was of course informed that a lot of courses were coming up and there were going to be a lot more hungry mouths to feed.

Things were changing at Worthy Down, instead of doing the NAAFI break in the morning I was allowed to take part in 'buttie bashing', which started at 06.00.
I was amazed at how many loaves of bread we were going to get through. Sandwiches were to be made for the local shop, our bar, the officers and Sergeants messes, the post office and for vending machines that were dotted around the camp.

Now buttie bashing is a scientific process. Every sandwich had to be made with the correct amount of ingredients; there was even a weighing scale on the table.
Tomatoes, onions and eggs had to be sliced into exact amounts. Chickens were boiled and then ripped apart. This all had to be done on a timescale as well, to be ready for people's break times. The sandwiches had to be delivered to various shops or units. I first started off by buttering the bread, we would have massive tubs of margarine and only one side would be buttered. The fillings were left to more skilled personnel though I did graduate after a few days. Eventually all those butties would have to be distributed so they had to be put into trays and would be transferred to our little van.

My buttie bashing went on for about a week. Of course, during all these preparations there would be talk and humour. One day my career in this field ended abruptly. I said something to Marge that she took out of all contexts. I said women are much better at making sandwiches than men because they are natural at it.

Now Marge had to make a fuss about this "oh so you think it's a woman's role to make sandwiches do you". My days of buttie bashing came to an end.

So, it was back to the NAAFI breaks in the morning. Now there was a new intake of students that had arrived after finishing basic training, they had come to Worthy Down for their B1 trade training. They were a great crowd funny polite respectful and **Magic**.

A new girl arrived out of the blue in the NAAFI, I took it she was Hazel's replacement. Her name was Donna, and she was going to help me run the bar, as things were now getting busier with bigger and more courses coming in.

To begin with we used to sell basics like crisps and the more traditional 'toastie' a great delicacy of the Squaddie. Recently we had a new pizza oven, and this is where the focus of trade was going to be. It was very basic with frozen pizza bases, and we would have to add the pizza sauce then add the ingredients, to order by the customer.

Surely, enough the bar was getting busier with students, we needed more staff and fair play to Bryn, he took on some permanent staffes wives.

Donna and I ran the bar every evening and the amount of pizza we were cooking was phenomenal, there were always two pizzas on the go in the oven, it was clear that we needed another oven. Apart from that we had to keep the permanent staff bar going as well. We had a tray of chocolates kept aside for them. One day a regular in the bar asked for a bounty but we had run out, this upset him, and he started stamping his feet. Donna and myself started taking the pee out of the permanent staff bar customers; we started making names up for them like one I called D form head. We started a saying whilst making a baby face "but I don't like this".

We were running the bar quite well until one day Bryn summoned us into his office. He said that he had informants and had been told that we had been drinking behind the bar, he told us that it had to stop 'now', if not you will be sacked, he kept on lecturing us. We didn't know who the informant was, but we suspected it was a member of the permanent staff bar. There were other members of staff that were doing worse things than us, so we started to call him blind Bryn.

Donna and myself were having a break one day and I asked her what music she liked "Oh you won't like my music. I like the Clash and punk" I told her I loved the Clash and met them once when I was a porter in a hotel in Swansea. We soon become close friends. Having said that I was working behind the bar and Donna was on a night off, she was drunk and got a bit nasty and the next day I wouldn't talk to her. After things cooled down, she said that she was really upset "when you didn't talk to me you are like my big brother". After that our friendship really blossomed. Being a young pretty girl she soon got involved in a relationship with one of the permanent staff.

In the canteen one morning I was working with Joanne, and for some reason I started calling her Newage. I suppose she did look a bit like a new age traveler; this too became a great friendship I will always remember these girls with great fondness. **Postavanje**. Newage was a typical scouser full of mischief but there was no one more honest than her. When we were together the place was always full of laughter. How we never set the accommodation on fire I will never know. When we weren't working, we would get howling and cook something in the kitchen nearly every time setting the fire alarms off. I went into the kitchen one day and the dish in the microwave was so hot it was bright orange. Newage showed me how to cook great meals cheaply, a specialty of hers was shepherd's pie simple to make and delicious.

In those days CDs had just started on the market, and I had bought a cheap CD player, most of the time you would hear Rod Stewart being played, nice music and never too loud.

There were two other members of staff, but they had boyfriends and kept to themselves. Sometimes I needed a haircut, I had brought along my own hair clippers. Now one day I decided to give myself a trim, as it happened there was a busload of Squaddies parked outside of the accommodation. Without thinking I started to use the clippers, and they made a racket. Newage said to me later that she happened to look out of her window and the squaddies looked back at her at the same time, it looked like she was using a xxx.
I couldn't help but notice there was a sign on the staff canteen door.
Join the British army's most active TA unit.

I asked Newage what this was all about "oh its EFI" a lot of the NAAFI staff join this, and the money is good. So, I decided that I would make some enquiries about it. I went to see Bryn and he said he would get in touch with them to see if there are any vacancies. A couple of days later Bryn told me that Colonel Smith would like me to come for an interview in Bulford camp. All I had to do was arrange a time to suit Bryn. So, it was not long after that a date was arranged.

I figured out the best way to get to Bulford was to get a bus from the married quarters, which were on the camp. There was a service that went to Salisbury, as it happens the bus passes through Bulford camp.

In July this is exactly what I did. I arrived at the camp and asked the driver to drop me off at Picton barracks. The bus stop was just passed the main gate, so I turned back and walked to the main gate, I told the soldier on duty that I had an interview with a Col Smith, 148 Sqn EFI, I showed my NAAFI id card and sure enough my name was on his, the guard pointed the way and I was let into the camp.

The EFI HQ was only a short distance up the road, I noticed a few Corporals walking about, then a Warrant officer approached me and asked me what I wanted, I told him that I had an interview with Col Smith, he told me to take a seat, and he would be with me shortly. Minutes later a tall grey-haired officer with a smile on his face appeared, with a strong Scottish accent said, "hello Miles" I replied, "hello sir".

I suppose I was a bit nervous, but it was really an informal interview. He asked me what military experience I had, I told him I was in the TA 4RRW and had also did one year with the Cheshire regiment including six months in Belize. He asked for my army number and that was nearly enough the interview was over with. He asked me how I got to Bulford, I said by bus, he then called one of the corporals and told him to take me back to Worthy Down. The Corporal went off and soon appeared driving a blue minibus. I got into the vehicle, and we were on our way. I asked him his name, and he told me Baz. I then asked him how many countries he had been to; he told me Croatia Norway the Gulf war Saudi Arabia I was quite impressed. At that time, I didn't have any decent clothes the best I could muster was a blue pair of trousers and a brown shirt, I suppose I looked a bit strange. I had a feeling Baz seemed wary of me. Within an hour I was back in Worthy Down. I thanked Baz and said, "see you soon".

Around this time the NAAFI had won a three-year contract to supply all the armed forces with their catering supplies. Apparently, the NAAFI's main computer had broken down and supplies to military catering establishments were late, some orders were wrong, and some orders didn't even turn up, this was causing chaos. Some units had to buy supplies from supermarkets. Indeed, this happened to us, Marge had to go to many supermarkets in Winchester to buy our pizza bases. She also bought ready-made pizzas; we could always add more ingredients. There were stories of Chefs having to do the same but on a much bigger scale than us. There were rumours that some military units had to go to McDonalds for breakfast. For some of the haters of the NAAFI this was great news.So it was back to the usual routine in the bar. There was a new course starting every week. We were even running out of pizza bases, so Marge had to go into town to buy some more.

One evening a strange looking bloke arrived at the bar, and although he was in civvies I could tell he was a Para, for he looked like he had been in a boxing ring a few times. A lot of the time I can tell what part of the forces a person is from, by the way they act, dress, haircut etc. This evening Donna was working with me, This Para type ordered a pint with Donna and started talking to her, sat on a stool at the bar and started to talk to her, he soon got up again, leaving the room only to return a short time later, returning to his seat. I don't know what Donna said to him, but he quickly got up and sat somewhere else. Later a few of his friends came into the club, came to the bar, got up and joined them, started talking about P Company.

P Company. This is where you do your pre-Parachute selection course training. You don't have to be in the parachute regiment to do this course, but you have to have a role with 16 Air Assault Brigade, but you had to do this course to get your wings.
For some stupid reason he said, "I would like to see someone like him do P company" referring to me of course. I immediately responded with "how do you know that I haven't done it" "have you" he asked. Anyway, Donna said to me later. "That really peed me off, he came into the bar with a wedding ring on, disappears, then comes back with no wedding ring.

In the meantime, pizza sales were rocketing, and every customer that came in ordered one. I asked one of the customers why they were hungry all the time, he told me the food in the cookhouse was awful.

Marge told me that she was still waiting for references from my old job, six months had passed, she said it didn't matter much now, as I had proved I could do my job, I wasn't the manager, but I was practically running the bar. They even sent me on a visit to the fosters brewery in Southampton for a day. At the end of the brewery tour we could have drunk as much as we wanted, indeed a few people did, I didn't bother, I had given up on daytime drinking.

Bryn had a little chat with me one day; he said that the NAAFI were short of managers, he asked me if I was interested in becoming a trainee manager. I said I would but after a couple of weeks I lost interest in the idea, as this would distance me from my friends that I valued. Also, I was more interested in joining EFI.

I was getting a bit frustrated waiting for Col Smith to get back in touch with me, so I decided to give him a ring to find out the score. Col Smith answered the phone, I asked him what was happening, he then told me that they were waiting for an exercise to come up in November, he would request that I be freed to go on it. So, things were looking up.

It was with some luck that a soldier got posted away from Worthy Down, he sold me his CD player cheaply, it was a newer make than the one I already had. Apart from the Rod Stewart album, I bought REMs greatest hits, and I was playing it over and over again.

Although there was a civilian bus service going into Winchester every two hours there was an MT section, they would regularly go there as well. The problem being that they were all civilian drivers, mostly ex regulars, what they hated the most was the NAAFI. We were able to use this service, but it was up to the discretion of the driver, inevitably some driver put a stop to it. Though it was handy we could live without it, it was no life changer.

September came around, Marge told me that she had a phone call from Col Smith, he wanted me to go on a two-week exercise to Denmark in November, which was great news to me. It was at this time that Bryn was going to take some time off work and Marge was going to be running the place.

November soon came along; I was going to be picked up by an EFI driver then taken to Bulford Camp to get some uniform and settle in. I didn't have to take any civvies, as we weren't going to have any time off. Someone who was a stranger to me picked me up. He told me his name was James; he went on to tell me a few things about EFI, like the lowest rank was Corporal and the places he had been to. We arrived at Bulford; he showed me into a barrack block then into a large room where there was a bed ready for me to sleep the night. We were going to get the ferry on Saturday evening from Harwich. Also in the room was Baz. We had to get up early in the morning to go to HQ EFI but before that though, it was breakfast. The cookhouse was within walking distance from the block. It was a busy old place, I would say there was enough room for 200 people to sit at any one time. It was very basic, with bare tables and no tablecloths. In those days all the cooks were ACC (Army Catering Corps). The usual system was to pick up a plate, then go to the serving area where a cook would give you the main food, i.e. breakfast would be two sausages 2 rashers of bacon, then you would walk on a bit further, help yourself to beans or tomatoes if you wanted an egg (which I didn't) you cook it yourself on a separate hotplate. There would be an area for bread and soft drinks and of course cutlery. In my opinion the food was top class, but some people were not happy. *Careful what you wish for.*

After breakfast we had a short walk to EFI HQ. We had to be there at 08.00, Colonel Smith was in his office but first I had to see the clerk who then was a civilian. She was going to process me into the system. The first thing she did was to give me a chit in lieu, which is a temporary id card, which in fact is a signed piece of paper. There were loads of forms to fill in, they had to be in detail but as I had an Army number anyway things would be a lot simpler. What I was basically doing was re-joining the TA. Even in this small establishment they had a military computer, which was called PAMPAS, this had a direct link to the main Army system. While this process was going on I was taken to the storeroom to get a uniform, which was all second hand even down to the socks. I managed to find combats that fitted me. Saying none of it was new was not strictly true, I was given a beret, a badge and a pair of boots, which were actually new, these I could keep after the exercise. I never thought that I would ever be in a military uniform again and here I am plus Corporal stripes. James and Baz were away most of the morning; they had come back for lunch via HQ, to pick me up for lunch.

Again, I could not complain about the food, for lunch it was normally things with chips i.e. fish, sausages, chicken, burgers etc., we had to queue for a few things but that was ok with me. It was the back to HQ where I had another talk to Col Smith, where he explained the pay and leave with EFI. We would see how I got on in this exercise.

There was to be an early start the next day, as we had to get a ferry from Harwich. In the afternoon I met Neil who was the Sergeant that was in charge of our unit in the exercise. He had been somewhere and had brought back a Landrover with a trailer, which was full of our stock that we needed for the exercise.

At 17.00 we finished for the day; we had to be back in the morning at 07.30 to leave for 08.00. James said that they were going to Amesbury, which was the nearest town, for a few beers in the evening, if I wanted to come along, great of course I would it was a chance to get to know the boys and get to see what the thought of EFI. It turned out to be a quiet affair, James told me about his time in the Gulf war and about a few tours in Croatia. After the pub we got a kebab, then a taxi back to Bulford.

Next morning it was a quick breakfast and into the Landrover, making our way to Harwich. It was a good-hearted journey everybody seemed to be happy to get away for two weeks.

We got to the Ferry in plenty of time. There were all sorts queuing to get on the vessel, civvies and military vehicles, this was a new experience for me. After parking the Landrover, we made it upstairs to the cabins. I had to share a cabin with James, we were free to do what we wanted, the first thing was to eat. With our tickets we were issued with a dinner voucher, which included a beer.

We were told that in the evening there was going to be a disco, so we headed back to the cabin for a shower and changed clothes. First Neil, Baz, James and I went to the buffet, then visited a few bars. We were having a chat and a beer, an announcement came on, to my amazement it said, "Can a Mr. Miles Rees come to reception", I thought, what the hell was this about. I went to reception and told them that I was Miles Rees. "Oh, mister Rees you left your passport in a shop". Well, I would never have known anything about it when I needed it. I dared not tell the boys what I was called for, especially Neil, I knew by then he was very strict.

This ferry journey was crazy, all sorts mixing together. We made our way to the disco, there were people with their smart clothes on, mixed with soldiers in uniform.

One of the units going to the exercise were the Worcester and Sherwood foresters better known as Woofers, by late evening James was becoming worse for wear, he was sitting at the edge of the dance floor eyes staring but his head not so steady he kept saying ' effin woofers' effin woofers' Neil was watching and he said "James go to bed" to his credit this is exactly what he did. A while later I went back to the cabin, passing out.

Next thing I knew I could hear the engines getting louder, this was having a soothing effect on me, I was out for the count. Suddenly Neil comes barging into the cabin "what the eff are you doing, we are docking, get up", so of course we rapidly got all our stuff together. We got down to the Landrover where Neil had the sternest of faces, then he laughed, this was how he was.

Denmark isn't a massive country, so it wouldn't be far to where the exercise was going to be held. We could see Military vehicles coming our way and others in front of us. Neil was reading the map, whereupon an MP (Military Police) vehicle stopped us, the MP asked if we were part of the exercise, of course we were, he told us it wasn't far, putting us in the right direction. We turned into a side road, there was a guard at a barrier, this he immediately raised for us and around the corner was this massive circus tent.  It was a built-up army camp, so we didn't have to build our own tents. Neil went off to look for the liaison Officer, soon came back and quickly found where our shop was.

We unloaded our military gear and the stock from the trailer, which mostly consisted of sweets chocolates cigarettes and perfumes. In the morning Neil was going to take delivery of the beer and minerals, which had been pre-ordered by himself.

The next morning, we went for breakfast, which was in the massive circus tent. It was very basic wooden tables chairs in a grass field but hey the food was good. Our first task after breakfast was to set up the shop and storeroom. There were two parts to this we had a hard building for the shop itself, a tent for the stores and our accommodation. We were getting bread rolls delivered every morning. The shop was set up in no time, it was very basic, and all the stock was put on makeshift shelves made from cardboard boxes and trestle tables.

People are strange

Business was very slow to start with; we would get in a group or a few stragglers. There was a particular customer, who was in and out, a Belgium Corporal he was a strange fellow. He kept coming out with strange sayings like "I was in the shower and in came a lady, I was completely naked" (in of course his Belgium accent). On another time he was looking at the perfumes that we had on sale, situated on a shelf behind me, he pointed at one and said "let me look at Anal-Anal" what in fact was Anais-Anais.

Some of our customers were Americans, not the politest of people in the world. A female officer came into the shop, she had an unfriendly look about her, she looked at the chocolates and abruptly said "snickers", I felt like picking it up and throwing it at her, needless to say I didn't get a thank you, this was my first lesson of pig ignorant customers. In the evenings we sat in the tent- come storeroom, we would have a few beers, we didn't have to pay for them as they had been written off as damaged stock. Neil, Baz and James had all been to Croatia few times, they recommended that I did a tour. I was told that it was a six-month tour with full Corporals pay, with leave (holiday) at the end, and in between get R&R (rest and recuperation), this sounded good to me, I was interested.

I was mainly in the shop, the rest of the guys were in the B.I.S. (bulk issue store), Baz and James kept going on about K.P. I didn't know what this meant, they told me that it was kitchen production; the Col insisted they do it, I suppose it was a profit maker. All it consisted of was making filled bread rolls. I must admit the function itself didn't look too hygienic, I don't think they even washed their hands.

These two weeks went quickly by, the next thing we knew we were waiting in the Landrover, in a queue to board the ferry. There was no disco this time just a quiet trip back. Neil kept saying "Troops

Herforder". I think he was trying to make us look like Special Forces. (In a way we were). Herforder was the beer that we sold, Hereford is where the SAS are located.

We arrived back at Harwich, and we had to go through customs, no problems there. It was back down the road to base as it was Friday evening when we got back. we had to wait until Monday morning to unload our gear and see the Col. This was going to be another drinking session first to the Kiwi pub in Tidworth. This was a strange set up, a civilian manager ran the kiwi, it was a proper pub but mostly everyone in it were soldiers. There was a jukebox, pool table and dartboard. After a few pints in the Kiwi, we got a taxi into Amesbury and did a bit of a pub-crawl, some pubs quite nice and some not so nice, they had one thing in common, all of them were full of Squaddies. You would have to be a special person to run one of these pubs, but I suppose the customers were good spenders.

I was then introduced to the local nightclub, which was nicknamed sticky carpets, and it stood up to its name. On Saturday we went into Salisbury, a longer journey but much more civilized. Sunday was quiet on the camp, as most soldiers had gone home. The cookhouse was quiet but more comfortable, with a roast dinner on offer I found it lovely, but people still moaned. On Monday morning I had to see Colonel Smith, he asked how I liked the exercise, I of course replied that I enjoyed it.

He told me that he was pleased with my performance. I told him that I would like to do a tour of Bosnia. The Colonel told me he would keep me in mind and would be in touch. I was told to hand in my uniform, then given a lift back to Worthy Down.

In these two short weeks away, things had changed. The rumours that Bryn was retiring were becoming more fact. Marge told me that Brian was going to take some time off work, and she was still going to be the assistant manager.

There were a few new faces in our staff. Main thing was that Donna and Joanne were still there. Christmas time was looming, Marge asked us to start thinking about what we wanted to do for a staff Christmas party.

I got to talk to one of the students, he told me he was from Swansea and would give me a lift home at the weekends if I was interested. When I saw Marge and she told me she was fine with that. My job had now become a Monday to Friday week. It was ok the new staff could cope at the weekends, it was a training camp and most people would go home. There was only need for one person to run the bar.

Meanwhile Janice's boyfriend was increasingly becoming a pain, he was frequently knocking on the outside door, it was always me that would have to open the door for him. One day there was a knock on the door, I was getting a bit fed up, I opened my window and shouted out 'eff off', the trouble was, it wasn't him, it was the camps RSM.

The RSM was fine about it though, like most RSMs he was a fine fellow. At the end of November, I was told that there was to be a permanent staff Christmas ball, it was to be run upstairs in our rarely used function room.

Normally the troops on the courses were well behaved, one particular busy evening we were running out of glasses, so I went out collecting. I went to one table and reached for a glass, a customer was getting abusive, I talked to him, and he replied, "you call me sir" I got really angry and said back to him "no you call me sir and don't come back to the bar as you will not be served". Later one of his friends came to the bar and asked for a beer, I said to him if it's for your friend you can't have it, really, I couldn't refuse to serve anyone, but I was trying to show a bit of authority. This was a rare occurrence though. The funny thing about this though was the next evening the abusive one was back in the bar with a broken arm. I asked him what had happened; he told me that he injured himself while training. Then he said "sorry about last night" 'I said it was ok and all was forgotten, well until now that is. As it was getting closer to Christmas, we, or should I say Marge decided that for our Xmas do we would go to Basingstoke for the evening, she would book an aisle in the ten-pin bowling Centre. I had never bowled before in my life. We got a minibus, which consisted of nine ladies and me. I wasn't too excited about bowling but when I got into it I realized that I was a natural. We had a great time making fools of ourselves. After that we went on a pub-crawl, happy days. As an aside, a year before when I was working in a pub, we had a Christmas do in a laser dome. We were firing lasers from guns at virtual enemies I must admit for an infantry soldier I did abysmal and came last.

The day of the permanent staff party had arrived. I hadn't met any of the Officers before, when I did on this day though I was not impressed by the way they were looking down at me. I hadn't really talked much to the RSM before either, but he was quite pleasant, his job was setting up the party. Another first for me was a visit to the cookhouse, I had to go there to pick up some cakes. There was a lot of grumbling about the food there, I wanted to find out what the cooks thought about the Squaddies. The Sergeant chef was there; I told him that the troops were always starving and wanted pizzas all the time. The chef assured me that there was nothing wrong with the food, there just was no pleasing them, I understood where he came from.

In the evening it was all hands-on deck, all the top brass and their wives some snobs and some not. We were out to do our best and I think we excelled. In the evening, they had a raffle with some expensive prizes, scores of them. At midnight it all came to an end, people had gone within half an hour. Donna and I were left to do the clearing up, we were amazed that all the raffle prizes were left, with the doors left wide open, having said that Worthy Down was a safe place to leave anything.

Worthy Down NAAFI was going to be shut down for two weeks over Xmas, so of course I went home and stayed at my friend's house.

Just after the New Year, we opened again, Bryn had not come back but had retired, leaving Marge in charge. It didn't change anything except my attitude to her. One day I wanted to ask her a question, she sat down, as I approached her, she came out with 'what do you want little boy' I could have gone through the roof but I restrained myself. Until now I couldn't understand why the staff disliked her so much.

At the beginning of February, I had notice from Colonel Smith. It stated that I wanted a six-month tour of Bosnia, of course I gladly accepted the offer. At the beginning of March, I was to be at Bulford to start training and get kitted out. It was both a good time and a bad time as I was going to leave my friends behind.

I had nearly been at Worthy Down for a year now. NAAFI had to keep my job open for when I returned from my tour of Bosnia, I assured Marge that I would be back, I doubted that I would though.

RUN TO THE HILLS

I was given leave and went home to Swansea this time staying at Moorside road where I used to live. There I received a travel warrant to get me to Andover where I would be picked up by James, then be taken to ward barracks HQ EFI.

Bulford camp is split into two camps with a main road going straight through the middle of it. Ward barracks to the south and Picton barracks to the north. I was taken to the barrack block and shown my pit space. I was to report to HQ EFI at 0800 next morning. At 0730 James and I went over to the cookhouse for breakfast then a short walk to work. First task on arrival was to make a cup of tea, I also had to make one for the Colonel and the Clerk. The second event of the day was the start of the processing back into EFI in the clerk's office. Here I had to fill in more forms to join the TA, next of kin forms and most importantly the pay forms. After all the forms were filled in, I had to see the Colonel. He told me that I would be going to Bosnia at the beginning of April, there was to be a lot of preparation. He was going to send Brian and myself on a forklift course at Bicester on Monday next. This soon came around.

Bicester is one massive ordinance depot. Red bricked buildings everywhere. It even has its own

railway system.

It was in one of these buildings that we would spend week training on the forklifts. Baz was on a reach and tier course, whatever that was, I was on a basic counterbalance forklift, to be honest I didn't know much about it, I just got on with it.

The first thing the people on our course was to learn was the 100 safety rules, and I mean you had to know 100 %, there was to be a test on this at the end of the week, in reality it wasn't that hard common sense had to come into it, things like always face in the direction you are travelling in, sound the horn at every entrance, this would drive some people mad.

One important thing you had to learn was to first parade the vehicle. The Army does this every morning with every vehicle for good reason; prevention is better than the cure should we say. Check the oil levels, the hydraulics, the tyres, there was a list that had to be ticked off. Then the fun would start, learning how to pick up loads and then how to stack them, it was a bit daunting, but the instructors had a few tricks up their sleeves to make things easier. We would have a NAAFI break in the morning, unfortunately there was no NAAFI just a kitchen for us. The mornings were all theory, and, in the afternoon's, it was hands on the machines then back to the Billet in the evening to do a bit of studying.

There was actually a NAAFI that we could go to in the evenings with cheap beer, a pool table and a TV to watch football if you were into that. There was a Scottish soldier who was on the course with Brian, birds of a feather stick together, I felt like an outsider.

It wasn't a particularly interesting week, Friday soon came along, in the morning, we had the 60-question exam, It was not hard and we all passed. In the afternoon we had a practical test on the forklifts again we all passed. So, I was issued with my new forklift licence. The tutors and students were all nice people, which made it a pleasant week.

I had a little problem in getting back to Bulford as Baz was going to stay at a friend's house. The Scottish lance Corporal said I could stay at his house that was actually on the garrison, not that I wanted to it, was my best option. I had an evening meal and a shower at his house and watched a bit of TV. He had a little dog that was nice and friendly I said a few things to the dog as you do. The bloke came out with "you can talk to the dog as much as you want but he is not going to answer you". I couldn't wait to leave that house. James came to pick me up in the morning then picked Baz up at his friends' house.

Bulford camp, I will elaborate a bit more on. The main thing you would notice about Ward barracks is the accommodation blocks, which would all have a name to them like Ypres and Salamanca, probably because they had battle honours with them. These blocks were solidly built with two stories each, containing four large barrack block rooms catering for about 24 soldiers, 12 bunk beds, two lockers, two-foot lockers. When you arrive, there will be blankets and pillows neatly stacked, you will have to go to the storeroom to get sheets and pillowcases. Just outside the rooms were the ablutions, separate toilets and showers where there would always be a sign saying 'don't wash your boots in here' sometimes you would get hot water and sometimes not. In the winter the billets would be very warm, around April the heating would be turned off for the summer. These blocks were to be kept spotlessly clean.

Now what I noticed about army camps is that they are very depressing, there seems to be an air about them, probably over the years many men would have made a one-way journey to a war. Central to all the blocks is the parade square. Where only the brave (or naïve) would dare walk on, for if the RSM or MPs caught you, there would be a Guardroom awaiting you. The grassed areas were always immaculate; again, you do not walk on these areas.

If you wanted to go to the shopping precinct you would have to leave the camp via the main gate, this was manned 24 hours a day, it would be a ten-minute walk, or you could be there in 2 minutes by a smaller gate which was manned only at certain times of the day. The shopping Centre was a square with all sorts of shops the main one being the NAAFI, you could always get what you wanted there. The NAAFI specialized in tea, they even had their own company, called aptly the NAAFI tea company. For years the NAAFI had supplied the forces, in my opinion there has never been a better tea. I remember a tea bag that would make a pot enough for ten people.

NAAFI was not the cheapest place to shop but sometimes they would have special offers, and they had their own cheaper brands. The main thing was they were always there for the Servicemen and Servicewomen. Us EFI staff could get 10% discount as well. Other shops in the precinct were Military oriented, mainly the tailors who would be making a roaring trade. What made this precinct different from any shopping Centre, it was on military grounds, you would always have to wear your beret and salute officers if you couldn't avoid them.

While Baz and I were in Bicester there were a few new arrivals that had completed their basic EFI training, in those days EFI trained their own soldiers, thank God I was spared that ordeal. Two girls had arrived and of course were put into the female accommodation, another male who seemed to know Baz from an exercise they had been on before. On Monday morning I would meet these people that were to be my colleagues in the six-month tour of Bosnia. The first thing in the morning was to issue everybody with lightweight tropical combats, of course all the uniform was second hand, it was more like a jumble sale. Eventually we all got something that just about fitted us.
For a new recruit there is nothing worse than a new beret, you have got to learn the art of shaping them or you could end up looking ridiculous.

From the start there was a divide between us boys on one side and the girls on the other, this week to me was just an admin week sorting out id cards and NOK (next of kin) forms.

At the weekend we were to go to Grantham (Lincs), which is the TA training camp for the RLC. Here we had to do a bit of military training. As we were going to Bosnia, we would have to carry weapons so of course we would have to be trained in them. Neil drove us on the long journey to Grantham in a big blue minibus, which belonged to EFI. We would have to be there by 1600 to get our bedding and be shown our billets. Of course we would be in separate accommodation. Male, female and senior ranks. There was to be an early start on Saturday morning, so we had to have our breakfast early. This was a full Army fry-up of bacon sausages eggs etc., although it was a TA camp they had Regular Army cooks.

Our first lesson of the day was in first aid and how to treat casualties that we might encounter in Bosnia. It was a light-hearted affair but there is no getting away with mouth-to-mouth resuscitation. For this task there was a model called resuscitation Annie, a half human figure cold and lifeless. I have got a terrible weak stomach and when it was my turn to do mouth-to-mouth I nearly brought up my breakfast. All the rest of the morning we had to be trained in all sorts of medical situations. We all had a little test on each subject and of course all passed.

The rest of the weekend was now concentrated on weapons training. So, after a bit of lunch, we went to the armoury to collect our SA80s, then into a classroom where we would be taught in stripping down and cleaning, sometimes this can be awkward as parts have an habit of flying off. Then onto safety precautions including how to deal with stoppages and firing positions, this you had to learn, then pass a test to be able to go onto the ranges for live firing. We had a female Corporal arms instructor, bearing in mind I had been in the Infantry, and it was most unusual for females to handle weapons let alone instruct in them. It was in the afternoon that I made a big mistake, saying to my colleagues that I found it a little strange to be taught by a female instructor, by the end of the afternoon I could tell that the instructor had taken a dislike to me.

The day's work had been done, and we were free to do what we wanted in the evening. We all decided that we would go into Grantham and have a look in the local pubs. So that is exactly what we did, booked out of the Guardroom and walked down to the Town that was less than a mile away. We didn't get past the first pub; we settled in and got to know each other a bit more. Ruth and Kate worked for the NAAFI in Germany, Luke had been lucky as he had been working in a military hospital, Baz was in the CADRE an elite unit in the NAAFI who were on hand to be sent anywhere at short notice.

Next morning after breakfast we went to the armoury to collect our weapons as we were going on to the range for live firing. The instructor was absolutely nasty to me all morning and was waiting to play her trump card. When I was about to fire my last shot, she shouted 'stop' and in that split second, I fired off the round, she shouted at me with a bit of obscene language. I looked at the boys who both had smirks on their faces. This is where I might have coined the phrase, Nasty And Awful Fin Individuals. In hindsight it is clear that someone had mentioned to the instructor what I had said the day before.

Well at the end of the day we were proficient in the rifles, and we could be let loose in Bosnia. We were making our way back to the minibus, Kate and I were having a bit of a laugh, it was a bit too loud for Neils liking, he told us off in no uncertain manner, I can't blame him as the training camp had a RSM who could put us all in jail. That was one poxy weekend at Grantham finished.

It was to be another week at Bulford, and then we would have to do what is known as CATC training. We would be spending two weeks at Warminster training for Bosnia. Baz told me that we would be meeting people that we would be working with in Bosnia.

At the start of the CATC training we had to meet up with the supply Sqn that we were going to be attached to, they were stationed at an old RAF base, now an Army camp at Hullavington. Here the RAF used to train parachutists, apparently this was the worst sort of training, as they had to go up in a balloon and jump from it. In a airplane you can't see the ground when you jump out a balloon is a straight drop, not for the faint hearted.

It was on a Sunday afternoon that James took us up to the old airfield. It was the first time I set eyes on our new comrades; Baz knew a lot of them that was quite clear.

We were not going to be staying at Hullavington for very long as we were going to be taken to Warminster by coach, which was waiting for us.

It took us about two hours to reach our camp in a place called Copley Down. This looked like a WW2 training camp, no doubt it probably was. Red brick buildings with metal-framed windows. Hot in summer and cold in winter.

The bus pulled up on the old parade square, where we disembarked, here we had to fall in, (get in line) then our names were called out and we were allocated a room number in a building, now we were truly integrated with the Squadron. We were told to fall out and put our Kit into our building, this is where we going to get to know our new colleagues, I must admit they welcomed us straight away I knew we were going to settle in quickly.

It was an early start in the morning first thing we had to do was go to the armoury to collect our weapons. We will be using the Sqns weapons for the upcoming training, which will be for two weeks. Of course, our weapons were the basic SA80 (small arms 1980) we were also issued two magazines and a BFA (blank firing attachment).

The training was going to be in two parts. The first week we were going to do training in a FIBUA (fighting in a built-up area) village. Basically, we were going to learn how to do patrols and what to do if we came under attack. We were constantly reminded that we were under the UN mandate so therefore we had to be unbiased.

The first couple of days it was mostly patrolling and coming under attack, Luke apparently saved the day on one occasion, when he put his rifle into machine gun mode.

Now here EFI are equally blessed and equally cursed, when you go on deployment you are a Corporal. This is mainly because we are in charge of handling money, but the Army didn't look at it that way. As we had the rank of Corporal, we were meant to be able to run a section on a patrol, or even at times a section in a fire fight. at times this was to cause havoc.

In the evenings we would be harbouring in a makeshift building. On one particular evening we were told to get our heads down, so we all got out our kip mats and sleeping bags, we settled in comfortably for a good night's sleep (yeah really).

Bang !!

All hell let loose, we were under an artillery attack. It was now pandemonium; people were trying to run whilst still in their sleeping bags, falling over people that had already fallen over, running into people who were running the opposite way. We were told to get to the basement, wherever that was. The only way was down; people were still trying to run in their sleeping bags. I could see the terror in Ruth's eyes as she passed me, oblivious that she passed me. Eventually we all got to the air raid shelter.

In another evening there were six of us on patrol, it was pitch dark where we stopped, excellent place for being inconspicuous, it was silent and calm, all of a sudden someone struck a match, it was only Ruth lighting a cigarette, you could say we were immediately compromised.

Later in the week we were in a rescue role where we had to do some FIBUA, we had to storm a house using ladders to get into the windows, after a bit of a struggle we managed to get into the house but unfortunately there were still enemy alive in there. So, a firefight broke out and by some miracle we managed to clear the house from bottom to top.

Unfortunately, the Regular Army girls weren't seeing the funny side of things, they were curious as to who we were and asked Kate and Ruth, they told them we were NAAFI; our cover was blown.

By Friday evening all the dry training was done, we all could go home for the weekend. The bus would take us to Hullavington; anywhere else, it was a case of finding your own way home.

Luckily for me I was invited by one of the Supply Squadrons Corporals to stay at his quarters, I of course I took up his offer and the hospitality he showed me was second to none thanks Jim McCabe **postavanje**.

The second week was a bit more serious as we were going to be using live ammunition.

We had to prove that we were proficient on the weapons, this was all done on the Monday, we had to strip the rifles for normal daily cleaning, put them back together again, then go through stoppage drills, to be fair to the girls, they did the drills perfect seeing as they had never used a weapon prior to going to Grantham, they excelled.

So, on the Tuesday we were going to the ranges. Where? We were not told.
As it happened, we ended up in Tidworth, which is the next garrison to Bulford.

We were issued with 20 rounds (bullets) to put in a magazine; we would have to wait our turn to go onto the firing line, this always seems an eternity. You would be told to load the magazine with 5 rounds, when It came to our turn, normal procedure is to walk to the firing point, get told to adopt the prone position, (on your belly) then wait for the order 'load' that is when you put the magazine onto the rifle, make ready (cock the weapon) then given orders of what to do next, in this case fire five rounds. You would probably hear, "with a magazine of five rounds, in your own time, carry on". Fire the shots off, then walk to the target to see where your rounds had hit and what sort of grouping you had got. You should be able to tell if you are aiming high, low, left or right this is called Zeroing. Then the instructor would normally adjust the sight for you, depending on your experience. Same process with the next five rounds if all was ok you fired the next ten rounds. However, there was one thing the poor girls had never anticipated, we were wearing helmets, when you get into the prone position the helmet would slip down, making it impossible to see the targets, this is a lesson we all learn i.e. fasten the straps properly, the girls got there in the end with a bit of coaching.

On the Wednesday we were back on the ranges, this time it was to see how accurate our shooting was, I must admit I never really liked the SA80, my groupings were not too accurate,this seemed to please the guys who had been made aware that I was former Infantry.

On the Thursday we went to Warminster; this time the ranges were different, we were going to be doing live firing section attacks, this is no mean feat with live ammunition. I had to do it very often with the T.A.

RUNNING UP THE HILL

The equally blessed scenario comes into effect again, as we in EFI were Corporals; in any part of the British army, to become a Corporal you would have to go on a course. On this course you had to learn how to be a section commander. You could be anywhere in the world and called on to run part of a platoon, which is a section, thus a section commander. You would be expected to run a section in a firefight. I managed ok from my experience in the T.A.

There is one sight I will never forget in my life. Poor Ruth was leading a section attack, - bearing in mind this was live firing-, up a hill and to her credit she did her best, it was funny to see, there ended up five guys pushing her up the hill, whilst live firing to the enemy position, but hey she did it. To think a couple of weeks ago she was in a NAAFI in Germany, having never been in a military uniform in her life. **Postavanje**.

Friday was an admin day, cleaning weapons and handing them back into the armoury. Cleaning the ancient Billets, then handing back bedding which we hardly used. It was back to Hullavington with our newfound colleagues. Here we were being picked up with the big blue minibus, again with James waiting for us. James asked me if I would like to stay at his home in Swindon for the weekend, so of course I did. We had to go back to Bulford first.

His mother showed me great hospitality, and I wanted for nothing. We went into Swindon for a Saturday night out, and I was curious as to why James was leaving EFI.
He told me that he was fed up with all the travelling and not having a life. I tried to talk him out of leaving to no avail. We had a good evening, and I got hold of some girl's addresses to write to while I was in Bosnia.

It was a two-week wait before it was our time to go on tour. On a Monday morning, we were told that we were leaving for Croatia next Wednesday. Many cups of tea later Colonel Smith gave us a briefing on timings. We would be going to Brize Norton Wednesday afternoon and would be flying to Croatia early Thursday morning. I was really disappointed; we were not going to Bosnia but staying in Croatia. Looking back, this was an awful time to be in Bosnia. So we had a couple of days to sort out our admin.

We went to the Kiwi in the evening. Luke told us of his times in the warehouse, at Amesbury. Because of the debacle with staff messing contract EFI staff were seconded to work in the warehouse. Luke had to work in the frozen section.
The time soon came along to leave for Brize Norton, Colonel Smith bade us farewell with his great smile. It was into the big blue minibus. It was about an hour and a half travelling time, passing through Tidworth and the ranges that we had been on not long ago, passing over the M4, through country lanes eventually seeing signs for Brize Norton.

The driver will have to show the armed guards a pass, then we could make our way to the terminal, where we would hand our luggage in and get our boarding pass. As this was not my first visit to Brize Norton, I knew this could be a long affair.

We were then free to go to Gateway house, which is like a Motel just in a military way. We would go to reception, and the staff would ask us where we were flying to. They would check our names from a list that they received daily. When our names corresponded, we would have to hand over our boarding passes, we were then given the keys to our rooms, we were advised that we will be called at about 0300.
All the rooms were twins; there was no way you would have a room to yourself. After going to the room and putting our cabin luggage away we could go back downstairs for a few beers, in a fantastic bar which was duty free, I would say the beer was less than half price of a NAAFI bar. Then it was to bed.

"Good morning the time is 0300, this is your early morning call, please press the transponder to acknowledge this call' 'transport will be leaving for the terminal at 0400'.

The chances are that you wouldn't get much sleep, that was unfortunate, from now until the next evening, you would not find anywhere comfortable to rest. We made our way down to the restaurant, where we could have toast and cereals. After breakfast we had to hand in the keys in exchange for the boarding passes. The buses turned up on time for the short journey to the terminal. When entering the building there was more queuing to be done, as we had to show our passport or ID card to be able to enter the departure lounge.

In those days the RAF had two squadrons for transporting troops around the world. One was flying Tri-stars, the other was flying VC10s. I had flown from here times before going to America with the TA and Belize with the Cheshire regiment. So, it was not new to me. Today's aircraft was to be a Tri-Star; they were second hand; British Airways were the previous owners. They were ideal for the RAF because they were designed to fly over mountainous areas. They proved their worth in the Falklands conflict.

At around 0600 we took off and made our way to Split, passing over the Alps then over Venice, then onto the blue skies and blue sea of the Adriatic. Halfway through the flight there was an announcement. " Ladies and Gentlemen, we will shortly be providing you with breakfast. It was a welcome meal, of bacon, sausages, beans, egg and a bread roll, plus of course a hot or cold drink.

Turning around to make our way onto FRY (Former Republic of Yugoslavia) the weather was beautiful. On this day, looking down, we could see many islands as we approached Split. Split is a coastal city, as you come into land all you can see is the blue water below, all of a sudden you will see strange looking houses and cars. We landed with a bump, the engines going into reverse, taxiing and stopping. We could see the steps being brought to our aircraft, then the doors being opened. Welcome to FRY.

A bus arrived to take us to the arrival terminal; here we had to show our passports or ID cards. Our luggage would be taken to a building for us to collect later.

Once through this procedure we didn't know what was going to happen next. Baz disappeared without saying a word, which annoyed us all a bit, as we were all a bit confused. Well of course Baz came back with our boss, a Captain, none of us had met him before. We had to collect our luggage, which was on a pallet that had been brought to us. A white painted Landrover turned up and we were told to put our luggage in the back. We were then instructed to get onto a bus that was waiting to take us to our final destination DWC. Dalma warehouse complex.

As it was April the weather was quite pleasant, sunny but not too warm. The bus was basic; the dusty windows needed a bit of a clean. This bus took us down to the main road, which was a dual carriageway. There were some lovely looking houses, but the more prominent buildings were the high-rise flats, this was my first experience of what the old communist buildings were like. We were soon on the coast road; I could clearly see a submarine in the middle of the bay. We had the city behind us after a few miles and we were now on a two-way road, which had a distinct odour of car fumes. After about a half hour on this road we came to a junction with traffic lights, this is where we turned left onto a narrow road, we ended up to what looked like a large warehouse, which was surrounded by a barbed wire fence.

A Ghurkha soldier lifted the barrier, and we entered the compound. It was now early evening, we got off the bus and we would have to wait for the Bedford to arrive with our luggage, which seemed a long time. Our OC arrived on the scene and told us to follow him to our part of

the warehouse, which was behind a massive steel door. The male accommodation was actually in a cabin in our part of the warehouse, the two girls were then taken away to their accommodation, which was upstairs in the warehouse. In our accommodation there didn't seem to be much room for three blokes. On the door was pinned a notice which read 'welcome to Dalma, you are all going to die' which was obviously left by our previous tenants. Luke had the notice in his hands, with a look of distain said 'charming'.

Understandably our part of the complex was very secure; we had very expensive goods like, TVs chocolates cigarettes Bose music systems and digital cameras that were new on the market. The only way into our warehouse was through the massive steel door, which was secured with a chain and a padlock from the inside. There was a camcorder looking at the door, which was probably broken and had been written off but could still be used to show a picture on the TV. The noise the door made would wake anyone up anyway.

We were told there was not much going on for the rest of the week as roulement (exchanging regiments) was on and only a few units had accounts still running, so we were allowed to go to the bar.

We were reminded that there was a strict two can rule in force, yes, we were only allowed to drink two cans of beer this evening. The two girls had come back to the warehouse, and then all five of us went to the bar, which was just around the corner from us.

The bar was very basic, wooden trestle tables, a few chairs, table tennis and a pool table. When I say basic, there were not any glasses, so we had to drink out of the cans. The best part about this was that we didn't have to run the bar.

I started talking to the person behind the bar; a Ghurkha, he explained that he was part of the 10 Queens' own Ghurkha transport Regiment. (10 QOGTR) they had been given the task of running the bar. I asked his name, I will call him Eka, which is number one in Nepalese. Reason being he was the first Ghurkha I had actually talked to. Eka told me that he was the only barman but could get help if needed.

I have always had an interest in learning other languages, tonight I would be given my first lesson in Nepalese, I asked Eka "how do you say thank you in your language" and he told me what sounded like Dundee bad. Well, it seemed that tonight Eka ignored the two-can rule; the main part of the supply company hadn't arrived yet, so there was no one to enforce it anyway.

I had a few more beers and was looking at the lovely view of the snow-covered mountains, through the door that was open; well, that is what it looked like to me, at the time.

The first breakfast at Dalma was a welcome one, it was lovely, the usual English breakfast, however the main thing to mention was that there was no cutlery or crockery, we had to use plastic knives and forks, and paper plates, the reason being there were no facilities for washing up and probably hygiene reasons.

At 0800 we started work in the warehouse and were shown the routine. We were given a printout from the Sergeant in the office, which would be from a unit who had an account with EFI. What we had to do was put together the items wanted this is not as easy as it sounds. The first orders were a learning curb it was no good putting boxes of crisps on the pallet first even if it was the first on the list (most orders would normally go on a pallet) basically heavy items go on the bottom and lighter items go on the top. Also, if we had orders of cases of pop you would have to count in tens or nines then decide which sort of pallet you would use. If you had ten cases of pop (or beer) you would use a chep pallet which would easily take ten cases, if you had only nine cases you would use a euro pallet which would take the exact amount. We would have to wrap some pallets in shrink-wrap, which is like giant cling film. I found this a bit of a challenge to begin with as there was no one to show us how to use it.

Lunchtime would come along; we would close the warehouse and go to the cookhouse. The menu for lunch would be items like pies sausages and chips. We even had bread and butter and of course tea and soft drinks. The cookhouse was very quiet at the moment because the old supply Sqn had gone, and the new Sqn was on its way. We were told this would be for about a week.

Back to the warehouse for the afternoon's tasks, all the pallets that had been put together would have to be put onto the unit's transport, normally a Bedford. This is what my training on the forklift course in Bicester was all for. Of course, now this was the real thing, so I had to take my time. We had our own forklift, but it was apparently always breaking down.

We could always use the supply Sqns Hyster if it was available, well there wasn't anybody here to use it anyway. There is a law regarding using a vehicle in the forces in that if you use a vehicle you have to 'first parade' it. This means checking oil levels etc. a form has to be filled in, ticking all requirements. This, we were taught in Bicester. When I did this, I helped load up all the orders. The last task of the day was to take all the rubbish out to the skips, which were on the main yard.

At 1700 the day's work had been done, it was to the cookhouse again, of course now it was the main meal of the day, there was a roast on and all the vegetables and a sweet after. Things were good. For the rest of the week, it was the same routine getting a little busier but manageable.

I noticed a few things were not quite as they should be. We were getting told off for orders not being right, inevitably as we were learning things would go wrong but there was a dark side to this. We had to start double checking other people's orders for mistakes, instead of telling us of our mistakes, Luke would go straight to Nigel to point out people's mistakes.

I hadn't realized that wrapping pallets with shrink-wrap was important. To be honest there was no shrink-wrap to be found at this time, naively one day I tried to wrap a pallet with a bit of old Shrink wrap, the customer watched me but didn't say anything, it was a pathetic attempt.

Out of the blue some wrap appeared, I had to learn how to secure the pallets. The wrap was surrounding a large cardboard tube, just put some wrap around the pallet and it sticks to itself or tie some wrap to the bottom of the pallet, then wrap around, keeping it tight was the secret. Trouble being it burned my hands with the friction so I started using a broom handle while walking around the pallet, then another problem arises it makes you dizzy, I remembered watching some dancers when they spin around, they focus their eyes on one object then turn around looking at the same object, it worked wonders providing you remembered to do it. In the first few weeks I was still learning the forklift, taking it steady. At one time I was loading pallets onto a truck and going a bit slow, Baz was making all sorts of faces to the customer showing his disdain. I soon picked up speed and got more confident.

The rest of the supply Sqn started arriving and we were told that we would soon have to be on parade every morning. The Squadron Sergeant Major, (SSM) was very strict, so we would have to look smart with our uniforms pressed and boots highly polished. So, it was polishing and ironing every evening. Our new comrades were getting the Forward rendezvous point (FRV) ready for their tasks ahead, making sure all their equipment was working properly. One day we heard an almighty crash in the courtyard, it turned out that one of the forklift drivers was trying to put a metal cage containing tank tracks on top of another two, he misjudged and pushed it right on top of our white EFI Landrover, rendering it U.S. (unserviceable).

Before the rest of the supply Squadron arrived, things were quite relaxed, we were getting to know each other, would have a good chat in the bar at night, they were nice fellers and made us outsiders welcome.

Back in our accommodation things were a bit cramped. I know I snored a bit, one night I got woken up with a boot thrown at me, I looked up and it was Baz, I picked the boot up and was going to throw it right in his face, I didn't let go but is face was a picture. Something had to be done; the answer was for me to find a pit space in the warehouse somewhere. I asked the boss, and he said it was OK; so I found a place and surrounded myself in boxes of television sets, it was ideal.

Time waits for no one, the rest of the Squadron arrived but without the SSM. They had a lot to do as now they had a backlog of orders to sort out. I was told that their job was to supply all the units in Bosnia with everything they needed, like parts of vehicles tank tracks in fact anything an army would need, this is why it was called the FRV. The army can't run without it. We started doing the parades every morning, it wasn't strict yet as the Squadron were running it themselves. By now there were about forty of us on the parade.

There was enough stock in the warehouse to last for a few weeks, it wasn't so busy yet, we would be getting our first delivery very soon. The deliveries would be a NAAFI lorry that would have to drive from Germany or even the UK. It was going to be a challenge for me on the Forklift truck as I was the main man.

One evening all the senior ranks arrived and now we had to behave and observe the two can rule. Next day the SSM did his first parade, he told us that we would have to be in three ranks at 0800 every morning, he expected a good turnout, as he would be looking for people to do extra duties. He explained that he was not going to do an inspection every morning, but random ones. This actually worried me a bit, as when I was attending a parade with the Cheshire regiment, just before our deployment to Belize, the RSM specifically picked on the TA volunteers to march them to the guardroom. If a button was undone or boots weren't up to scratch anything; they were picked on. I was lucky, probably because I was a bit older than the others, he passed me by. The ones he did pull up were marched off for a beasting that I had never witnessed before. Making the poor lads run around with rifles or artillery casings over their heads around the parade square until they dropped, it was not a pretty sight to see hardened men crying. From that day I would absolutely dread a parade with the army. Another thing we had to do was fitness training every evening as we were going to have to do a BFT (basic fitness test) in a couple of months' time.

The delivery from the NAAFI was going to be every Wednesday; this would probably be only one lorry. Now the time had come, this was going to be a great learning curve for me. The lorry backed up to the loading bay in the main yard, I would simply have to pick up the pallets with the Forklift truck, then take them to the main door of our Warehouse, drop them off, for Baz to pick them up with his reach and tier, to be put away on the shelves, in the warehouse. Some of the shelves would be quite high. The reach and tier is exactly as it says. This all sounds easy, I found that the more pallets I picked up the deeper I would have to go in the lorry next time, I found this was not for the faint hearted, as it was dark and creaky, I thought that I was going to go through the bottom of the lorry. I had to be careful that I put the forks under the pallet and not into it. Some of the pallets contained TV sets or sound systems, broken beer crates made one hell of a mess.

The first few weeks were all about learning the ropes and luckily it wasn't too busy, we got into the routine of working all week and have a half-day Saturday then be off Sunday.

The parades were going ok with the SSM, only picking on trivial things, we would be in the usual three ranks and he would just walk around us, one day we were in for a shock the SSM shouted ' *In open order right dress'*, this was not the first time I have heard this, as we used to do it in the TA. We would be in the usual three ranks upon hearing the order the first rank would do one step forward, right arm up onto the shoulder of the soldier next to you. The middle rank would stay where they are and be in line with the soldier in front of him or her. The last rank would do one step back and be in line with the soldier in front now everyone should be looking to the right, with arms on the shoulder of the soldier on your right, and you would wait for the order '*eyes front*' sharply look forward and arms to the side and you would be standing to attention. This first one was absolute bedlam, I couldn't help looking at Ruth's face, it was in utter disbelief, she didn't have a clue what to do or where to look, the poor thing, to be fair on her she hadn't done any drill before.

Another unfortunate thing about Dalma was that we had a little shop just outside the big doors; it was in a converted steel ISO container with a door and a window. It had to be open every day and of course my time came along. We sold all sorts like sweets pop cigs and other essentials. My shift started off quietly selling random things, all of a sudden a large group of Indian soldiers arrived and they were so awkward, one in particular was being a pain wanting to look at things but not buying, the queue was getting bigger, he wanted to look at cuddly toys, I told him to hurry up as he was holding everybody else up ' I am wanting to make a purchase' repeatedly in his Indian accent, I suppose the British soldiers in the queue were finding it all amusing. I told him to get out and took the cuddly toy off him, I literally threw it in the corner.

Something else happened that day which I have deeply regretted since. A civilian man and woman came into the shop and asked to buy 200 cigarettes, I refused them because they were Croatians who, they not really allowed to buy any tax-free goods, they practically pleaded with me, but I still refused. I went to see Neil in the office, I asked for his advice, he told me if they were locals not to serve them, I asked "how do I tell" he replied, if their names end in ch, they are probably Croatians. They left with utter disdain in their faces. I thought about it later and I started to think that the cigs were not for them, they could be used for bargaining tools for some reason, who knows? I know I should have called them back and sold the cigs anyway. The next morning, I was called into Niels's office, I was told that Luke had complained that I had left the shop in a mess.

The second delivery arrived and by now we were all getting more competent and understood what our jobs were, my skills on the Forklift truck had improved a lot. One thing was new to us though, we had to check the delivery off to make sure that we received everything that we were billed for, it would upset the computer system if it were wrong. This initially was a painstaking task, as we had to find the item listed and match it with the product, Neil could then accept it and input it into the computer and therefore be able to issue it out. Some things were simple like cases of pop sweets or chocolates.

Ruth was struggling with one of her items, she was looking for orange digestives; we often would have special edition goods. Now we were all in search for these packets of orange digestives, turning everything upside down. Someone decided to check her invoice and noticed that what we were really missing was *orange Rennie digestive*.

After a few weeks all the Squadron were in theatre, they insisted that we do everything that they do which was not a bad thing, as we were invited to their BBQ every Friday, also invited to their fitness programme. Every evening after work we would have to go out for a run out of the Warehouse and around the local village, by now it was hot and smelly, I had realized, the snow I had seen on the mountains was just the reflection of the moon. At least we had found some local shops around the area what I didn't need was some old lady shouting at me 'schnell' while I was struggling by, but maybe this was a first sign of what I was to learn about the reality about this awful war.

We had all settled into the routine, Breakfast- parade- work- lunch at 1200, then we would shut the big metal door and go to the cookhouse. The food was great, the usual pies fishfingers etc., all served with chips on paper plates, simple just eat and throw away the dishes. The big problem now was as the temperature was rising, flies were getting more abundant. I wouldn't dare leave my table place because the flies would be on my food in seconds. Back to the Warehouse for the afternoons work, then change into running gear for a hours run around the village; to be honest sometimes it would be a walk, this is where I would learn my first Croatian words. I was walking with one of the Squadron boys, he said Dobra Dan to a local, I had a good idea that it meant Good day; he confirmed that when I asked. Back to the Warehouse for a shower and then to dinner, which was the best meal of the day. As we had Ghurkhas naturally there would always be a curry on offer, nothing-wasted bones and all. I wasn't too keen on the goat curry but that is discrimination.

The girls were finding the demands of the Warehouse a bit too much; they were given the chance to run the shop, which they did, much to my relief.

In the evenings I would go to the bar and have a chat with the Squadron lads. One evening a disturbing subject came up; they were talking about the coffin that was in one of the rooms of the Warehouse, for some reason they thought it was a source of amusement, one of the boys, had even got into it. I never saw the coffin myself, but I did wonder what the hell is a coffin doing here, there is no war where we are. Such is the naivety of the British people; more of this subject will come up later.

Things were going great in the Warehouse; the work wasn't too hard I was going great guns with the Forklift truck; I even had my own system of taking the rubbish out of the Warehouse with little effort.

One thing worse than unloading lorries- that was loading them. The ISO containers were no problem as they were easy to load, there was no rush for them, and they were static on the ground. This would be a two or three-man job Baz was the main man with this job because he had the experience, so he taught us how to do it. We got to know that these containers would carry ten pallets, they had to be put in a certain order, the heaviest pallets would go in first so it would be cans of beer or pop. I would drop a pallet in the container with the Forklift truck, then it would be maneuvered with a pallet truck which was quite an art, simply pick up the pallet and do a 180 degree turn on the spot, it wasn't that hard to do, the next pallet had to be put in the opposite way, or else all ten pallets wouldn't fit. When it came to the last two pallets they were simply put into place and then shunted in. the last thing that needed doing was to pack empty pallets so you could only just about shut the door. A padlock and seal would then be put on the container, then the key would be given to the driver.

One day the boss came up to me and told me that the RSM wanted us to contribute to the regiment's guard duties, a good thing was for someone to be the duty Corporal in the guardroom. It would be a 24-hour duty; he told me that I had been picked for the task. It would be in a couple of days' time, when I finished I would be able to have the morning off.

Meanwhile I was getting annoyed by this woman in the Warehouse, she was everywhere that I was, loud mouthed, I couldn't get away from her, I hated her.

The stud-lies, as they liked to call themselves, loved her because she couldn't say a word wrong, her name was Celine Dion, they played her nonstop, I hate her music to this day. We had a Bose surround system; it was so loud it filled the warehouse even at half volume.

Baz decided one night that he was too good for the bar and wouldn't bother going there again. I don't know if it was because he had a bit of a scrap one evening. One of the regulars had a go at him, well Brian is over 6" and a big bloke, he punched the bloke once and he went down. Baz stopped going to the bar and anything he did Luke did.

We were allowed out in the evenings, providing we booked out at the guardroom when we left and booked back in before curfew time of 2200, not one minute later. A few of the soldiers took their chances and got caught, then charged; they were then sent home, I doubt that their wives were so happy about it. We were allowed to go out to the local town of Stobrec'. It wasn't too far from DWC, a twenty-minute walk once we booked out from guardroom, out of the main gate then onto a road that led to the main road, Split to the right and Dubrovnik to the left. Straight over, then we would come across a leisure complex, well that is what it used to be; now it is a refugee camp, not surprisingly the occupants didn't seem to be enjoying their holiday. Now we were on the coast and would come to a ww2 defence bunker to the left of this was some derelict hotels and empty swimming pools, to the right a few bars, of course not too busy and awaiting better days.

On Sundays we would spend the day on the beach, in the evening go to the bars drinking pivo. The locals were ok with us; we never had a problem. Indeed, we knew we could leave our possessions, go for a swim with the absolute confidence that the locals would not touch a thing. One thing I learned quickly was that the oldest boy's name was Mario and the eldest girls name was Marina, that is all the names we ever heard being shouted.

At one time we were walking back from the beach, we stopped at a bar for a bottle of beer, sitting minding our own business and a shaven headed guy came along and approached us, muttered something in Croatian, he must of known we were British, he said "welcome to Kroatsia (sic) many times, even in the early days I knew that Croatia to the locals was Hrvatska, it was all in good humour though, he had probably been drinking, he was no problem and left us, then went on to harass a few girls sitting near us.

On the Saturday after we had done the morning shift, we were able to go into Split. The old town was so beautiful and immaculate, no doubt in my mind it had a Roman history after all Italy was only just across the Adriatic. All the buildings were made of white marble and the streets were cobbled. In the city centre

there were exclusive shops and bars, even a peep show?
The harbour was busy with passenger ships, embarking and others disembarking I wondered where they were all going; it was so frantic. I remembered all the islands we could see on the approach to Split airport. Not far from the city centre there was a market, the first thing I needed was a pair of sunglasses, there were many stalls. I started browsing, in one particular stall I tried on a pair, there was a lovely girl running the shop. She said "Dobro", I had a good idea of what it meant, she was a fantastic salesgirl, I bought the glasses,. The few little words of Croatian were coming together, Dobro is male, and Dobra is female, to me the simplest way to remember is a girl wears a Bra. Next thing I needed was a t-shirt, there were plenty of those stalls around and instantly one caught my eye, there was a picture of a shark on the front, on the back the words BIG BLUE BEAUTIFUL CROATIAN SEA. No hesitancy in buying that one. I was looking to buy presents for my sister who lived in Bristol; I was also very fond of her mother-in-law, so I wanted to get her something as well. There were two of us that had split from the larger crowd, Ruth and Myself. We came across a plate stall; I thought this would be perfect, the vendor was talking away to us and a plate caught my eye, I asked if I could look at it, I liked it so I asked how much it was, remarkably something had appeared on the vendors head, Ruth was sniggering, I thought it was blood maybe; he hit his head when he

picked something up. I bought the plate, and we went on our way, I asked her why she was laughing, she said I was a bird dropping.

There were a lot of bars to choose, all the beer was sold in glass bottles, no draught for some reason. It was fine with me in DWC all the beer was sold in cans and there were no glasses. There were plenty of restaurants around, most of them specialized in pizza that was also fine with me. The only trouble with going to Split was that we had to be back before the 2200 curfew, this didn't stop some people though, they would climb the fence risking getting shot, this included one of our staff.

My duty came around, I had to report to the RSM at 0800 I wasn't the guard commander though, just the duty Corporal so I was free in a way. Unfortunately I had to keep an eye on an idiot who had been charged and was in detention, he had to be escorted everywhere, unfortunately I had to march him to the cookhouse, it was so embarrassing, I got out of step at one stage and the clown said to me 'do you want me to show you how it is done. In his little mind it would be funny, it would look like the prisoner was marching the guard, it didn't work with me I suppose some EFI idiot would fall for it. At around 1700 I had to report to the RSM for a briefing, it was simple really I was in charge of the security of the camp while he was off duty, " you are the RSM this evening" this was the closest I would probably ever get to being an RSM.

One of my duties was to go to the bar to make sure, all was ok; I had to go there at 2200. I had to tell some mouthy sod to leave the bar, he uttered something, thinking I didn't know what he said, he mentioned STAB which is a regular army acronym for Stupid TA Basket, he then ran off, I chased him down the corridor and shouted at him to stop, much to my amazement he did, I gave him a mouthful, then told him to eff off.

Luckily the rest of the evening was quiet, I knew there were people still out who were going to climb the fence to get back in, they were not a security threat, so I was not too bothered. I had my breakfast in the morning and then waited for the RSM to relieve me of my duty. I went back to the warehouse and the boss said I would have to be up at 1200, go to lunch and start work at 1230. To be honest it would have been better if I had gone straight to work and not go to bed, I felt like Sheisser when I did get up.

From then on I disliked the bloke. I knew what the self-named studlies were up to and he was colluding with them.

There was a new arrival at DWC, and it wasn't one of our Sqn, but to the transport Squadron, I knew the bloke well, as he was a son of a good friend of mine, Don in Swansea. He was only just passed 19. He had recently joined the army; it so happened his first posting was at DWC. It was such a young age to be driving a lorry into a war zone, he was also working with girls, who had to do the same; I respected them so much. As happened, the Welch fusiliers were passing through DWC on their way up to Gorazda in Bosnia. Of course, I got friendly with them in the three days that they stayed with us. Sadly, for them one of their soldiers had recently died of a heart attack, it was obvious that they were deeply upset. They told me that he was a lovely bloke; he was only in his early forties. I got on great with them and was sad to see them go. Little did I know at this time everything was about to go pair shaped.

SILENCE IS GOLDEN

Unluckily for the Fusiliers when they arrived in Gorazda things had turned nasty. The Serbs had just taken over the town, so they we forced to take the Fusiliers prisoner. I couldn't believe that the boys that I had been talking to a few days before were now on television.

They were all eating something the Serbs had cooked up for them. To be honest they had the typical Squaddie attitude of not giving a fig. **Postavanje** Sparkie.

Youtube link (v=V_7cblzRO0) Bosnia British hostages.

Their captors were obviously treating them ok. The Serbs said that they would look after them and no harm would come to them.

The British said that they were going to send a Battle group to Bosnia to rescue the Fusiliers if they had to. This event soon turned into a crisis. We could tell in the warehouse within a week that things were getting busier, our workload turned into reasonable to ridiculous. It was decided that we were now going to have to work 12 hours a day seven days a week to keep up with demand. Before the recent events we were getting in a routine of going to Split on Saturday evening and to Stobrec' on the Sunday, just lying on the beach all day, then going to the bars in the evening but the good times were put on hold.

Although things got harder we had new customers which included an Engineering Regiment, they were ordering about twelve pallets of goods a week, I really had my work cut out, but they were good guys, they were worth it. There was a flip side however, a REME Staff Sergeant came up to me and asked if I would put a small pallet on the back of his hired transporter van with my Forklift truck, there was not a great deal of goods on it he was just being lazy. Unfortunately for him I damaged his back door, and he wasn't too happy about it. For the next few weeks he kept complaining, saying his Squadron had to pay for the damage because of me. He couldn't help but to say to his friend with him "these guys come out here and make a lot of money, and we can take it back off them". I was only doing the bloke a favour and it went wrong. I hope he eventually recovered from his ordeal.

The crisis with the Fusiliers and the Serbs was going on for weeks, I was still seeing pictures of my friends on Serb TV via BFBS.

I was so busy on the Forklift truck it was ridiculous all I kept hearing was people shouting out Taff- Taff – Taff, my only redeeming factor was that I was about to go on RnR soon, it couldn't come quick enough.

Things were getting worse in Bosnia, a crisis had developed in Gorazda, and the Serbs were warned that if they harmed any soldier they would be bombed. The Battle group had been set up in Bosnia; we were struggling to cope. One day though we had relief and four more staff were sent out to us; our burden was lifted somewhat.

The day of my RnR had arrived; we were civvies again for two weeks. First thing to do was to have breakfast then go to the admin office to get travel warrants. A bus was waiting to take us to the airport at Split where of course we would check in with the RAF and drop our bags off. After this procedure we would end up in the departure lounge overlooking the runway and wait for the incoming aircraft.

It's a silly sort of thing but I suppose it can't be helped. Obviously the returning troops would get off the plane, they would have to pass us to get out of the airport. Their faces would be down to the ground, a lot of banter would be directed at them, but we all knew that in two weeks we would be in exactly the same position, but for now who cares.

I was so glad to get away from the bedlam of DWC. We would have to wait a while for the Tri-Star to be refueled and cleaned it seemed an eternity. It was now midsummer, and Croatia was roasting, it was nice to get on the air-conditioned aircraft. We tend to think that FRY was a long way off, but the reality was the flight was only three hours. Our flight was not going to Brize Norton but to Stanstead, where a coach was waiting to take us to Hullavington.

I decided that the best thing to do was to go to Bristol and stay at my sister's house, as it wasn't too far. Next day make my way to Swansea.

There were buses laid on for us non-permanent staff, taking us to Swindon Rail station. From Swindon I got the train to B.T.M, then a taxi to Linda's house it was so lovely to see her. I managed to get a few cans of beer from the local shop, we had a chat, and all the family went to bed.

It then struck me, **the silence the beautiful silence**, oh my god I have never been so happy to be on my own with no noise, no hearing Taff- Taff- Taff, it was bliss. In the morning, I opened my luggage to get the plate out for Pat, it was on top of everything in a hundred pieces thanks to the RAF handlers. After saying goodbye to the family, I got a taxi to BTM then a train to Swansea.

My friend Pete let me stay in his house, but all available was a couch downstairs but I didn't care. At the beginning of RnR two weeks seems a tidy time. I soon got back in the routine of my local the White Rose seeing my old friends. Pete my Landlord had arranged a Gower run, which was basically a pub-crawl around the Gower. Some of the guys would drink all day, happy in the knowledge that beer was food and they wouldn't eat anything; those days were over for me I had to eat. I had a good day out with some hardened drinkers.

Before I knew it the days turned into a fortnight, and then it was time to go back Croatia. There were mixed feelings about RnR, some people say they don't want it, some say it is a waste of time it breaks up a routine. It brings great expense to the military but tell that to the kids.

Some poor souls were forced to take RnR in the first few weeks, making their tour seem longer, well five months without a break. One good thing about RnR is that if you didn't get along with someone at least you will get a month without him or her.

It was going to be a long day travelling to Hullavington, before I got to the railway station in Swansea I bumped into a friend of mine, Terry, who happened to be a Professor at Cambridge university. He was on his way back to Cambridge, he always stopped off for a pint in the Adam and Eve, before getting his train. I thought it would be terribly rude not to join him.

Terry and my other friend Don Collier were war kids, and they often told me stories of their escapades in the war. Terry told me of the times when he would sit on Mumbles hill watching Swansea burn. Don told me of the time in the blitz when some German plane dropped a bomb and only killed a cow causing much distress to the farmer. Don also told me about the time he sneaked into the US army camp, found the kitchen, there he stole a tin of butter and then got chased by some angry Army cook.

One way or another I got back to Jims's house in Hullavington, Luckily Jim was on RnR the same time as me and he invited me to stay the night before we were taken to Stanstead, I was looked after in a fine Scottish way **Postavanje** Jim.

It was an early start to get back to Stanstead. I was told the reason we didn't go to Brize Norton was that the main Army Regiments were from East Anglia. At least we didn't have to stay at Gateway house in Brize Norton.

Over the Alps and Venice and out to the Adriatic and make our way to approach Split looking at the beautiful islands in the deep blue sea. I swear that we never landed at Split runway it was more of a thump. It was now our turn to face the cruel reality of our return to FRY. Our faces down to the ground with banter being thrown at us, they knew in two weeks' time it would be the same for them, but for now, they didn't care. It is strange you dread going back, but you have got new friends now and it is nice to see them.

One thing I did dread in the mornings was the awful parades, even though this was only at Squadron level. Especially on a Monday where I would usually have a hangover.

Every week the SSM would have a different duty Corporal to call the parade to attention. Sometimes he would have an inspection, one particular day an MT fitter was on parade with us and the SSM asked him why he hadn't polished his boots, he replied that he had polished his boots but there was diesel on them, the SSM said back to him "well I use boot polish on mine". I dreaded these parades so much that when I was on RnR, I went to see my doctor and got prescribed Beta-blockers to calm me down.

I soon got back in the routine of the warehouse, luckily no one had stolen my job as the forklift driver. In time you get to know your customers, I must say most of them were great. There was one in particular that was a pain. He was a Turkish officer he was a fussy man; he seemed to think that the world revolved around Turkey, you either loved him or hated him though I couldn't think of anyone who liked him. A troop of Kenbat (Kenyan Battalion) turned up at our warehouse one day, bless them although it was +30 they were all wearing woolly pullies and they still were cold. Some of the customers i.e. the Engineers would bring their lorries to be loaded. By now I had perfected the art of getting the pallets on to their lorries, the one thing I could not prevent was the bottles of Beck's beer rolling down the road. The Germans would use as little packaging as possible this made their crates weak and they would split easily, especially if they were wet, it was a nightmare. Richard the son of my friend Don would come to collect his Squadrons' goods, he told me one day, he was very popular because they always seemed to have more than they ordered: strange that one.

The war was hotting up in Bosnia, Nato had bombed the Serbs for violating something they had made up. Then the Fusilier hostages were released with no harm done to them, although some of them did need counselling. And then there were reports of a massacre in Srebrenica.

Apparently the Serbs artillery was in Range of Split, they were told that if Split got bombed the Croats would in turn bomb Belgrade, it's a worrying feeling when you know you are within a killing zone.

The warehouse resupplies were now getting three lorry loads a week, as soon as the shelves in the warehouse were filled they would start emptying again. The four new members of staff were a godsend, I don't think we could cope without them. We were able to go out a bit more and even able to have Sunday off again.

Unfortunately, Baz took a dislike one of the guys. On one occasion Corporal G started answering back and it turned into a bit of a scuffle, he knew he wouldn't be a match for Baz but threw a token punch at him, then Baz said " is that the best you can do" just to humiliate him more. There was no hope of the boss intervening, as he would always take Baz's side, as he did with me on a few occasions. For instance, when I would have to do another duty Corporal shift. I asked him why? he came out with some bullshit. I found the new guys ok at least they were sociable unlike the studlies who had self-banned themselves from the Junior Ranks bar.

Walking back from Stobrec' one afternoon after a few Pivos Corporal G picked up a Gecko that seemed quite happy to stay on his hand, he comes out with "A Gecko is for life not just Christmas". Talking of pets Ruth was looking after some pups but as they were growing up she couldn't manage them anymore, they become a nuisance, one happened to urinate in someone's room and ruined a carpet, a Sergeant decided to kill them all, this ruined Ruth's day.

The Ghurkhas were a lovely bunch of men but sometimes their antics were a bit funny. They would have a goat kid and walk him around on a lead, soon the kid would grow up and get to trust the Ghurkha and would follow him around without the need for a lead, that then was his death knell, as he would soon end up in a curry.

I have always loved a curry but the goat curry I really didn't appreciate, as the bones were included, well of course in Nepal nothing goes to waste. One evening in the bar a Ghurkha bought a pot noodle, filled it up to the line with water, waited for a while and looked surprised that the noodles hadn't absorbed the water, he waited ages for it to soften, the problem was that he filled it up with cold water. A crowd of Ghurkhas were walking along the delivery ramp, for some reason there was an emergency escape ladder hanging about head height, one of the Ghurkhas was walking backwards, talking to his friends, it became clear that he was going to walk straight into the ladder, I was about to shout out to stop but too late 'crack' it must of hurt.

NEEDLES AND PINS

One memory I will always be fond of, we had a CSE (combined services entertainment) show, which was at a Royal Engineers camp, and the main attraction was the Searchers. I suppose a lot of people wouldn't have heard of the Searchers they were even before my time, but I knew a few of their songs like needles and pins etc.

The first act was a magician who was excellent especially when her top came off, I was thinking it was a pity her assistant's top hadn't come off as she was gorgeous, though she didn't leave much to the imagination. After that show was a dance troupe who were called under wraps and again the three girls were stunning, I didn't understand why they were called under wraps as they too didn't leave much to the imagination.

Of course, the highlight of the evening were the Searchers. At the beginning of their show the singer Spencer James said " I know what you are thinking, a bunch of old farts" then they rattled off hit after hit, by the end of the evening everyone was dancing on their chairs and clapping to 'sugar and spice, Sweets for my sweet' etc. they went down fantastically well with the crowd. Looking at the Ghurkhas they were really enjoying themselves, practically all of them were dancing, on their chairs, what a fantastic evening. The singer was practically crying at the end of the show because of the response the band got. Everyone started bowing down to the group and saying " we are not worthy" like a scene in Waynes's world, this was a film that was out at the time. Adding to that there was a thunderstorm going on outside. The fun hadn't finished yet though, when we were on the bus going back to Dalma the toilet door on the coach had broken. I looked up and Corporal G was walking down the aisle with the broken door taking it to the driver.

I always thought the Ghurkhas were really proud to be in the British army, but I found out this was not always the case. I was talking to one of their Corporals and he was telling me how bitter he felt at the way they had been treated, their pay was low, and they would not be getting a pension. He was telling me that his grandfather and his father both served in the British Army, when they left they got nothing from Britain. He told me that boys in Nepal had to walk to a selection camp, to get even a chance of an interview, sometimes it took days, even hundreds of miles, they could be turned away without so much as a cup of tea. The selection in Nepal was really hard as hundreds of them would have to go through a rigorous selection weekend, then only a handful of them would pass that stage, the remainder would then have to walk back home again; I bet some didn't even make it back, and that was even in the good days when the Ghurkhas had Infantry Regiments. Even his own unit the Queens own Ghurkha Transport Regiment was going to be disbanded on their return to the UK. You will never find no more loyal friends than the Ghurkhas and they were my friends, especially as I had an interest in learning their language. **Postavanje**.

DIRTY OLD TOWN

I was given a chance to have a break from the vigour's of the warehouse, as I could go down to a place called Ploc'e with Gary Britt, one of the relief staff, he was going to do a mobile (shop) for the troops  down there. They didn't have anything, only local shops that only had the basics of life. Gary had obviously been down there before on a previous tour, so it was lucky for the troops that there had been an incident in Gorazda.

Gary knew exactly what was needed for the trip; he filled the trailer with all sorts of gadgets. Of course it would be an early start. We hitched the trailer onto the Landrover, booked out of the guardroom then onto the TTTS road and instead of turning right as we usually did, we turned left towards Dubrovnik.

This was my first experience of the holiday side of Croatia, the main road was always high up from the coast, I could see little roads leading down to little villages and their harbours. Further along the coast there was a sign saying The Makarska Riviera. We picked a fine day for the trip Gary told me that this road could be treacherous, he told that a part of the road coming up a convoy was on its way down the coast and one of the lorries lost control, and veered over the edge onto the sea killing the driver. When we reached the scene I could easy imagine what had happened, the hill was so steep there was no way that lorry was going to stop. After a few hours Gary told me that we were approaching Ploc'e. All the way down so far it was all pretty coastline and villages, but it changed as this port was stinking.

We drove to a building that was unused but in good order, as happened Gary had a key for it. We unloaded the trailer and put all the goods onto a trestle table we had brought with us and made use of a unit in the building. A few soldiers came along and bought cigs beer and sweets. There was some interest in the digital cameras that were new to the market in those days, and to give Gary credit he knew what he was talking about when selling. In the afternoon things went quiet, so we decided to pack up and leave. A little bit lighter going back than we came down with. There was no way we could sell all of our stock, but you had to take plenty of everything.

As we were leaving the port we were involved in a road traffic accident, for some reason Gary had bumped into a car, which forced a head on with another car causing a fair bit of damage.

As it turns out the drivers of the cars were Croatian Marines, so their Military Police had to get involved. Poor old Gary was being interviewed by the police, so I decided to get in the back of our Landrover and took photos in case anything went wrong. Things were soon sorted, and we made our way back to Split.

`One week I was appointed by the SSM to be his orderly corporal, this meant that I would not have to be on parade with the soldiers but bring them to attention every morning. I thought it would be great to call an open order inspection.

Three mornings passed and the SSM didn't call an inspection on the fourth morning the SSM was late, so I decided to call the Squadron to attention, then told them to fall out. I waited for the SSM to arrive, he was ok about me falling the men out but this morning, he said that he was going to call an inspection, just my luck so in my term of orderly Corporal I didn't get the chance to do an inspection.

The supply Squadron had taken us in as one of their own. With them we did parades BFTs and on a Friday to give the cooks a rest day, there would be a BBQ. This would normally start in the afternoon with a bit of sport like five a side football. One of these fridays I was forced to play on the side of the cooks. I never professed to be any good at football, even when I was in school I loved football, but I was crap at it and today was no exception. We got a hammering from the supply Squadron team, and one of the Corporal cooks gave me a hard time, blaming me because they lost, I hope he eventually did get over it. I must admit that after a while I did get fed up of the friday afternoons. It might sound strange to refer the cooks as just that, the reason being in the forces you are not a Chef until you reach senior rank i.e. sergeant. On one weekend it was decided that we would have a Squadron sports day, and by this I mean a lot of beer was involved while we played table tennis table football and netball to name a few, we were divided into ten

teams and if I remember correctly my team came in at about tenth.

I forgot to mention that the QOGTR were also involved and they were outright winners in the netball. It was a scorching hot day and a good day.

Fitness was a big thing with the supply Squadron and we in EFI were not exempt. In the early part of the tour it was an evening run around the local town, to begin with I found it quite hard but at least my fitness had improved, and I even got to enjoy it. As the summer got hotter it was decided that we would have to go running in the mornings, so we had to get up really early. As our workload got heavier the boss arranged for us to do our own sports, when we had the time, which meant after work but it suited us fine. A group of us would run to the beach at Stobrec' go for a swim and then run back, well that was the theory, because it was fine running into the water and having a bit of a swim to cool down, when you get back out and start to run your legs feel like lead, making it hard to run, so we mostly ended up walking back, this was time consuming and we didn't have much of it. After four months we had to do a BFT and if you didn't pass this you would have to go on remedial PT, you were given two chances, the first BFT I failed with ten seconds lapsed the second one I just passed. This was good enough for the Squadron the girls were not so lucky.

My second stint at orderly corporal had come around and by the heartfelt kindness of the boss, he arranged it so I could start it after my day's work. I got to the Guardroom and signed in, luckily today there were no prisoners. I asked the RSM, who by the way was a Ghurkha, why it was me that had to do the duty again, he replied that he had asked for someone else but was told that I was the only one who could do it, say no more. The night passed with no incidents, so I went to breakfast before I finished my duty. The RSM took over from me at 08.00 and by the grace of the boss I was granted four hours of sleep, so kind of the grunt. The tour was nearing its end; again we talked about the coffin, earlier I didn't understand why it was there, now it was clearer, there were road traffic accidents, heart attacks, murders and suicides. It is hard to imagine how some people reacted to what they witnessed up country. There were some horror stories that we heard about. These were never reported about in the newspapers. Rules of engagement were of no help to some people. The worst side of humanity had been witnessed here. One thing I learned, the coffin served a macabre purpose.

There was a new phase in the Bosnian war now. The massacre at Srebrenica was fresh in the news. The Hvo had rearmed their army, regrouped and had taken much of their land back in operation Storm. The next phase was to take back the Krajina that the Serbs had taken and held, the main town was Knin, and it was not very far from Split. Apparently the only Serbs left there were elderly, and they couldn't leave. A couple of days after the Hvo 'Liberated' Knin a few of us went to the beach at Stobrec', it must have been on Sunday.

It wasn't very pleasant as we passed a platoon of heavily armed HVO soldiers, who were wearing scrim net bandanas, one of them looked me straight in the eye, not a friendly face, it wasn't a nice encounter. When we actually got to the beach it was empty apart from our British squaddies, they were sunbathing face down. The usual throng of locals was missing. I asked one of our guys what had happened, he then told me that the beach was busy, these soldiers started shooting into the water, making all the civilians scatter. They did not frighten away our soldiers, they stayed there defiant.

The brave HVO soldiers loitered around threateningly, they could have shot a few of our guys but I think the defiance made them think twice, although none of us were armed (not that I knew of). The HVO wisely left us alone. What they wouldn't know is that there was always a QRF (Quick Reaction Force) not too far away. Operation Storm was a decisive event.

There was a conference going on in Dayton USA. The most likely outcome of this would be a ceasefire; NATO would step in to keep the peace.

I spoke to the boss and asked him if he could arrange for me to get a posting to Germany after this tour. He obviously had influence in this as after a short while he told me that all had been arranged, I was quite happy about it.

One of the last major events was to be the medal parade, of course we would have to practice the parade and get our uniforms up to scratch.

The parade went well with no hitches and nobody fainted. Some of the soldiers would already have a UN peacekeeping medal so they would not get another one, instead they would get a much smaller no 2 medal. Well of course this was going to be my first. A high-ranking Officer inspected us, when he got to me he said, " you must have lots of those" (medals) I said yes sir, I didn't really, this was my first.

Before we handed over, we would have to have a stock check of the warehouse, it would be shut down for the day. On our last day the boss told us that he had a message from Colonel Smith, asking if Luke and I would do another tour, I politely told him to eff off, however Luke bit his hand off. Ruth and Kate went back to Germany. Luke and Baz went off into the sunset. I went home the Swansea and by now my bank balance was quite healthy and we were to get a £800 bonus for finishing the tour.

DON'T STOP BELEIVING.

While I was at home I got a letter from the NAAFI telling me that I was going to be posted to Gutersloh, Germany, in the middle of November. By the time came along I was not so keen on the idea. I was filled with anxiety and just wanted to turn back but I knew I couldn't do that; I just had to go through with it. My air ticket was to RAF Bruggen, I had to travel to Paddington by train then go to LHR via the underground, I was really feeling sick the entire journey.

It seemed an eternity before I got to Heathrow, when I checked in I started to calm down and accepted that there was no turning back. After a two-hour flight I arrived at RAF Bruggen, here I had been told someone would meet me after got through customs, of course this is what happened. The person was called Mrs. L; she was the big boss in HQ NAAFI Germany. I was taken to a NAAFI hostel in Monchengladbach. Normally there was to be a week's induction and for some reason I was told that I didn't have to go through that hell. Of course I would have to stay the night, I was shown my room and given some bedding. I was also allowed to use the facilities and have a few beers. I would be picked up in the morning and taken to the railway station. I had a little walk around, went passed the famous fish and chip shop, which was unique to Germany however it was closed. It was nice to have a few beers it helped me relax and get some sleep. Mrs L had told me that I had to meet her at 0800, I would be give my rail ticket and be taken to the railway station, true to her word she met me at the hostel and took me to get my train.

Everything seemed bigger in Germany even the trains. I didn't have long to wait for my train, which arrived precisely on time. I was in a six-berth cabin, which was empty, so I took a window seat. A little later two elderly ladies entered the cabin, one said something to me, but I didn't answer them, I got a look of disappointment, and they sat down. I later realized that they had said Gutenmorgan, which is of course Good morning, I was ashamed of myself.

The scenery at the south was stunning, getting more to the industrial north there was a stark contrast, what I noticed was the graffiti; everything but everything was painted, some were a piece of art, and some were just pure vandalism. This surprised me about my new German home.

Well after that long journey, that to me was not long enough, I got off the train at Gutersloh. Mrs. L had told me that she had given the person that was going to meet me my description. True enough when I got off the platform I was approached by a lady who asked if I was Miles. She told me that she was the manageress at Mansergh barracks where I was to be posted. Now this was a great relief to me as I thought that I was possibly going to a camp called PRB (Princess Royal Barracks) and to a facility called Club 47. This was probably a thought that was giving me anxiety.

We left the station and walked a short distance to her car, we got into her car, this is when she told me that Mansergh Barracks was home to an artillery regiment, and also Kings school.

We arrived at the camp gates; I noticed that security was a bit lacking. I asked the manageress what her name was, and she said "Just call me Mrs. M". She told me that I was going to be working in the kitchen to begin with. I asked her about Xmas and stated that I was promised that I would be able to take it off. She replied that I would probably have to work, as it was a busy time.

We have all got to start somewhere, it was early in the morning when I went down to the kitchen. We had to prepare for breakfast. A member of staff Steph was supposed to show me the ropes; I could tell straight away that he was not going to be much help. I had to learn how to cook breakfasts quickly, the NAAFI break is always at 11.00 and there would be a lot of hungry men around.

When the rush happened, Steph was in a hurry to get things plated up. I was appalled by the way they were doing things; everything was cooked fresh except for the sausages that were the first under the grill. Now this place was the king of portion control i.e. one sausage, one rasher of bacon, one egg, beans or tomatoes and of course toast. The process was to put a sausage on a plate, microwave a rasher of bacon (which I have never seen been done before); in seconds it was cooked it did look a bit raw though. Add a ladle of beans, fry the eggs and add a cup tea. I thought these men must have been starving to want to eat these breakfasts, but it seemed to me this is Germany; everything was in a rush. Well at least there was little waste in the kitchen.

Things slowed down after the NAAFI break, Steph was still not interested in helping me.

At least I was given time in the evening to settle in a bit and to do some shopping. The NAAFI shop was ok, but it was very basic. I needed to buy a TV; Mrs. M said she would take me to the 'big NAAFI' on the weekend. My second day in the kitchen was hectic again Steph was supposed to help, now he was more of a hindrance. He did cook a few breakfasts, one person complained that he didn't have any bacon, that rasher of bacon was about 20% of the meal. So, I had to cook another rasher of bacon, I rebelled and cooked 2 pieces. I apologized to him and told him that cooked two pieces, I said, " for the price you pay, you should have two pieces anyway".

The first weekend couldn't come around soon enough. The canteen wouldn't be open, as the Squadron didn't work weekends, however the bar was open. On the Saturday I had the chance to walk around the camp. As with all army camps the place was pristine, it became clear to me that this must have been a German army camp, there were still signs in German pointing the way to the air raid shelters.

There was a football pitch near the main road; it was still a relatively small camp, in a populated area. So, It was off to the big NAAFI, PRB (Princess Royal Barracks) was pointed out to me as we went past.

We got to the NAAFI and indeed it was big and busy. The first thing I needed was a TV and an Ariel for it. I had a fair bit of money spare from my tour of Croatia. I decided to buy a large set and also some groceries, so at least in the evening I had something to accompany my cans of beer. I went to the bar in the evening; there were only two people there, the barman and a squaddie. Later the bar got a bit busier, Andrew (the barman) told me that it was usual, as the beer was a lot cheaper in the NAAFI than in town, the troops would get their fill then go into town later. Anyway, next week it was my turn to work in the bar.

One of my main reasons for wanting to work in Germany was to buy a motorbike, here they were tax-free for the soldiers, this included us NAAFI staff. There were all sorts of forms to fill out and I would have to send off for a German license. This was a relatively easy procedure; Mrs. M would help me out.

Of course, the main thing to do was to find a motorbike. I was told that there was a good bike shop in Bielefeld. On one of my days off I decided to set off and fulfil my dream. I needed to get an early bus; according to my map Gutersloh and Bielefeld were not far from each other, in all it took me two hours to get there, for some reason I managed to find the shop quite easily, being on the main road helped.

There was a good selection of bikes to buy. The last bike I had was a Yamaha xs250, which was adequate at the time. I needed something bigger for Germany, I thought a 750 would be too big for me. I decided to go for a black Kawasaki z500. Needless to say, I was unable to purchase the bike there and then. I gave the shop owner a deposit, all I had to do was to get the necessary documentation.

The law had recently been changed in Germany regarding number plates, up until recently you could get British number plates. An unfortunate incident had occurred where a British soldier had been murdered, by terrorists, they had been following him, it was highly likely that someone driving a car with British number plates, would be a British serviceman. You were able to get British number plated if you exported the vehicle back home. It didn't matter to me; any number plate would do. I had all the forms filled out and had to take them to PRB, to get processed by the NAAFI finance there.

My shifts in the bar passed without any hitches. There were three of us full time NAAFI staff who were living in, all the rest were soldiers' wives, they all worked part time. The only two exceptions to this were Lurch, the assistant manager, who happened to be Mrs. Ms husband, and Sam a five-star supervisor.

I was ok working in the kitchen and the bar, but I didn't have much experience with the shop. At the third week in Mansergh it was time for me to work in the shop, I knew this was going to be a challenge. The shop was busy straight away, but I was mainly filling shelves and helping Lurch. As we know the main shop was a few miles away, Mansergh shop was more of a convenience store. One morning Lurch decided to put me on the till it was not a problem until some customer produced a credit card, which was new to me. In Worthy Down and DWC we would use a swipe machine which embosses the card details onto a voucher slip, which makes a few carbon copies, this was crude but effective. I was stumped with this card, the queue was getting bigger and frustrated, so I rang the bell for help, an angry looking Lurch came onto the till and sorted things out, but that is all he did, he didn't bother to show me how to remedy the problem, he just disappeared naturally another customer came along and produced a Credit Card I tried to finish the transaction but I was doing something wrong, so I rang the bell again, this time no response. The queue was getting bigger and the faces angrier, in the end along came Lurch throwing a tantrum, he got another member of staff to take over from me.

After that, my main job was to work the bar six nights a week it was fine by me at least I could talk to people I could relate to. As happened, the NAAFI staff were not well liked.

I enjoyed my nights off when they came around. However, one evening I heard the phone ring underneath our living quarters, I heard Mrs. M answering, and all things went quiet. I knew there was something wrong, my instinct was to hide. I heard Mrs M shouting up the stairs, "Miles" ' I foolishly answered, "You are working tonight" no please or do you mind, I certainly wasn't going to get a thank you. I was beginning to regret coming to Germany. The woman who was supposed to work the bar went sick, that was what the phone call was about.

Christmas time was soon upon us and one morning I decided to have a look around the shopping centre of Gutersloh, it was not too far from Mansergh Barracks. It's always cold in Germany this time of the year, the reason I know this is about ten years previous I helped a friend who was a DJ. We worked in many an army camp doing the Xmas parties, it was a crazy time, and this was when BAOR was in full swing.

The cold added to the character of Germany; there were many stalls open selling hot food and beers, they certainly made an effort here in Gutersloh.

Mrs M came up with some good news, telling me that I was able to go home for Xmas, with a bit more luck a member of staff offered me a lift to the UK. I was so glad to be able to go home, at least I could get away from Germany for two weeks.

The time soon came along, and we and we started off early in the morning it was going to be a long Journey to the ferry at Calais. There was not much chance of any sleep though, I was in the back seat of the car, and I could witness the driving, the driver was in some kind of mad rush to get home all the time in the fast lane doing at least 100 mph, when he approached a car in front he would be up their rear, and would flash his lights until the car moved out of his way. Before we arrived at the Dutch border we went to a place called Vankum, which was the last filling station in Germany where you would fill up with petrol and use your fuel coupons. The next stop was the Dutch border where there was a service station, what astounded me about this place was that it was full of Gorgeous women; I mean every one of them was pretty. Then it was the mad rush to get to Calais, and nothing got in our way. The plan was to get to Reading railway station, there I could get a train direct to Swansea, this worked out fine.

Now I was on my own and would have to make my own way back to Gutersloh. This was a straightforward task all I had to do was get a coach back, in those days there were many of them daily. Well Christmas and the New Year flew by, and it seemed a non-event.

It was quite simple to get a ticket back to Gutersloh but there were going to be a lot of coach changes involved. The first part of the journey was to get the coach to Dover quite straightforward so far, just get onto the ferry and have a few beers on the crossing, for some reason it seemed a long passage. When we arrived at Calais things started to get a bit more complicated and by now it was cold wet and dark. I got on a coach and was assured that it would get me to Gutersloh, at least then I knew I was headed in the right direction.

Now I could smell the familiar smoke and cheap perfume. This was going to be a long bus journey, I didn't care I was in no rush to get back to Mansergh. We stopped off at the service station at the Dutch border, this time it wasn't as pleasant as on the way home. It was here that we had to change coaches, there were four to choose from all going in different directions.

In those days there were a still a lot of military garrisons and still two RAF bases. It all seemed chaotic but soon enough the massive crowd thinned out and I was directed to my coach and again, I was assured that it would take me to Mansergh barracks, this was going to take at least eight hours. All the while I was thinking that I should have stayed with EFI and gone to Bosnia, where NATO had taken over from the UN in the peacekeeping mission.

In my heart though I felt my mission was to get a motorbike and see the countryside of Germany. Eventually we reached Gutersloh where the first stop was PRB, most of the people got off there, and then onto Mansergh where by now it was early in the morning. I got into my room without anyone seeing me, I could have gone downstairs to see if I was needed for work, I decided to stay in bed, if they wanted me they could knock on my door, luckily no one did. I waited till late evening before I showed my face, by then it was too late to start work. Mrs M happened to be around, she told me that I was working in the kitchen in the morning, also I would be working the bar sometimes in the evenings.

It was as if I had never been away after a few days. In the afternoons I would go out for a walk, on one of these days I saw what this place was all about. I knew that the camp hosted an Artillery Regiment, I happened to be walking past a Squadron workshop and right in front of me was a Braveheart AS90 self-propelled gun  which was apparently very effective and accurate. Another day I walked past the playing fields and there was a large crowd despite the cold January day watching a football match I thought it must have been important, but I didn't get very close.

One morning I had great news from Mrs. M. She told me that I was going to be posted to Dempsey Barracks in Sennelager in a couple of days' time. Now I was quite happy about that, but it caused me a bit of a problem with the motorbike, how was I going to be able to get it delivered? I decided to make a journey back to Bielefeld and pay for the bike and take all the forms that had been sanctioned. I made my way back to the bike shop again, I give the manager the money for the bike, I also bought a biking jacket and a pair of boots. I told him that I required the bike to be delivered to Dempsey Barracks, and he agreed; that problem was solved. One good thing about the NAAFI in those days is that they had a delivery system. When we moved they would allow us to put our things into boxes, they would send them to us, it would take a couple of weeks though, at least it was free and made life easier. I was soon off and given a train warrant to take me to my new home.

My father was posted to Sylt in Germany, when he was in the RAF, he often talked about the massive Philips display that was in Hanover railway station, as it happened I would be passing through and changing trains there. There it was, larger than life right in front of me, of course I would have to take a few photos of it to show my father that I had been there.

The train ticket was for a place called Schloss Neuhouse, I arrived there and again one of the managers was waiting for me. She told me that I would be starting work there in the morning in the kitchen. She also told me that I would be the only male there, and there were another 15 staff. Some people might think this was a good thing, after a few days I realized it was not. I was taken full advantage of, if there was any heavy lifting or dirty work I was always called out. I soon realized that this place was not any different to Mansergh Barracks and in some ways it was worse. As it happened though I did have a friend amongst the staff and it was Kate, who was with me in EFI at DWC, she was going to prove to be my window into the goings on in the NAAFI. She told me that she was asked to if she wanted to go back to EFI for another tour but declined the offer. She also told me that Ruth was posted somewhere near Gutersloh. I was also to be working in the bar in the evening, which wasn't such a bad thing as I got to know the squaddies; they were quite friendly to me, I mentioned to them that I was getting a bike; I was then invited to go out with their club when I was on the road.

After a few weeks at Dempsey, I was told by the bike shop manager that my bike was ready, it would be delivered to me in a couple of days. The main problem now was the weather, it had turned much colder, and it started snowing, this made me a bit nervous with having a big bike and the icy roads, I thought that I would come a cropper straight away. One of the squaddies told me I would be ok, and he would help me out when it arrived.

Well, the morning arrived when the bike was going to be delivered; I was told that it was going to be there at about 9 am. It was a freezing cold day, it was snowing, I waited outside the Barracks expecting the delivery to be on time, but I was wrong. I waited for two hours for the bike, that I was assured would arrive on time. I was cold and a bit peed off. I decided to ring the manager of the bike shop to ask him where the bike was. He answered the phone, I told him that I was still waiting for the delivery, I was shocked with his response, instead of apologizing that the bike was late he became very rude, raising his voice at me and abruptly told me that the bike was on its way; at about midday the van arrived. The driver took the bike out of the van, gave me the keys and to his credit he pushed the bike to my accommodation building. The squaddie that promised to help me arrived on the scene, got the bike and parked it up safely for me. I wasn't going to ride it until the ice had gone from the roads.

I had been at Dempsey for about a month, when the area manager gave us a visit. I asked him if I could have word with him. I told him about the way I had been treated by the staff, I asked him if I could be posted somewhere else or if I could go back to EFI.

They were not very keen on people leaving Germany to go back to EFI; he said he would see what he could do.

In the next few days the weather had improved, the ice had disappeared from the roads, but they were still wet, I decided to give the bike a bit of a run around the camp, with a bit of help from my friend. I soon picked up the confidence and was ready to go onto the road. We were entitled to petrol coupons, as we didn't have to pay tax on the petrol, so it actually cost next to nothing to fill the bike up. Of course, with a new bike I had to run it in, for a few hundred miles, it was a slow start.

After a few weeks the area manager returned. He did what he came here for with the manageress. He called me to one side and told me that the manager in the big shop in Gutersloh was looking for a store man, I said I was interested, he told me that he would have a word with him.

After shaky start besides the roads being icy, I started getting used to riding a bike again. Going out further and further every time, one of the most interesting places local was Schloss Neuhouse, by now I got to know that Schloss was a castle. Some of the soldiers asked me if I wanted to go out riding with them. They all had bigger bikes than me; indeed, one of them asked me why I decided to buy a 500 rather than a 750 I said it was a step up for me. It wasn't that I was ungrateful that I was asked to go out with them, they would mostly go out on the weekends, and I would be working. I also didn't want to hold them back, but that probably wasn't the case. It only took me a few days to run the bike in, I was really impressed with speed, it would reach 125 mph in a few seconds that was its top end though.

WHITE LINES DON'T DO IT.

After a week or so the area manager came back to visit us. He told me that the manager in the big shop in Gutersloh was offering me the job as storeman; it was mine if I wanted it. I told him that I would accept the job and was very grateful to him. He gave me two weeks to get my things together, I could then put them on the NAAFI transport.

My biggest problem now was, how was I to get my bike up to Gutersloh. Well, there was only one solution and that was to ride there.

It was a happy day when I left Dempsey barracks. All my things had been sent to Gutersloh, and the day came for me to make my way.

It wasn't a long journey to make but it happened to be a rainy day. Once I got out of Sennelager I hit the main Autobahn, it was a fast road, but it was quite safe, it wasn't the first time for me. I decided to take the direct route, a little bit on the Autobahn then onto Hovelhof head onto Kaunitz then onto Gutersloh.

On this day I was to learn a valuable lesson. I was doing about 60 mph when I changed lanes to get off the Autobahn I accelerated at the same time, I did this on a thick white lane marker, it felt like I was on ice, lesson learnt don't accelerate or break on white lines, especially when wet.

I got into Gutersloh, now my second problem was to find the big shop. I thought I would try the old method of asking someone. I stumbled upon some married quarters and asked someone at a bus stop, as it happened I was not too far away, I quickly found my way.

All I had to do now was to find the food store manager Mr. Tyne. I asked at the customer service desk, someone came along and showed me the way to the warehouse where I was introduced to Mr. Tyne. He told me that I was going to be driving the big green van delivering all sorts of things in Gutersloh and further. He took me into the yard and showed me the green van, I was astounded, as it must have been one of the biggest vans I had ever seen in my life, this worried me a great deal. I was told that I would be taking over the job from a person who was leaving in two weeks' time and he would show me the ropes.

I was introduced to the assistant manager whose name was Simon and his wife Deli, she also worked in the storeroom as an accountant. I could tell straight away that he was a decent bloke. I was to start work first thing in the morning. In the meantime, I was to be taken to the accommodation a few miles away in a hostel. I thought this was great not having to live in NAAFI accommodation. I pointed out that I had a motorbike with me so was told that I had to follow Simons car. We went for a few miles on a dual carriageway and turned right down a small road, there was a Honda motorbike shop where the hostel was above that. There was plenty of parking space for my motorbike. We went up some stairs, which were on the outside, there were two elderly men already in there who also worked for the NAAFI, Cedric and Clive, they told Simon that they would look after me and he could go. I said that I would see him in the morning. I was shown to my room, it was a tidy size, then the bathroom and the laundry. We then went back into the living room, I was shown the bar, and a fridge that was full of beer. The idea was that I could help myself and just write it down on a tab. I knew already that I was going to like this place. They told me that there was a pub just up the lane and a hundred yards on the main road, they also told me that there was another lodger living here, that he was a butcher, at the time he was in work.

The next morning, I took my bike to the big shop! That's what the staff and customers alike referred to be. Simon gave me a tour of the storeroom and explained what my job entailed. Like keeping the place tidy and checking stock rotation. Another part of the job was to check in deliveries and make up small orders.

Already my life was better, and I only had to work Monday to Friday. However, my main job was to drive the big green van, currently a man called Stan was working his notice. I had two weeks to learn the ropes.

Mondays were delivery days to satellite shops and to a few homes. Tuesday in the storeroom then Wednesday we would have to deliver items for the leisure department, which was next door to our grocery store. Thursday was delivery day and Friday back in the storeroom. There was one thing that was scaring me, it was the big green van it was massive and more like a lorry.

The first day Stan showed me the ropes we were to go to a place called Harsewinkle, just north of Gutersloh where there was a little families' shop that we had to keep supplied. There was one hell of a shock awaiting me, for the person running the shop was no other than Ruth from the warehouse in Split. It was a small NAAFI world.

Here the shop was on the second floor of a block of flats, so we had to take the goods up bit by bit it was difficult enough for two people.

The time I spent with Stan was very awkward; he was very bitter about the NAAFI for some reason. He told me that he was going to refuse to show anyone the job, but he seemed ok with me. He told me that when he first arrived in Germany he couldn't speak any German and had to learn very quickly. At least on the first day he spared me the turmoil of driving the monster. Wednesday though I would take over the reins and we would be delivering washing machines to customers. Most of the married quarters in Gutersloh were in blocks of flats, only the officers seemed to have houses. Now I was to learn something peculiar there was a phenomena that I was to discover, the heavier the washing machine the higher it would have to be delivered. I must admit I learned a lot on this day, and my biggest learning curve was to realize my best friend was going to be a sack truck.

Stans' two weeks' notice turned out to be a week, I never did know why he was so bitter about the NAAFI, I was soon to have a few ideas. In the short time I knew him I did learn a lot about the job, I was sad to see the last of him. Now the monster was mine.

One of my first jobs was to do a delivery to Harsewinkle. It was a hard slog delivering the stock as there was no lift and the stairs were quite narrow. the parking space was quite a distance away. Eventually I finished the task, and Ruth offered me a cup of tea, which I was not going to refuse. I went back downstairs to park the green monster in a safe place.

Returning to the shop it was catch-up time with Ruth. After about fifteen minutes I thought it was time to make it back to Gutersloh or they would be wondering where I was. There was one last thing though, Ruth gave me the cash box to give back to the cashier in the big shop.

A funny thing happened on this day, I was recalling talking to a friend of mine, Terry Mullins, while I was on leave in the White Rose in Mumbles. He was talking about an advanced driving test he did. Now part of the test was that he had to ad lib to himself so the examiner could understand what he was thinking. Now for some reason I decided to give it a try, I was talking to myself about what I was doing. "Looking in the back mirror", signaling to turn left, going down the road at fifty kph "looking in the rear-view mirror"'. Oh, my Mein Gawt, the back door of the van was open. I must have driven 5k with the back door open.

I stopped the van and looked in the back and luckily nothing had fallen out. The sack truck was there, the cardboard boxes, and other rubbish was there, then I realis
zed that there was something missing, The Cash Box. I turned everything over and realized that now I was in the proverbial Sheisser.

I got back to the storeroom and told Simon that the cash box had gone missing. Simon was ok with this, but he told me that he had no option but to tell the store manager, well at least I hadn't been sacked on the spot. The next day I went back to work in the storeroom, I was tidying up when Simon approached me, he told me that I had to report to the shop manager. Well, this is it then I am about to be sacked and on my way back to Swansea. I knocked on the manager's door and he shouted, 'come in' 'sit down''. what happened' I told him that I didn't know as far as I knew I had locked the doors. 'Do you think that someone had stolen the cashbox'? Of course, I couldn't tell him that I was chatting to Ruth. I told him that all I can remember is that I was driving back and looked in the mirror and the doors were open. I went back the way I came and there was no sign of the cashbox on the road, it would be easy to see if It had fallen out. Ok he said, ' I understand this was only your second week in the job and the cashbox only contained petty cash'. Well, that was lucky for me. "I have no alternative to give you a formal warning" he then told me to leave. A lesson learned. I didn't know and will never know what happened to the cashbox. Did it get stolen when I was talking to Ruth?

Did someone open the back of the van while I was stopped at the traffic lights? Why the eff was the back door open?

Things settled down and I started getting into a routine.

With the evenings and weekends off I felt I had more time on my hands, I had a few plans. I bought a new PlayStation and of course some games to go with it.

I also had plans with some trips on my motorbike, one was to go to Berlin, and another was to do my own personal dam buster raid of, course these would be on a weekend. The bike was so cheap to run, there was no road tax to pay. I had to go to PRB weekly to collect my petrol vouchers, which basically gave me about 80% off the fuel.

I was picking up the German language slowly, I would watch German films on the television, buy magazines, especially children's ones as it was very basic. I was quite friendly with the lady behind the counter in my local petrol garage, she could speak fluent English. One day I was getting low on petrol, I thought this would be a good time to learn a new word. I asked her what empty was in German; she replied Leer, some words you never forget. this would be one of them. A peculiar thing about Garages in Germany is the petrol nozzle; when you put it into the tank you can press a button, and it will carry on discharging until the tank is full then automatically stop. I wondered why they never used this system in the UK.

Gutersloh had a great traffic system at least on the main roads there would be a sign saying Grüne Weller, which I soon learnt, meant green wave. The speed limit around town was 40 KPH, now if you kept to this speed you would never have to stop at a traffic light as the green light would always be on for you.

The assistant manager in the leisure department told me that there was a motorbike meeting every Wednesday, he told me the Germans called it a Motorrad Treff. Sometimes there would be hundreds of bikes there, in peak season there would be thousands.

Workwise things were going well I got over my fear of driving the green monster, although there was a fault with it, as it kept cutting out and stalling.

I went Harsewinkle one morning and told Ruth what had happened with the cash box, I couldn't understand what had happened to it.

I said it might have happened when I was talking to her, but I think she took it the wrong way, and I was blaming her for it.

I liked Wednesdays as it meant I was out of the shop for at least half of the day. We would deliver white goods and the majority of these would be washing machines, and the biggest and heaviest of these would be Meille, it seemed that people that lived on the top floor of a high rise flat preferred them. Some of these flats had a lift and some did not, if they did it wasn't guaranteed to be working.

    A lot of handling these goods depended on who was my assistant. To lift a washing machine upstairs requires a bit of planning. I always had a sack truck in the monster, which is like having another helper. Two people and the sacktruck would make a good team but a good assistant was essential. A common mistake when pulling a truck and a washing machine upstairs is that the assistant would lift the machine, which would pull it off the sacktruck, and potentially lose control and it could cause expensive damage. The idea is to lift the sacktruck itself. Another thing to take into account is the assistant himself, if he is good it makes life easier but if inexperienced he could make things awkward by fighting against the puller and that was me, you know at the end of the day by the backache. At other times lady luck would play her part.

On one occasion a reliable assistant and I had to deliver a washing machine to a top floor flat, of course the lift didn't work, I had to take the old machine out and take it downstairs, it was no easy task. Then we had to take the new one up, when I got back upstairs the flat the customer said that I hadn't taken his washing machine away this, baffled me, he showed me his old one, what had happened was, his neighbor was throwing his old machine out and I took it out by mistake. Logically I thought I could leave the old one downstairs, but I couldn't, as it was not ours to move so I had to take it back up, a heap of work for nothing.

A PICTURE OF YOU.

On another occasion we were delivering goods and heading back to the shop, we came to a set of traffic lights, as I was turning right the light was on green, I moved forward behind a car who was also turning right but the Sweinne didn't move till the last second and the light's changed to red, I had to go as I was in the middle of the junction, suddenly there was a horrible flash, which gave me shivers down my spine. There is no doubt in my mind that the driver in front did this on purpose. Of course, when I got back to the shop I had to report the incident. I told Simon what had happened, his first reaction was to laugh, this was no sleight it was just his personality, and it was fine by me. He told me that this was a serious offence in Germany, and I would probably get a driving ban, I could then lose my job.

Soon I would be going home because I was told that I had leave to use up. A couple of days after the traffic light incident Simon told me that I had to report to the manager's office. When I got there I was given a document that had a picture of me driving the van and a prosecution will be following. Though the incident was serious there was a bit of humour attached to it, in that my assistant's face had been blacked out.

Apparently some relationships and marriages had been ruined because these documents had been sent to the recipient's address and the partner had opened the letter, revealing that the loved one had someone else in the passenger seat. I had to sign a form saying that I admitted to be the driver, the manager told me that the punishment would take a few weeks, so I could go home for a fortnight's leave.

HOME IS WHERE THE HEART IS.

For my journeys around Germany, I needed to buy a map, none better than a foldable map that I could put on my tank bag, that I had recently bought, of course it had a see-through cover. As I had already taken the journey to the UK as a passenger I had a good idea of the way home, it wouldn't be too difficult as most of it was motorway. I was advised that if I did 80 mph all the way it should take me six hours to get to Calais, although my bike was only a 500cc it was quite capable of cruising at this speed all day long. The bike could do about 120mph, but I could feel it loved being at 100mph. To begin with, driving on the right side of the road was a challenge, it soon became second nature.

I set off early in the morning with all my bike gear on, waterproofs etc. and the map on the tank bag. Of course, the first thing to do was to fill up with Benzin, as the Germans called it. It wasn't a bad journey the weather was good, and I did a comfortable 80mph most of the way, through Germany and to the border with Holland, of course stopping off at Vankum, where I filled up using the petrol vouchers, which would be sufficient to get me to Calais, it was a busy old place.

It was good to have a bit of a rest before the next leg to Calais. The roads were now getting busier in Holland, so I had to have my wits about me, a few hours later I arrived at Calais, where I had to find the ferry, but it was simple enough. I had to ride the bike on the ferry, the marshals led me the way and secured the bike. I thought to myself that I would have a few beers on the crossing as it was going to be a few hours at least. I waited out a bit and was glad that I did because before I knew it we were docking in Dover. Now I had to get used to driving on the left-hand side of the road again, not a great worry as it was mainly motorway again back to Swansea. I arrived in Mumbles at about six in the morning, I thought I would have quick look at the village. I was driving down the road, I couldn't comprehend why a car was driving straight at me, I quickly realized that I was on the wrong side of the road. I didn't have to worry about a place to stay as PG let me stay in my old lodgings, but I had to stay downstairs on a single bed.

Pete had pre-arranged a Gower trip, which was a day long drinking session. He had hired a minibus, and it was an early start, we were going to have lunch in one of the pubs. Not all of us though, because to some people, eating got in the way of drinking, one person even said, 'beer is food isn't it', though the driver said he didn't drink, he managed to sink a few pints along the way. It was a long day and a good day as it was nice to see some of my old friends. It didn't end there though as when we got back to Mumbles the second wind kicked in and the hardened drinkers carried on and that was most of us.

I thought that it would be nice to go back to Worthy Down for a visit to see my old friends, it wasn't too far as the weather was good, and I could stay the night in Bristol on the way back.

I got into the camp at Worthy Down no problem because I had a NAAFI ID. I made my way to the worthies' club and the first person I saw was Marge. We had a bit of a chat, she said that she had left my job open because she thought that I was coming back after I finished in Bosnia; I told her that I had a chance to go to Germany, then I could buy a bike that I had wanted for years. It was lovely to see Newage, she said that she was chuffed for me that I had got a bike. I stayed and chatted for a few hours then made my way back to Bristol. It had been many years since I last went to Bristol on a bike westwards.

Back in Swansea I was chatting to one of the barmaids in the White Rose, I told her that I had got a new bike. I said it was outside and asked her if she wanted to look at it, well if course she did, she was very impressed. I told her that I would take her out for a ride if she wanted, she told me she would love to. A couple of days later I kept my promise and picked her up at her house. We went around the Gower Worms head etc. and were out for a few hours. One funny little incident happened when I got back to Mumbles. I stopped off to fill the bike up at a garage, then went on to pay in the shop. When I came back out I put my helmet back on, also I was wearing a leather jacket. As it happened someone I knew by the name of Dai the farmer, a well-known character in Mumbles was filling his car up. I went up to him and said "we are greasers" his reaction was hilarious. I was expecting him to recognize my voice but he didn't. "Greasers by eff" he said and stopped filling his car and stormed off to the cashiers. He never did find out it was me.

The leave time soon passed and it was time to head back to Gutersloh. The epic journey went without a hitch and I was soon back in the hostel. When I got back to work the next day I had a surprise in store for me. There was another person being employed to help in the storeroom. We got introduced to each other, he told me that he was a pads brat, which meant that his parents were living in married accommodation, one or both of them were military. He told me his name was Yuan and he could speak a little German, that I thought would be helpful for me in the quest to become a master in the language. Another thing he also had a room in the hostel.

It was back in the old routine in the storeroom. After a few days I was told that I had to go and see the shop manager. He informed me that I had been banned from driving, for one month. It did seem strange that I had not been given an official notice of the ban, I presumed that a deal had been struck with the German authorities. I don't think the Germans had the power, to take a British persons driving licence off them, but hey it suited me. The manager told me that my job was secure I would just have to work the storeroom for a month, I had to hand my driving licence over to him. Who was I to complain? This meant that I had more time on my hands in the evening. I decided to buy a new playstation game and was advised that one of the best current games was called Resident evil. I found the game so addictive that I spent most evenings playing it. The last time I had played a games console was on a Sega mega drive playing Sonic the hedgehog. Now this playstation was a different kettle of fish. I was getting used to acquiring new weapons like the shotgun and blowing the heads off the Zombies even doing this with two Zombies with one round. I didn't find the game too frightening until one day when I was walking past a window, two rottweilers came crashing through a window killing me instantly. I thought I was getting the hang of the game but one night I got into a room and couldn't find my way out for six hours the cans of beer didn't help much.

I started going to the local pub with Clive and Cedric. I found it to be a nice pub and the locals were friendly. Frugie the landlord was the image of meatloaf. There was a great variety of German beer and I soon discovered Weisenbeer, which was made from wheat, and after a couple of Steins of this you knew about it or in some cases you didn't know about it.

Chris and Cyril had planned a trip to Amsterdam for a weekend and asked me if I wanted to go along, well why not?

The manager of the leisure store got wind of this one day and came out with the remark "why have you got to go to Amsterdam to get a woman". I thought to myself that it was not even worth bothering to tell the anusol that was not the reason why we were going there.

We made our way in Cedric's car; I was not too confident that it would make it all the way but he felt sure it was ok. We had to set off early on the Saturday morning as it was going to take about six hours to get there. Cedric found his way, all the way to the suburbs, he wasn't too sure of the rest of the way. We stopped in a lay-by and tried to figure the way. A lorry passed us and Clive had the bright idea of following it. I said to Cedric that the lorry could be going anywhere, so don't take any notice of him. I was glad that he heeded my warning because we certainly would of got lost, as it happened a bit further up the road there was a sign for the centre. We found our way to central Amsterdam and Cedric parked the car up. I now had to find a place to stay as C& C had already booked a hotel. It wasn't too long before I found a Pension, which I learnt on the continent, was a cheap boarding house. This was fantastic I had found a big room at the top of the building  with a fantastic view.

I had a shower and a change of clothing, then went to find the hotel that the others were staying in. We were all pretty tired so we decided we would only have a few beers, after all we had all day tomorrow.

Early on Saturday morning I did what I always did in a new place, went out for a walk with my camera. Well Amsterdam didn't disappoint as there were strangely dressed people, cats with bow ties on, bright coloured houses with odd shaped wooden windows and thousands of cycles. Of course the canals would be on my list so I had a stroll along then with my camera in hand.

I even went into one of the famous cafés and had a coffee I didn't want to start drinking too early. The first thing that struck me was the awful stench of cannabis smoke. I didn't stay too long to embrace the culture of the Hippies.

I had a good day out, then went to find the other two, we arranged to meet up later in the evening. Every bar we visited smelled of sickly stale cannabis smoke and the people who smoked it weren't much different. Amsterdam was as it said on the tin, legal cannabis smoking and the girls in the windows. Clive and Cedric went back to their hotel I presume, I wanted to stay out a bit longer. I went out doing a bit of window-shopping and there were some pretty women to be had on the streets, I didn't take one.

MOTORBIKING

With that adventure over it was back to the routine of the storeroom. Yuan was employed solely to help out in the storeroom. It turned out that he was good company after work, as we went out on our motorrads. He also knew Germany quite well and could speak a fair bit of the language. From the hostel there was a junction leading to the main road, here there was a set of traffic lights, we worked out exactly when the lights would turn green, because there was a crossing where the lights flashed 30 times, that was the cue. We must of terrorised some of the car drivers who out of the blue would have two motorbikes whizzing past them. Every Wednesday we would go to the motorrad treff, which was held in a big field. In this field there would be all sorts of bikes, choppers, vintage, scooters, big bikes, small bikes and all had one thing in common, a proud owner. Some Wednesdays there would be a few hundred bikes but in its peak in the summer one day I reckoned there must have been 3000 vehicles.
There would always be the show-offs thinking that the crowd were waiting for their grand entrée.

There was an unfortunate incident one evening, a soldier from PRB got killed. Odds are that at some time that there was going to be a fatality with all these bikes criss crossing junctions. Yuan had a friend who often rode pillion with him to the treff. One day I asked her if she wanted to have a ride on my bike, she was interested, to cut a long story short I borrowed a crash helmet, we went onto a main road I don't think she ever knew that I got up to 100 mph, anyway she enjoyed the ride. One evening there happened to be a lot of flies around, Yuan and myself mentioned it when we stopped off at some shop. Literally minutes later we had to slow down, I lifted my visor and in that split second a fly went straight into my eye and by eff it hurt, if I expected any sympathy from Yuan I was out of luck as he found it hilarious. Yuan asked me if I wanted to visit a monument, which was just past Munster so of course I was interested.

As we were both off for a weekend and the weather was good we decided to go for it. It was a good few hours away but it proved to be worth it. It turned out that it was a monument built for Keiser Wilhelm. I had never seen anything like this before or even heard of it. We had to park our bikes and walk up to the monument and a slog it turned out to be. At the top was a fantastic view of the beautiful scenery.

On a Sunday I would give my bike a clean, however one of those days Chris told me that there was a law  making it illegal to wash a vehicle on a Sunday.

Those days of biking in Germany were fantastic. The roads were perfect with no potholes anywhere. I would go out on a random bike ride and I knew I would find something interesting. Towns with strange names like  Groin, Fuchtorf and I even found a town named after my family.

It was a lovely summers day when I was riding through the countryside, I could see this vehicle in the distance coming in my direction it seemed a bit unusual so I slowed down as I passed, I realised what it was; an immaculate red tractor which was not so unusual in the countryside but the person driving it was, it was an elderly lady, I thought to myself that I couldn't let this go by without taking a few photographs. I immediately turned around passed the tractor, parked the bike and waited for the lady to pass me. It worked out perfectly and the smile on her face was terrific. On this day two absolute strangers made each other's  days. These things cannot be bought..

Everyday I had to go to PRB to collect mail and parcels for the shop. In the office there was this pompous ex officer who thought that he was still in the cavalry. I was told at a later stage that he was going to report me to the police because he thought he could smell alcohol on my breath.

Sometimes I would have to go to the bulk issue store (BIS). This is where units would get their beer. It was away from the main bases. Now this is where I got friendly with a giant of a man who was in charge of the place. I was told his name was John By The Way. One day he asked me if I wanted to meet up with him for a few beers, sounded a good idea so I said give it a couple of days time. Sometimes I would have to go to the Junior Ranks Club, which was called club 47, as the address of the camp was BFPO 47. It was notorious as a rough place. I had heard of this place when I was told that I was going to be posted to Gutersloh. If I had I don't think I would be writing this story now. PRB used to be RAF Gutersloh; they had recently deployed two of the Fighter Squadrons back to the U.K. The Army then took over the camp. Now at Gutersloh were the Army Air Corps and the RLC. One particular day I was to learn a valuable lesson. I was taking the green monster back to the hostel after a days work. I saw one of the girls who worked in the leisure shop and I asked her if she wanted a lift home, " Are you sure" she asked of "course jump in" I answered. She lived quite a distance from the shop so I had gone way out of my remit. On the return back to the hostel I stopped at a junction and in the distance I could see a lorry coming my way, it seemed safe for me to pull out. As I said earlier the van would cut out sometimes. I put the van into gear pressed the throttle and the bloody thing cut out, leaving me stranded in the middle of the road. Luckily the lorry swerved, narrowly missing me. I had nearly caused a serious crash. Ok the van started again and I carried on back home. The next sets of traffic light were on red so I stopped. Meanwhile the window was open and this bloke came up to me with his fists in the air and he was threatening to punch me in the face. I thought to myself that I have got a nutter here, and then I realized that this was the driver of the lorry that had just missed me. I tried to say sorry and out came ' enshuldi gung' he repeated what I had just said and looked bemused. The lights changed and I left the scene.

From that day on I promised never to go out of my way to help someone, because it will backfire on you.

My job was not all driving sometimes I would have to work in the shop storeroom. You would not dare break anything, as the food store manager would be down on you like a savage rottweiler, as if it was his money being lost. One day Yuan broke a bottle of wine, Mr Tyne came running out of his office ranting and raving. Yuan turned round passively and said "calm down I didn't do it on purpose" I had to give it to him as Mr Tyne had probably never been answered back.

The assistant manager Simon was a great guy; also his wife Deli worked in the office as an admin assistant. He told me that he was with EFI in the Gulf war. At this time there had only been one Gulf war. There was a cage that waste meat was kept, and in the summer the stench would be awful. Simon told me that in the gulf war that smell was constant. Most people don't understand what war is really like, you can't smell things in a film and you only see one side of the story and that will be the victor.

Although we only worked weekdays there was the option to do some overtime on the weekend, I would often see Yuan working on the tills. Sometimes I would help out cleaning the warehouse or doing a stock check. It was at this time I coined the acronym (N.A.A.F.I.) Nasty And Awful Effin Individuals. And there were a few around. Upstairs in the big shop were the offices and also a large canteen area desolated with plenty of seats and tables. There were also a few microwaves that were very useful for cooking bockwurst that I put in a crusty roll with plenty of mustard.

One day while I was working in the storeroom I had to get something from the walk in freezer, I was always wary of this, thinking how easy it was to get locked in there and be found days later stiff as a statue and with a terribly unhappy face. On this day I went into the freezer and minutes later the door shut so I shouted out, a young female member of staff opened it laughing as though it was a funny thing to do. A bit later I was back in the storeroom and Ian passed singing frosty the snowman of course he found it funny. What I felt like doing was to grab the girl by the hair and dragging her into the freezer and locking her in there for ten minutes. I resisted the temptation.

Another day there I was involved with a conversation between a few managers and I put in my opinion of the matter, the leisure manager said to me "who the eff are you, you are only a low-down storeman". And that was not the only time. I asked one of the girls if she wanted a ride on my motorbike and she was interested so I told her I would pick her up in a couple of days time. The only problem was I only had one crash helmet so I thought it would be useful to buy another for any occasion that would arise, so I went and bought a new cheap one. When I went to pick the girl up a few days later I went into the leisure shop and happened to see the manager he said, "that's a bit ridiculous to buy a helmet for the girl".

One evening I met up with John from the BIS on PRB, in a military clubhouse for a few beers. We had quite a good evening and a good chat. He said my surname is Bytheway but people call me John By the way. I don't suppose many surnames come out that way. He told me that he had a drink problem, one day he went to the doctor who asked him how much he was drinking, the doctor asked him how much he had drunk the night before, john told him two bottles. The doctor replied to this and said "two bottles of beer isn't too bad" "no not beer, vodka".

I learned from john that on the weekends you could go anywhere in Germany on the trains for a pittance. He asked me if I would like to go on a trip somewhere, of course I thought that was a great idea. I told him that Dresden would be a great place to visit.

HAPPY TALK

Wherever I go I like to try and learn a bit of the local language and I seem to have quite a bit of a gift in this area. Probably the first German that comes to most people is Bitte (bitter) then comes bitte sern . You hear this in all sorts of places like shops and pubs. A lot of people recommend that you buy childrens books and of course that was the first step I took. A dictionary and a phrase book are essentials, I also bought a little booklet named 5000 German words and another named 1000 German phrases. Good for things like Traum Frau – dream woman. And from this little book I learned my favourite of all time "Ich kan nurien bisien Deutshe sprecken" which means "I can only speak a little German", in the years I found this to be very impressive. Watching tv and the films or programmes was another path I took. One evening I watched a film it was quite sad and morbid. Fred ist tote, so I learned tote meant dead. Then Mord he was murdered. Every weekend I would stop off my local garage and buy TV magazines my favourite one always had the caption Alles Drin, Alles Dran, Alles Klar. I never found out what it meant but the last bit is obviously, all is clear. Another great way to learn the local language is to drink beer. One evening in our local pub I started talking to a local, with the little German I knew, and he couldnt speak much English either, but by the end of the evening we were communicating, it was at this time I realized that we talk a lot with our hands and eyes. At one time he mentioned 'mein auto' in my drunkenness I quickly deciphered the meaning. We arranged to meet again to further our conversation but unfortunately I drunk so much I couldnt remember when and where.

Some english and german words are so similar like vor (where) est (is) Das est(that is). I later read that english is derived from the German language. Now the strange thing is that the German word for window is Fenster it is very similar in Spanish French and unbelievably Fenester is welsh for window. I remember in the old commando booklets the Germans would often say schwein hund, that's easy- pig dog. Sometimes you only need one word for instance 'Berlin' put your forearms out and fingers turned up this obviously means 'where is Berlin' . you have to always be polite and learn the basics like bitte shern , enschuldegung =excuse me. Still if you don't even know any words at all , hands together like in prayer and head bowed , universal language.

You might think you are getting on in the language but you will get a knockback now and then. I was out on a bike ride one day and was making my way back to Gutersloh but I couldn't see any signs, I didn't even know if I was going in the right direction. There werent any people around and it was getting dark, eventualy I saw someone walking on the pavement. I stopped and got off by bike, waited for the man to approach me , I said to him "vor est Gutersloh" he didn't seem to understand me, I repeated it a few times, no joy. I decided to write the word Gutersloh on a piece of paper and handed it to him, he read the paper, looked up at me and said 'ahh GUERTESHLO' I am sure that he knew what I was saying and anyway he pointed me in the right direction and soon I was on the right track.

At one stage I thought that I was getting on quite well with my Deutsh learning, until one day I heard a three year old girl talk,I realized that I had still a long way to go.

Simon asked me if I wanted to join a darts team, although this was 'verboten' because management were not supposed to socialise with staff. This was a great help in learning the numbers obviousy if you a chalking you have got to think quick, or be made to look thick. I learned that when you had to think quickly your mind takes shortcuts, when you get to know the basics things get simpler. The Germans don't say the numbers like we do in the modern day, they say them like we used to in old English, for instance we say twenty three the Germans would say drei unt svanshish which means three and twenty. A spanner in the works is the Amluet for instance Gutersloh to us in english is straight forward but when you put two dots on top of the u, it changes the sound and the s is a sh.

Being with a friend who can speak german is a great help. Mark; one of the butchers in the big shop showed me around the town, he had been in Germany for a few years. After a few beers we went to get a Greek kebab shop, he ordered a giros and a flashen of coke. I said to Mark "flashen means bottle does it" ,yes he replied. And another time when we were out we we decided chicken was on the menu this day. He ordered halb ein henchen , half a chicken. These things stick in your mind.

Yuan could speak quite a lot of german but didn't profess to know it all. One Saturday evening we went to a disco in Beilefeld, we decided a great way to get chatting to the girls was to ask for a light for a cigarette. He told me to go up to the girls and say 'habben zi fire bitte', this I did but I got a negative response, in fact I got no response at all. Obviously she didn't like the British I couldn't blame her I suppose.

OUR HOUSE

Life in the hostel was quite good of course. We had our own rooms.
 There was a Butcher named Phil who didn't socialise with us at all so we didn't see much of him. The only time I would see him was at work, as the butchers was on the same floor as the canteen. His room was on the first left as you entered the accomodation. He didn't socialise with us at all. Of course the lounge was the centre of the accomodation, all our rooms were around it. There was a lovely view of the Meille factory  to the front.
 It was very quiet, although there was a motorbike shop underneath us but we never heard much from that either, also we were at the end of the street. Our local pub was not too far away, a short walk to the main road and a few hundred yards to the left. It was a nice pub, some nights it would be quiet and other nights it would be busy. Frugi the landlord was always there to serve us. I normaly drunk the local lager then got introduced to Weisen beer, which is wheat beer. After a few of these you knew you had a drink, sometimes you didn't. There was a juke box which played British and German records. What surprised my about the German pubs was that the staff were still allowed to smoke behind the bar, back home that was banned a long time ago.
 Sometimes there would be parties one particular night was a hallowe'en party and a great effort was put into it by some people. Clive dressed up as Dracula, saying that, he didn't have to put much effort into it. Same with me, all I had to do was put some paint on my face and I was a Zombie. Cyril was dressed as the walking dead , it was remarkable that he looked like the picture that was to his left .

HOLIDAYS IN THE SUN 2

On a fine weekend I decided to take a ride to Berlin, I knew that it was a fair distance away so I knew that I would have to stay overnight. The way to Berling was really straightforward when I got onto the Autobahn. All I had to do was to get onto the A2 and stay on it until I reached Berlin. The main thing on my mind was the distance, which was more than 405 K. It is odd that when you think in kilometers, you tend to think that the journey is going to be quicker but of course Kilometers or Miles it's the same distance. Once on the motorway the signs were already telling the distance to Berlin but it soon got monotonous, at times I thought I was never going to make it. My bike had a relatively small engine being a 500 cc, but there were not many bikes that overtook me and I passed many a Harley Davidson or similar bike, that were just cruising along. Well, I finally made it to the outskirts of Berlin, my main aim was to get as close to the City centre as possible, then find somewhere to stay the night. This proved easier than I anticipated as I found the centre and a quiet road, then parked the bike. I looked around for a Pension and as it happened there was one just around the corner. I went in and enquired about the availability and price. It worked out fine, the owner said he had a room and the price was reasonable. I asked if there was anywhere I could park my bike, he told me he didn't have a space but my bike would be safe where it was. So I went back to the bike and put it on its centre stand and put the disk lock on the front wheel. I put all my gear in my room and soon went on my way to explore and look for the Brandenburg gates; there it was in its glory, only a short walk away. I however was in for a shock as there were hundreds of young men all sitting around, I suspected that they were not indigenous to the city. I had a laugh to myself, thinking Hitler was probably spinning in his grave, that is if he was in one. I was quite hungry and walked around looking for something to eat and came across a schnell imbiss which was a welcome sight and ordered a kebab. I decided that I wouldn't be going far tonight as I would have to leave quite early to get back to Gutersloh.

WINDS OF CHANGE

I was going to go through East Germany, as it was not long ago. In that sense I mean Soviet occupied east Germany. In the morning, I got up and had a bit of breakfast, I was wondering if my bike was still where I left it, of course it was. I had decided that I would head for Magdeburg and head for the A2 from there. It hadn't been that long since the Berlin wall had come down, so I wanted to see what East Germany was like before they changed it. Obviously Berlin was booming as all you could see on the horizons were cranes. I got to the outskirts of the city and in one place there were little shops, selling all sorts of trinkets, like medals and army training manuals. I bought a few medals and pinned them to my cutout denim jacket that I bought when I first got to Germany, at this time clothes were really cheap. On the back I also put a Welsh flag which I bought when I was on leave. In another shop I bought a WW2 army training manual which of course was in German, so I couldn't really understand, but there were plenty of photographs. I was quite content that I had visited Berlin and obtained a few souvenirs.

Well, what I saw while passing through Eastern Germany amazed me, I had just gone back fifty years in time. I don't think any public building had been painted recently, unless they had a surplus of dull mustard paint, everywhere the grass was unkempt even the telephone exchanges looked like they had no life in them. Luckily there is an advert for a hotel in the picture so I have been able to work out where I had been. Hotel Tannengrund not far from Potsdam. I could see the winds of change though as passing large towns at a distance I could see cranes dominating the skyline, just like in Berlin. It looked like to me that the Soviets had made these people suffer for invading mother Russia. There were plenty of towns that I went through, all interesting in their way. These days with google earth you can visit places again, but they are nothing like they used to be. I was lucky to see the places before they changed. It's a pity I didn't take more trips into Eastern Germany, hindsight is a great thing. After Magdeburg I headed back towards the A2 and came upon a sad looking Bahnhof called Hakenstedt. I thought that this would make a fantastic photograph. It had seen better days as the picture on the left shows. Out of interest I looked on Bing for photos of the station and I found some. My picture is at bottom, the picture on the top must have been taken within weeks of each other, even the trees and plants are noticeable, the picture in the midddle has to be later, the station name must be in someones back garden.

the return from Berlin was far more interesting than the journey there. Another free weekend had come up so I decided to do my own Dambuster raid. My aim was to the four dams in one day. The weather was perfect for bike riding and the roads didn't look too busy. I had already meticilously prepared my route, with the tank bag and map.

My first target was to be the Mohne Dam which is on the Mohnesee.

See; in German, seems to mean a lake a reservoir or even the seaside. I had found there were a lot of lakes with sand around them, I take it that most of Germany is landlocked so they made do with the lakes. I worked out the best way was to go past Rheda-Weidenbruck down to Soest and then south to the Dam. When I passed Soest the roads changed and it seemed as if these roads were made for biking. Winding bends uphills and downhills and the roads were immaculate, not a pot hole anywhere and not a bit of litter. Now I was also driving through forests and signs for the dam had appeared. All of a sudden over a hill I could see the reservoir and the dam, it was beautiful. I got to a carpark and went on foot to the dam, well I wasn't allowed to take my bike anyway. There were crowds of people admiring the fantastic views and marveling at the engineering that went into building this beautiful giant. After a while walking around and taking photos, I decided it was time to make my way to the Sorpesee, so I had to make my way to Arnsberg and down to Sundern, where I would get to the dam. Sure enough I found it, there was no comparing the two dams I had seen. The Sorpe had its own beauty but didn't have the architecture. Basically, it was a giant mudbank and that was the main reason this dam didn't get breached on Operation chastise. I spent a while riding around the reservoir and taking in the sights. My next step was to go to the Edersee, but not today it would be too late. It was dark by the time I got to Gutersloh; this was the time that I had to ask directions.

Next Morning I set off early to get to the Edersee I would go down the A64, just after I passed Paderborn I noticed a sign to Buren and Salzkotten, there was another blue sign, basically saying war cemetery, I decided to have a look. The place was immaculate and well cared for. I felt sad, all these soldiers had parents, siblings and maybe their own children that loved them. I had a respectful look around and then made my way towards the Eder. There was a sign for Stiftskirch so I thought this might be worth a visit. I parked my bike up and walked around the town which had a religious feel to it, I suppose the Kirch part of the name gave it away.

One of the things I most admired about riding around Germany was that if you took a detour off the main route is that you were nearly guaranteed to see something awesome. There were many stops on the way down to the Eder but I knew I wouldn't have the time to concentrate on them all.

Again the roads were fantastic, especially getting near the reservoir and the hills all had a special view of the Edersee on their peaks. This reservoir was massive I must of ridden around it for two hours. I went back to the Dam just to take a few photos and decided to make my way back home. I was going to cross-country on the A252 to a place called Winterberg and then head north back to Gutersloh, I was not going to go to the Ennepe as it was too far. Again today the weather was perfect and the roads were out of this world, makes you wonder why anyone would use a car. I got to Winterberg and again I was not disappointed. I could tell that it was a ski resort but today it was a bike haven. I got to the summit and there was a ski lift waiting; waiting for the snow to arrive. It was now October so it wouldn't be too long. I took some photos and made my way back down. Stopping every now and then to take more photos. I was enjoying myself so much I didn't realise how late it was getting. I would have to get back on the main road, it was easier than I thought and I was soon on the A480 then the A516 to Ruthen then up to Lippstadt and it was simply follow the signs to Rheda-Weidenbruck.

What a fantastic weekend of biking I just had, I didn't really plan to visit all these places but I am glad I did.

These were the most memorable bike journeys but of course there were numerous other rides which all had their special events.

Now there was another journey, but this one was by train with my dear friend, John By the way.

TRAIN IN VAIN.

It was now late in the year, and the bike riding journeys were over. I met John one night in the military club in Gutersloh; we decided that a visit to Dresden would be a good weekend out. There was no need to book tickets as you could go anywhere in Germany for a little sum of money on the weekends and buy them at the Bahnhoff on the day.

The trip started on the Saturday morning and we had to meet at Gutersloh Bahnhoff at the ridiculous time of 04.30 to get the 0500 train to Leipzig. First we had to buy the Woken Ende (Weekend) tickets and John sorted that one out. The Bahnhoff and the train itself were extremely quiet not surprising in that hour. We had bought provisions the day before i.e. cans of beer. At 0500 on the dot very quietly the train made its way to our adventure, for good or for bad.

I thought now was a good time to catch up on some sleep. I was starting to drift off, all of a sudden there was noise that put paid to that. It was only John opening a can of beer. I thought this was a ridiculous time to start drinking, I decided to join him.

Obviously the further we got the busier the train was going to get. We stopped at some Bahnhoff and a group of student type people got on our carriage. Now John was getting abusive and he shouted something in German at them. Now this was one of the times when you learn something that nobody could teach you. One of the guys seemed alarmed and said " vos est ist" (simply = what is this) and found a seat as far away from us as was possible, Classic.

A few stops down the line a scruffy looking bloke sat down opposite john. When the train had moved on a few miles I could see that there was something wrong as john was getting agitated. He was talking to the guy in German, I didn't worry too much about it thinking that john had probably upset him, so I just looked out of the window and hoped to drop off. A bit further down the line something alerted me and I noticed that this scruff had pulled out a knife, but was not really threatening john.

John quietly told me that this scruff had come on the train to kill someone who had started a fight with his friend a week ago. Really I didn't appreciate the seriousness of the situation that we were in. John carried on talking to the guy for a while and pulled something from his top pocket and gave it to the scruff, in exchange he gave John the knife. Luckily the guy got off the train at the next stop.

I asked John how he had managed to get the bloke to hand the knife over, he said "I told him I had some speed tablets and would exchange them for the knife". He then told me something more frightening; he thought that when the bloke bent over to hand over the knife he saw what looked like a gun; now that we had solved a problem we were now in a dilemma.

John showed me the potential weapon, which was a small-serrated meat knife; it had been sharpened by something like a lathe. The problem now was how were we going to get rid of the knife, we now had in our possession a lethal weapon. How the hell do you explain that one away?

We got off the train to make a connection; we had to think of something fast. John suggested that we hand it into the police, I didn't think that, a good idea as they would want to question us and ruin our weekend, there could be a misunderstanding and we could get accused of having an offensive weapon, it was not a good idea.

We were passing a litterbin and I told john to give me the knife, just throw the offending article away, that is exactly what I did. God knows what would of happened if John hadn't taken the knife off the scruff.

We found the connecting platform for Leipzig and didn't have long to wait for train. This incident took it out on John as when we got settled he broke down in tears, it had really frightened him. **'Postavanje'**, John.

We had a few more beers and John perked up again. Our next stop was going to be Leipzig; it was getting

dark outside.

We didn't have to wait too long for the train to Dresden, which was a good thing, as it was getting cold and wet. We finally arrived at Dresden and our first mission was to find a bar. The idea was to stay local and keep drinking until our train was ready to take us back to Leipzig. We got off the train and went outside the Bahnhoff expecting to find a bar straight away. We were out of luck. There was no sign of a bar, absolutely nothing. John approached a number of people and they all came out with the same thing, saying there were no pubs in Dresden. I was wondering if John could really speak German. In the end we believed them. The saviour of the day was that there was a shop open back in the Bahnhoff, which sold beer. It was a quite miserable affair though it was cold and dark and no toilet was open. Our survival instincts kicked in and we drank until we got back on the 05.00 train in the morning.

John was unaware that I took this photo and I was unaware John took this photo.

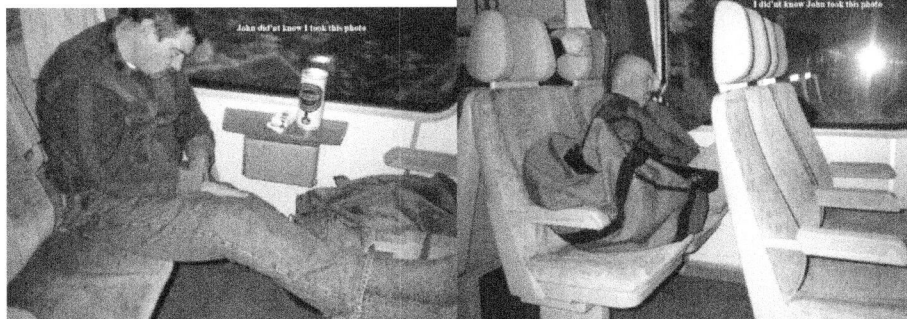

There were no incidents of note on the way back it was a can of beer and a nap, Hence the photos above. By the time we got back to Gutersloh I had enough of drinking and I thought John had too but he wanted to go back to the military club. I went back to the hostel and had a good nights sleep.

It was now getting late in the year and I had enough of Germany, my money was getting low and I didn't want to spend another year there. I talked to Simon about it and he said he would see what he could arrange. When he got back to me he said the consensus was that I was needed in Germany and I couldn't go back to EFI.

A few days later I rang the Colonel and told him that I wanted to come back. He said that I shouldn't worry and he would soon get me back. The managers underestimated Colonel Smith's authority and he would always come first. The biggest problem I had was where was I going to store my belongings? and what to do with my bike. I was soon told that I would have to do a months notice in Germany. A couple of weeks before I decided that I wanted to leave Germany I went to the Honda shop below our hostel and looked at the bikes, I took a liking to a silver VFR 750. I couldn't have the bike at the time so I ordered one with a small deposit. What I ended up doing was selling my Kawasaki 500 to the shop at a loss to myself. There was no way that I could take it back to the UK. I spent Xmas at the hostel and it was soon time to go home. I never regretted going to Germany, I met a lot of nice people and had a great adventure on mein motorrad. I achieved what I set out to do. It turned out that my belongings were no a problem, all I had to do was keep them in storage cage and come to collect them when I could. After a few leaving parties it was finally time to leave Germany.

    December 1996. I got a train to Hanover airport, here I was to get a flight to Heathrow, where I even had someone to pick me up to take me back to Bulford. Of course, in the morning I would have to have an interview with Colonel Smith.

SALISBURY PLAIN

I was dropped off at the accommodation block and the driver told me that I would be picked up at 07.50 and be taken to the EFI HQ.

In the morning I went to the cookhouse and had a good breakfast, I loved the food there, it was basic but it was good. A full breakfast was waiting for you and a hot or cold drink and all catered by military personnel. I then went outside to wait for the driver to pick me up and so he did at 07.50.

The driver told me the reason he had to pick me up was because the HQ was no longer on the main Garrison. it was now in a place called Double Hedges. We went out of the main gate, turning right, a few hundred yards up the road was a post office, this was not the run of the mill but a military post office. A few hundred yards further on was another turning right, about a mile up this road on the left was Double Hedges, the new

HQ EFI. A solitary building surrounded by grassed areas and barbed wire and beyond the gate was a large car park.

We arrived there at 07.58. Colonel Smith's car was parked in its bay. The Colonel was always the first to arrive in the mornings he opened everything up and put the lights on. The first thing I heard when I got in was 'Hello Taff', it was Dawn the Colonels clerk, she was now in uniform and had Corporals stripes. She told me to get myself a cup of tea, the Colonel would soon call me in, a little later he came out of his office with his usual smile and said " hello Miles, follow me into the office and we will have a chat".

First he asked me about Germany and then reminded me that when he rang me and asked if I would go back to Split I basically told him to eff off. He then told me that I would be going to Norway at the beginning of January but first I could have a few weeks leave and would have to report back here on the 2nd of January. This of course meant that I would have to travel back before New Years Eve.

It was nice to be back with my old friends in Mumbles, Don Collier, Terry Llewelin (Don at Cambridge university), Graham Durk my best friend, I had been his best man at his wedding, Peter my Landlord, Johnny Vie, Dai the farmer, Dai the drill (boring) and a lot more; the pubs were buzzing in those days, but the good days don't last long and next thing I knew I was back on the train to Andover, which was the nearest Railway station to Bulford Garrison. There I got picked up by the duty driver and was taken to the billet. The same old routine and I would be picked up at 07.50 on the 2nd.

In those days we didn't have a permanent uniform we would get kitted out before our tour, which meant everything was second hand except for our boots and beret. When I say second hand, that was an understatement it could have been used multiple times. And so it was on the morning I arrived back in the new HQ at Double hedges. It was like rummaging through a jumble sale to find uniform that fitted.

Now I had the time to look around the new HQ. The main building was built of brick, which of course was the original, dating back to WW2. Its main function in the past was to look over the tank and artillery ranges

on Salisbury plain.

There were steps that led to the top of the building, the view was stunning, you could see for miles. Netheravon airfield could be seen in the distance; sometimes Parachutists could be seen descending. It was a mystery to us what was going on there but we knew it was an army-training centre. On the opposite side was MOD Boscombe Down, sometimes strange aircraft could be seen coming and going, not far from there was Porton Down well known for NBC (Nuclear Biological and Chemical warfare) research. For a bit of extra pay service people could volunteer to be a Guinea pig and get injected with some sort of poison.

Not far away but out of sight of Double hedges was the local town of Amesbury, this is where a NAAFI warehouse was and not far from there was the NAAFI HQ.

Back at Double hedges there was the Colonel's office, Dawns office and a storeroom, in which was a red heavy-duty scales, I presumed they were to weigh baggage or equipment for transporting to exercises. There was another room that was full of stationary, stacked to the brim, here there was also a pile of books called NAAFI in uniform, it was nothing of the calibre of the book you are reading now though. By the entrance there was a large room that didn't seem to have a purpose, except for drinking tea and chatting. To get to the main storeroom we would have to pass through the most important part of the establishment, which was the kitchen. This kitchen led to a hallway that used to lead to a back door. In this hallway the walls were adorned with pictures of old EFI squadrons and basic training pass outs, needless to say I didn't know many of the people in the pictures. This hallway led us out of the brick building into what I could describe as non-solid construction. The first room on the left was the main uniform storage room; now, there was a strange object in this room in the shape of a headless mannequin, it seemed as if it had a life of its own; it was as if you could always sense someone behind you, I thought some mischief could be made with this. There was another room down the corridor on the left with more uniforms however these uniforms were more ceremonial. There were rank insignia on most of them; some had quite high ranks as well, which I never knew EFI had,this was the last room but then was a door which led to outside, this door was also locked. Opposite the ceremonial room there was another door, which too was always locked. The next room was the main classroom in which there was a load of tables put together surrounded by about twenty chairs. There were other desks in the room; one of them was full of photographs, of course at the time I wouldn't know most of the people in them, but they were in interesting places.

There were windows looking out to the grassed area, there were always rabbits running around. There were also a few ancient barrows to be seen here as well. Going back into the corridor with all the photographs, what struck me were the instructors in each photograph, they looked tough and mean. Back through the kitchen you would have to turn left to get to the Colonels office and the toilets that were to the right. The walls were adorned with artefacts mostly from the Falklands in particular a propeller from a Pucara attack plane. There were also souvenirs from the Gulf war. There was something about this place, the atmosphere was always stale.

It was soon time to get kitted out for the arctic. The first item would be a Bergen then items that would be packed into it, a smock, special boots that you could clip skis to, a white face mask, a furry hat and other thermal clothing and of course this stuff would take up a lot of room and be quite heavy. The next day we were going to start lessons on Norway and Arctic survival. In all there were about twenty of us, hadn't met any of them before but they seemed a nice bunch of people; the days work would always finish dead on 17.00, we would be taken back to Ward barracks of course separate accommodation for the boys and girls. However the first stop was the cookhouse. The evening meals were great you would have a choice of roast meats pies or sometimes Curry and a selection of veg. If you wanted you could have a soup starter and a dessert afterwards. For some pathetic reason some people wouldn't eat in the cookhouse I could never understand their logic. I do believe that some people felt intimidated by being in a military establishment. I suppose some soldiers wondered who we were. There was always a lot of grumbling going on about the food, but it was free for us and it was wholesome.

In the evenings we were free to do what we wanted ,as long as your uniform was pressed for the next day. On the camp was a gate that was only open for a few hours in the evening, it was a short cut to the local shopping precinct. After 1900 you would have to walk a fair distance to the main gate. The precinct was actually part of the garrison so you had to abide by the military law. If you were in uniform you had to be smart, and wear your beret to be able to salute officers. In the British armed forces you can only salute if you are wearing head-dress, if you are outside without head-dress you are in trouble and if you salute without head-dress you are in bigger trouble, if you are not careful you could end up in the guardroom, a situation you do not want to be in.

One of the shops of course would be the NAAFI and one perk we had was 10 % discount. Not that you would buy that much there. Though the NAAFI did have one unique treasure at the time, it was called the NAAFI tea company. I have no doubt they made the finest tea in the world. I know from my own past, they even had a teabag so strong it could make seven cups of strong tea. WIGIG. There were a few other shops in the precinct in particular a military tailor and for them in those days, business was good.

Not far from the shops was a pub called the Kiwi; unique because it was on military grounds, and it was owned by civilians, members of the public were allowed to use it though not many did, the exception to this would be family members who worked in the Garrison. It was good for family members and ex forces that worked locally. It was a bit more expensive than the NAAFI on camp but at least it was outside and a good meeting place. I noticed that there was never any trouble in the Kiwi unlike other pubs where Squaddies

frequented, overall it was a nice place. Out if interest on the way to Bulford camp from Tidworth there is a kiwi dug out on the chalk on one of the hills.

In June 1916, Sling camp was set up for the New Zealand Expeditionary Force, this was for the training of the NZEF before deployment to the Western front, above the camp was Beacon Hill and the Kiwi was created there. When the war ended naturally the NZ soldiers would want to go home, unfortunately there were no troop ships available. The soldiers were not very happy about this and did a bit of rioting. A lot of the soldiers were punished harshly and some who were decorated had their medals taken off them, others were demoted and some jailed, the thanks they got for going through hell. The commanding officers solved the problem by getting the soldiers busy carving the enormous Kiwi. I have often thought to myself, to always take advantage of adversity, this is what the Kiwi's did here.

There was a lot for us to learn in the next week. Ruth from the Dalma tour was in attendance; contrary to what the boys told her on the Grapple tour that she would never do an EFI tour again. There was another girl, Karen on the course, who I had never met but I knew about her, I got on well with her, as she was a nice person. Most of the lessons would be death by PowerPoint and our tutor was Neil who was the SNCO from Split. There was also a lot of practical training, which was done on the grassed area outside. Of course we had to learn how to keep warm, avoid frostbite and don't touch metal objects, for if you do your fingers could stick to them, you don't want to learn that the hard way, avoiding hypothermia, how to recognise it and then how to treat it. We were warned that when we get attached to a unit we might have to do further training, this could involve jumping into a hole in the ice and swimming for a while.

We would not be carrying and weapons so there was no need for any military training. Some of us would have to drive myself included; we had a bit of training for that.

One lesson we had to learn was how to put up tents and being as it was quite cold outside I decided to replace my beret with a bobble hat. Nobody really cared that much, except for Colonel Smith who happened to come out to see what we were doing. "Corporal Rees get your beret on, who do you think you are" and he wasn't joking. We were not told where we were going to stationed in Norway as they were playing it by ear. I wouldn't of had any preferences anyway as I didn't know the country. On the last day of training we were issued with our sleeping bags, they were in the room that had been locked, I noticed that there was a pungent smell coming from the sleeping bags.

8 Jan 97

LIKE CLOCKWORK

The day came to start our adventure. We were to fly from RAF Brize Norton (BZZ) but first we had to go to the Joint Air Mounting Centre in South Cerney (Gloucester) to check our luggage in. This was a massive hangar where thousands of troops could be mobilised. The reason for this was to ease the pressure on RAF Brize Norton, who didn't have enough staff or room to cope with a large deployment. There must have been a lot of planning involved to get people to their correct destinations. The RAF was not solely responsible for the organising but in conjunction with the Royal Logistics Corps (to put it simply) of the Army, this is why it is called the Joint Air Mounting Centre. It was a long boring day sitting around doing nothing, in the afternoon the Royal Marines arrived; they struck me as a good bunch of guys. I will now refer them as either Marines or Royals, as this is what they call themselves. At around 18.00 hrs we left S.C. for RAF Brize Norton, which is near enough thirty miles away.

When we arrived at BZZ we didn't have to wait too long to get our passports checked and were able to board the VC10, Karen and myself managed to get a seat together; we managed to leave Ruth at the back of the plane. By now she was getting annoying because she was constantly moaning, a bit of taxiing and we were soon airborne and into the clouds. We flew over Manchester, Hull, over Scotland and then across to Norway, there was some fantastic scenery and I could clearly see the oilrigs below. There is a peculiarity with a VC10 in that the seating is unusual as they are facing towards the back of the aircraft, in effect we were flying facing backwards. We soon were approaching Evenes airport, the climate had changed dramatically. There was no problem landing on the runway it was quite smooth, when we were actually out of the aircraft I was amazed how a plane could land on this sheet of ice. I was actually expecting it to be freezing when we got off the aircraft but it was not too bad. The RAF pilots are obviously well trained, as they have to land in all sorts of terrain. We were taken to a hanger to await further instructions. All the while we could see aircraft coming and going, I say that loosely mind, as sometimes we couldn't see the aircraft through the sleet. We waited for a while, and then someone came along and told us what groups we were in and where we were going. Myself, Karen and Ruth were going to Harstad. It was now time for our groups to go our separate ways, in a way it was sad because I had got fond of them. I had a good idea though! In my naivety, we would all swap our mobile phone numbers and keep in touch. It would have been a miracle in those days though if your phone rang. There were no contracts only PAYG and UK only. It was in the infancy of mobile phones and my phone could only receive about five messages before the memory was full. I did actually try to phone someone, nothing but blackness

9 Jan 97

AS COLD AS ICE

Our bus arrived to take us to Harstad, Karen and I managed to get a seat on the back of the bus. The bus ride was a few hours through some beautiful scenery made more impressive because it was dark and only lit up by streetlights. We eventually arrived at an army camp with a sign saying Asergarden. One person shouted out 'oh thank you God' the camp was plainly a Norwegian army establishment vacated for the winter. We were very tired by then, as we had missed a night's sleep. Our ordeal was not ever yet as we had to have a few hours of briefings. The officer running the briefings said to our group " Hello welcome to Norway" now Ruth replied to him " there's lots of snow here, isn't there" with a face of disbelief he said, " well that's the idea of being in Norway"

After these briefings we were told where the shop was and were free to go. We found Neil (now a Staff Sergeant) and a Corporal called Dell downstairs in the B.I.S. they had left a few days before us and they had moved all the stock by themselves, that had saved us a lot of work. I was told that I would have to go on a snow and ice training course in the morning. I was shown my accommodation and was able to have a lovely hot shower; I then went to bed and slept like a log. When I woke up in the morning, I realised that things were different here as it was still dark.

10 Jan 1997.

On the snow and ice driving course, it was mostly a day of hanging around but it was worth the wait. Driving a Landrover on a pan was fantastic and I managed to get away with only killing one pedestrian. Apparently the female drivers did a lot better than the males as they were a lot gentler on the vehicles. I had to drive the Landrover back to Harstad, unfortunately no one had shown me how to operate the heater and I couldn't shut the window, by the time I got back me feet and hands felt like they were frozen.

Before starting work the next morning Del asked me if I wanted to go to breakfast, it wouldn't of taken much persuasion as I was famished. He told me the Galley wasn't far. The Galley is the Royals speak for the restaurant. It wasn't far from our building, just an icy walk away. We had welcome bacon and eggs, he then took me back to our building and to the B.I.S. where I was going to work, this had already been set up. We had to go through the classroom to get there. The two girls were going to work in the shop, in which were all sorts of goods for sale, even things I had never seen before like trolls.

First thing in the morning things of course would be quiet. Del told me that he had arrived a couple of days ago with Neil and they set up the shop. He told me that he worked in the NAAFI Warehouse in Amesbury. He lived in a place called Durrington walls, which was not far from Bulford. He came to Norway every winter for the tour. He was a nice quiet chap.

Strangely the B.I.S was in the same room as the Royals had their briefing room. I would learn a lot about the Royals from here.

Whenever a camp is set up, it is military law that there has to be a fire drill. So the alarms went off and we mustered outside in the cold, when everyone was accounted for we could go back in the warm buildings.

The first couple of days were going to be busy in the shop because of course the Royals had to learn survival skills before going out in the field. Soon after the shop opened the class filled up with Royals. They had to do a roll call, which was done by a sergeant, this is where something fundamental struck me. The Royals were all sat down one of them had failed to answer his name, if this were the army there would be hell to play, this was not the case with the Royals, now in this situation the Army would say he was AWOL (absent without leave). The Sergeant who was doing the lecture asked if anyone knew of his whereabouts, a Royal said that Marine Smith was 'Adrift'; and that was that. Now this is where I realised that the senior ranks respected their soldiers.

The next few days we got into a routine in the B.I.S. I mean it was not busy at all. One good thing about Norway was that the Royals ran their own bars and we would never have to work in them. All we had to do was to supply the beer and this was Neil's domain. It looked a really complicated business. We of course had a delivery of beer from the brewery and they were all bottled and in crates. Neil explained to me that the Norwegians were keen on recycling so all the bottles had to be counted. Simple really, each case has 24 bottles. The problem was that every bottle came with a deposit on it, so Neil had to work out exactly every bottle and input it into the computer system. No money was handed over at this time but the invoices had to be exact. Well it looked complicated to me but Neil knew exactly what he was doing.

Another small unit was on this exercise that we worked closely with, this was the postal service or posties as they were fondly called, that is if you were waiting for a letter; and this was by everybody, and don't we all like to receive a letter. I was told that they always worked in harmony with us, they were part of the RLC just like us although they were regular army unlike us who were classed as T.A. There was a Sergeant a Corporal and two female privates. It just happened that we were natural companions.

Things went very quiet when the Royals went out on their training. At lunchtime we could shut the Bulk Issue Store and go to the Galley for scoff. Now there was one problem with the food in the Galley in that it was meant for the Royals, they after all needed the stodge to sustain themselves in the field. The food was not meant for us shopkeepers and I started to put weight on, it would prove hard to get rid of. The food was so good that it was hard not to gorge out on it.

As we didn't have to run the bar it meant only one thing and that was Skiing. It was all free, even the renting of the equipment, all paid for by 40 Commando Royal Marines.

I had done a bit of skiing before in Scotland so I had a bit of an idea. Obviously first we had to get kitted out getting a comfortable pair of boots was the first step the I had to find a set of skis that were compatible with the boots with a bit of changing around I was confident that I was suited up. Neil and the rest of the crew were experienced so they went ahead on the big slopes I would have to get some practice on the nursery slope for a few hours to get the confidence to get on the lifts to take me up higher.

One thing that amazed me was the little Norwegian children. Maybe as young as two-year-old just passing we without a thought, bless them. I eventually decided that I was competent enough to go up to higher ground. On the way up on the ski lift I noticed our crowd below me, I got off at the next stop. I went down the slope and whizzed past the group. Later I was told that Neil said " wow look at Taff go" little did he know that I didn't know how to slow down or stop. There was only one thing for it, before I crashed into something nasty. I had already tried a technique called snowploughing but I was going too fast for it to take any effect, the only thing I could do was to take a tumble. I must of rolled about two hundred yards before I came to a halt no harm done though, all I had to do was find my skis and poles. When I went back up the other bunch were still at near enough the same places. I decided to take it with a bit more caution this time around and wanted to see what was happening. As it happened Neil had taken a tumble and had a crack in the mouth so he decided to call it a day. It had been a good evenings skiing but I felt that I needed a bit of coaching. Later in the evening whilst we were having a few beers someone mentioned that a couple of years previous, a Para decided to take a slide down a ski slope, however he didn't use skis to attempt this stunt but a beer crate, he never lived to tell his story.

It was the time of the year in Norway when it was darker longer than it was light; the sun never rose above the horizon. There is a mental illness that affected people and made them depressed, it is called SAD (Seasonal affective disorder) apparently there were a fair amount of suicides this time of the year in Norway. There was going to be a few weeks since we were to see the sun, then there would be a festival called Soldagen I take it meant Sun-day. Sol (sun), Dagen (day).

When the marines came back from training in the field they were allowed to go into town but there the alcohol was expensive. The beer in their bar was cheap so most of them would get drunk before they hit the town. It was well known the local men resented the presence of the marines, (of course the local ladies loved them), they would try to start a fight with them, knowing full well that they would lose. The logic behind this was if a marine punched a local and the police got involved he would end up in prison, in Norway there was zero tolerance with violence. The best advice was to slap the perpetrator, which was allowed, apparently. There was no sense in going into town in the week, as it would prove to be financially unviable, so we would go into the marine's bar. This however had its risks. For instance if someone shouted out 'naked bar' that is exactly what would happen, yes you would have to take all your clothes off, even the girls, though they would be able to keep their underwear on. Luckily they never called this when I was in the bar. Sometimes they would have a fancy dress party usually the item most used would be the laundry bags, pillows and bed sheets.

Another weekend came up and we were going to visit Harstad again. I asked Del if he wanted to come with us for a drink, he declined the offer because he was friendly with two Royals and wanted to stay with them. Although it was expensive in Norway for alcohol, Harstad was bustling at the weekend. The posties and us EFI found a quiet bar to start off with, the price of beer was ridiculously expensive, spirits even more so. The locals were very friendly to us, so we got on well with them. Walking along the icy harbour was strange as it was minus 20 degrees at least. There were ships anchored in the docks and I was wondering why the sea wasn't frozen. Fred the Corporal postie (who knew everything) told me that the temperature in the water was about plus 6 degrees because of the jet stream. So if someone wanted to jump into the water they would not freeze to death, I don't think there was no-one silly enough to do so though. Getting closer to the city centre we came across a pub called the Exchange and it looked busy inside. The owner of this pub must have been a very clever person. There were flashing signposts with the price of beer, when a certain beer got popular the price would go up and others would go down, so of course people would start drinking the lower priced beer which would then start to go up in price. The pub was thronging, the music was good and the locals were friendly, what a fantastic evening we had.

One day the OC of the RMs decided that he wanted our Bulk Issue Store as a television room, Neil was not too happy about it, we spent most of the day moving our stock downstairs into a cellar, where we kept our bonded stock (tobacco and spirits), all this time Ruth was in the shop reading a book.

I was told at one stage that I would probably go to another location further up country, as it happened the two girls decided they wanted to go. Ruth was always complaining, she seemed to think she was on holiday, Karen was getting bossy, though I liked her and we got on well, I started calling her baby troll.

I think my bosses had plans for me regarding driving. Now that the girls had gone Del and myself had to work in the shop. One day it would be busy and another day it would be quiet depending on what the Royals were doing. They could be learning to ski, I could see the progress in this. At one stage they would be just in uniform and a few days later they would have C.E.M.O (Combat equipment marching order) then they would have C.E.F.O (combat equipment fighting order), they were quick learners.

Some units were isolated so we had to get to them as they couldn't get to us; that meant that I would have to drive our Landrover with one of the girls. We had to stock up with necessities and little comforts

that the military couldn't provide, for instance 'Pot Noodle a very popular item in our stock. Cigarettes, sweets, chocolates, crisps, boot polish, anything really.

My first mission was to a remote camp, this was in a field, obviously it was iced up. It was ok going into there and selling our goods but I couldn't find a way out. I could see the tracks that I made to get into the camp but getting out was not going to be so easy as there was a hump, if I tried going slowly there was a risk of getting grounded. What I decided to do was speed up to get over the hump, this I did but it was very risky, it seemed that when I got onto the main road I must of just missed a car as I could hear a horn being blown, no doubt by an angry motorist my assistant looked a bit shook up as well. Another part of my job as a driver was to take the manager in charge of finance to the bank, of course it would be time to do some shopping. We went into an outdoor pursuits centre shop and I was astounded how cheap things were, considering the high quality of the goods. I bought a pair of trekking boots and a warm pullover, of course there were food take away shops, the menus were also outstanding.

At this time of the year it got dark early but if it was a clear night the Northern lights were doing their magic. At times it seemed like a God had got a stick and whirled it in the sky. Sometimes though I would have to drive to some other establishments on my own. I would have to take some staff to another shop or deliver some goods. It was a bit dangerous to be on my own but I didn't mind. Even though it was dark it was still beautiful when the moon shone on the mountains. I very often passed a

mountain that looked like it had a face of an ape on it. The roads could be icy at times but we had special tyres that had ball bearings embedded, so they would grip the road better. The roads were never too busy though and I could go for miles and not see another car.

Back in the camp there was another fancy dress party, it could be any theme. A lot of the royals were dressed as animals. There is a rule that there are no cameras in the bar. On this evening though there seemed to be a few people taking photos.

I decided to go and get my camera and take a few photos. However the Royals that Dell socialised with took a bit of umbrage to me taking shots. One of them said to me ' No cameras' I said' there are people taking photos' 'No cameras' was the sharp reply. I felt that I had better not argue, as they were serious.

In early February there was a message written on the notice board outside the EFI shop saying that interflora orders had to be in by the second of Feb. Interflora for us was a pain in the backside. The customer would have to write a message and get the receivers address correct, we would have to get the exchange rate correct and the customer would probably pay by card. In 1997 in Norway we would have to use the old system of vouchers using a credit card swipe system. However it was an essential service that we provided

for the love stricken.

After Feb 2nd I put my own drawing on the notice board, I think the Royals liked it because it stayed there until the end of the exercise.

Running up that hill

One day I was invited to go on a visit, to meet a local lady called Barbara; she lived alone on top of a hill overlooking the sea. So off I went with a few more tourists on a short journey up a slippery road. There she was in all her glory; Barbara overlooking the sea in case any Russians dared to sneak in that

way. AA

At least it was warm inside Barbara with all those shells ready to welcome any unwelcome Russians.

A few weeks went by and the Royals were trained up enough to go out in the field for a (military) exercise so it would be quiet on camp. This meant a bit more skiing. I found myself a bit more confident and could get to the top of the slopes; I was given some coaching with the Sergeant postie. The views of the mountains and the Fiords were stunning, even though it was quite dark by the afternoon. Every time it was time to finish I was glad that I had not suffered a serious injury.

Although the troops were out in the field there were other things to sort out like the duty free allowances. For their hard work the Royals were allowed to have a litre bottle of spirits at duty free prices, such was the gratitude of the British Government. They would be allowed to collect their goods on the last day of their tour. Funny thing was and I don't know if this was true, the SAS were allowed to buy a pallet of Whisky. Someone told me that they had their own black market business going on. Sure enough we loaded a pallet of Spirits and took it to the playing fields and along came a Sea King helicopter and slung the pallet underneath, then were off in a Jiffy.

GIVE ME SUNSHINE

It was very quiet with the Royals being out in the field but we still had some customers. As mentioned previously the day had come, on the 18th of March *Soldagen had arrived,* the sun appeared above the horizon; and indeed I did witness that day. When I got up in the morning there was a bit of sunshine, not for long though.

After four weeks there was a bit of a change, Neil went back to the UK and was replaced by another Sergeant by the name of Dylan. This was about the time that the Royals were finishing their training exercise in the field. When they came back it would not be long before they went home. This would not be the end for us though as there was another unit that would be doing their Arctic warfare training, this was the RMR the Royal Marines Reserve. The RMR would only have two weeks training which must have been hectic for them, though most of them would probably be ex Royal Marines anyway so it would be routine for them. Of course before 40 CDO went home the RMR would send out a forward party to set things up and sign equipment over.

We went on our last skiing trip, as the RMR would not be paying for the hire of any equipment. I was glad in a way for at least I hadn't broken anything. On the last day of the day of the Royals exercise those that had ordered duty free could collect their goods they had paid for. It was sad to see them go as I had made a few good friends with them.

One of the main men with the RMR was a Corporal called Sparkie, who no doubt had his work cut out.

On the day that the main group of the RMR arrived Dylan decided that we were going to pack up and go home leaving the RMR with no welfare facilities. Sparkie tried to talk him into staying but with no luck. I didn't understand why Dylan would do such a thing but that was that, and we were soon on our way home. Maybe just maybe there was a reason for this as this worked out to a good thing for me though.

GUNS ON THE ROOF

10 Apr 97

When we got back to Bulford Colonel Smith had some good news for us, we were going to Turkey for a three-week training exercise with the Royal Artillery. It was myself, Kev, Sian, Helen and the Det commander Heather. There was not to be any training for the exercise as all we were doing was to work in a shop. So no weapons were required. We went to RAF Lyneham on the evening before our flight and were taken to our accommodation that was a much better experience than we were used to at Brize Norton. We were provided with a good meal in the airmen's mess and after that we were able to have a few beers in the junior ranks club run by the NAAFI. We were given an early morning call at 0600 and had to pack all our kit and put it in a Landrover. We were then free to have breakfast and wait to be taken to the Hercules. It wasn't long before we were on the aircraft and airborne. It was a cheerful flight, it was only our small group and some cargo. After we got to cruising altitude Helen and myself were invited to go to the flight deck where we were given a seat and a set of headphones so the captain could speak to us. When he finished talking to us he gave us a map with our flight path on it. After a four-hour flight we landed at Adana airport. And from there we were taken to a place called Pinarhisar by coach. Of course Heather had been given the agenda by Colonel Smith. It was mid-day when we arrived at the camp, we were taken to what was to be our shop, which at the time was a bundled tent in a big field. Kevin and myself were given the task of putting the tent up which proved to be a slow process, of course we got there in the end.

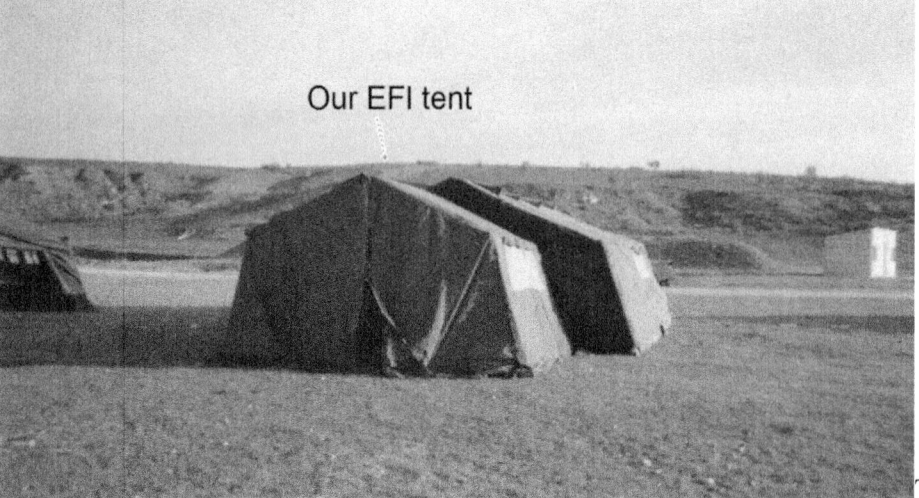

Our EFI tent

The next step then was to find the container that held all our stock, a safe, a till, padlocks, tables and paperwork, which was crucial for Heather to do her job. We found the container eventually so our next task was to get the container taken to where the shop was and then to transfer the goods into the shop. We were then ready to start trading. We were also given a Landrover for our use.

The staff, I hadn't met Kevin before but we got on great from the outset. Helen I had worked with in Norway. Heather the Det commander I also hadn't met before. As for Sian I knew her from way back before I even joined the NAAFI. Her family owned a shop about two hundred yards away from our house in Bishopston in Swansea.

It was to be a simple shop no fancy goods just selling cigs beer sweets chocolates and little luxuries, we were always obliged to sell necessities like toiletries. It was late afternoon when we were finished setting the shop up. The ladies were taken to their accommodation but myself and Kev had to put our own tent up

it didn't take long as it was not very big.

The only trouble our tent was quite a distance from the ablutions so it was quite a walk for us. Another thing about the ablutions was there was only one; so the boys and girls had to share, of course not at the same time. Kev and myself finished the building of the tent, then went for a shower and returned to our tent. We had no idea where the girls were. The tent was more than adequate for our needs but the age-old problem always comes up, Kevin snored for England.

So, on our first day of trading, Heather woke us up and told us to meet later in the shop for a briefing.

Heather explained that our main currencies were to be the Turkish Lira, US dollar, Deutsch mark and Sterling. As we were in Turkey the Lira was to be the default currency as it could be banked locally. At a guess then ,there was about four million Liras to the pound. People often asked why we always dealt in the local currency. There was a simple reason for it, banking. If we dealt in Sterling we would have to take it home with us and that was just not a practical thing to do also we would have to keep it in a safe. Efi used this system everywhere we went, bank it, and its out of our hands.

We were all issued with a calculator, we all had to practice exchanging currencies. It turned out quite easy; it just seemed more complicated than it was, for three quarters of us that was.

In the afternoon there was a grand opening of the shop and our customers soon started arriving. It turned out that our main customers were going to be from the Italian army, it seemed that they were the dominant force here. Sales were going great and the currency issues weren't much of a problem that is except for Helen, she just could not grasp it, so we all had to help her along. The afternoons trading came to an end and things seemed ok, the tills tallied. There was to be a bit of a difference in the evening though as we were going to be selling beer. All hands were on deck for the first shift. We opened the doors at 1900 and the Italians poured in, eager to sample our British beer. We were operating on two tills but, a problem was coming to the surface. Helen was really struggling with the exchange rates and she was starting to annoy everyone as she was holding everyone else up, as they had to stop what they were doing to help her out; something had to be done. I had a great idea; a crate of beer was a nice round number and they were selling well. I told Helen to stand by the window and only sell cases of beer, this worked a treat, the crowd thinned out and we could relax a bit. All we had to do was tell the customers if they wanted beer go outside to the window where Heather stood and she would hand them the beer, someone else would take the money. Problem solved; for now that was.

Heather decided to split the shifts into myself and Kev and the other one Sian and Helen. Kev and myself were to be the first shift in the shop. It turned out that we had a fantastic time with the Italians who were really friendly to us. I could speak a little Italian that I learned from a school trip to Sorrento and Rome.

Heather said she was happy and we could work in pairs rather than have us all in at the same time. The rota worked out that the girls worked the morning shift and the boys stocked up etc.

Heather allocated a job to Kev, he had to arrange the duty free allowance, take the money and store it away securely, simple, so Heather thought. All soldiers were allowed to take home a bottle of spirits at the end of the exercise. They could pay for the bottle at any time but it had to be kept in storage until the last day. I thought this was going to be a mistake by Heather.

Evening time came along and Kev and myself opened the bar. A great rapport had started with the Italians and us. I put a bit of a spanner in the works though, of course the Italians would greet us with 'cioui' when they were entering or leaving. I started to say to them goodbye when they entered the shop and say hello when we finished serving them. This started to become hilarious when the Italians fell for it, we were in stitches although it was done with great respect and it was all done with humour all round. Kev said, "I am into the Italians" I couldn't agree more with him.

The girls weren't having such a great time though. Helen was still struggling with the money, which was upsetting Sian. I had a chat with Sian and said we could meet up in the afternoon and go to the showers.

On the walk to the showers Sian told me that Helen was getting the money wrong all the time and it was causing big problems. I told her that Heather knew all about it and she didn't need to worry. Sian also said that she was concerned about the showers because there was always a male guarding the entrance. When we arrived at the showers sure enough he was sitting there. At the time there were no separate showers for males and females. When we finished and met outside Sian looked distraught, I asked her what was wrong, she burst out in tears and said she could feel the guard watching her. I told Heather about this and said something needed to be done about it. It later turned out that all the females were told not to go to the shower alone, there were to be three at a time and at an allocated time.

Things started quietening down in the shop so we started doing mobiles to remote units that couldn't get to us or have the time. One person could stay in the shop and the other was to go out on a mobile, a good idea you would think. Helen was given the task of getting to a location and sell what she could. So off she went with a little stock and a float, when she came back two hours later, she only managed to sell one packet of cigarettes and came back with less money than she started with.

When I first met Heather I must admit I didn't really like her. This was not personal, I just didn't like the Sgts who were in the EFI, as most of them were managers from the NAAFI. There is no other unit in the Army where you would enter as a SNCO. I soon changed my view on Heather though, as she was a nice person and fair. She was also a first class Manageress.

TRAGEDY

I will never forget the morning that Heather got us all together and said "good morning we have a new Labour government". A tragic day.

Later in the week she told us that she had arranged with the RAF for us all to go on a flight in a Puma. After the shop shut on that particular day we were taken to the Heli-pad and put into two helicopters two by two.

Heather didn't even fly with us.

They took us around the camp and then into the country flying under and over power lines, if the helicopter hit one of them we were dead. This was not my first trip in a Puma but it sure was one of the best ones,  though I had flown in one in Belize, which was an experience.

Fellow Puma

On another occasion Heather arranged for Sian and myself to go on Artillery range. It was quite exciting at first being next to the guns and watching them being fired. A strange thing about our position was we weren't on our own, there we hundreds of Tortoises. They were obviously indigenous to this area but they didn't seem to mind the noise and our company.

I asked one of the soldiers if I could fire one of the guns he said yes no problem. He told me to stand by the gun and handed me a cord that was attached to it, and he shouted 'pull' Bang, I had fired all sorts of weapons before but this was my first field gun. We had to stay all day with the Battery obviously we couldn't walk around while there was live firing going on. It got quite boring after a while and I was just sitting there minding my own business and all of a sudden I could hear Sian laughing. I asked her what was so funny

she said "you snoring".
After a week we had got into the routine, we were still having fun with the Italians; the screams of Artillery rounds were flying over our heads. I noticed something strange though. We were positioned in a valley and all along the hilltops were silhouettes of armed guards walking about. I thought to myself that there were some people out there who didn't like us.

PEOPLE ARE PEOPLE

I was surprised one day when Heather asked me to go into the local town to bank some money for her. Great I thought no problem; I had done this sort of thing in Norway not long ago. I was given the keys for our Landrover and Heather told me where the Bank was in the local town Pinarhisar. So I made my way into unknown territory. I arrived at the Town and needed to locate the bank, and then find a car park nearby. I was driving along the road when I noticed a young boy standing on a Zebra crossing; I don't know what the locals would call it. I did the decent thing and stopped to let him cross but he just stared at me and stood where he was, I beckoned him to cross and he did so with great caution. I realized later that in a place like Turkey the crossings are meant to be a safe place to stop and wait for no traffic, then cross.

I found the bank on the main street and deposited the money, no problems with that, now I was free to look around the town.

I was in my army uniform and obviously was not a Turkish soldier so people were looking at me curiously. They seemed nice decent people though, the song "people are people" a song by Depeche Mode came to mind; such a meaningful song. Another great pastime of mine was window-shopping. I looked into a few shops and a little market but I was not going to buy a skinned goat with its tongue hanging

out.

I had a pleasant walk around looking at the market, the man with his horse and cart who was quite happy to have his photo taken. It was great to see the real Turkey with no tourists. What a great day.

There was a trip organised by the detachment to go to Istanbul for a day. We were asked if we wanted to go, Heather was too busy Kev and Helen weren't interested. Sian and myself were keen to go so we put our names down. The day came along and a crowd of us met in the MT garage, the first thing we had to do was to find a volunteer to drive but nobody came forward. It was decided that a fair way was to put peoples name into a hat. I really was not confident enough to drive a mini bus of people on a motorway and drive in Istanbul. So I told a lie and said I couldn't drive, one of the guys said to me "you can't drive at your age" but at least I got away with it.

It was at least a four-hour journey when we reached the outskirts of the city, it was indeed a bustling city. There was a problem for the unfortunate driver as he had to find somewhere to park near the centre, it took a while but he found somewhere. We were told to be back at the same place at 1700. I found the city intriguing; there were men with big teapots on their backs pouring out into cups for anyone who wanted (to

buy) one.
over the bustling crowds

The big Blue Mosque dominating

There were Carpets for sale everywhere. Sian and myself were walking through a market and all I wanted to do was to carry on without stopping because I knew full well we would get pestered. Sian kept running ahead with her head down like a bull in a China shop, then the inevitable happened; before I had the time to stop her, she walked into a carpet shop, so I had to follow her in. The shop owner offered us a cup of tea, I politely refused, he then he asked Sian and to my dismay she said yes, she didn't realise when you say yes you are showing interest in buying a carpet. It was hard work trying to get out of buying a carpet, even if I wanted one I didn't have the money. I said to the salesman that I would have to go and get some money and dragged Sian out with me.

Istanbul was really exciting but it was relentless with nowhere to hide. I was glad I visited bit I wouldn't fancy going through that again. The mini bus, when we found it, was a welcome sight.
   Nothing good ever lasts forever and the exercise was coming to an end so we had to shut the shop down and put all our unsold stock away.
Heather had to sort out a calamity with the duty free for the troops, the assigned person for the job was not up to it. I think she realized that she had given the job to the wrong person.

ROCKAWAY BEACH

There was one more adventure in store for us. As we still had the landrover Heather decided that we should go out and find a beach, all we had to do was to head east and we were bound to find one. We didn't even have to book out of the camp, also we didn't even tell anyone where we were going. We kept to the main highway and eventually found some signs, hinting of a beach somewhere. We drove along some country lanes and stopped to look at the map we had. Nothing was clear so Heather decided to just carry on east, there wasn't anyone around to ask for directions. To our relief we suddenly saw the great blue sea. There was this massive white-sanded beach as far as the eye could see, without a soul was in sight. I learnt later the place is called Igneada.

Well when I say there was not a soul in sight, I was technically wrong, as there was a herd of cows grazing on the few bits of grass that was growing through the white sand, which was also covered in cowpats.

About half a mile away were some buildings that seemed to be unoccupied. We started to chill out a bit and even had a few cans of beer. The girls got brave and stripped down to their bra's, this was a bit naughty really as we were in uniform, well there was nobody to see us anyway, or so we thought. After a while, one of the girls said that she was sure she could see someone in the buildings and appeared to be looking through binos. The girls decided that it would be a good idea to put their clothes back on. Half an hour later a car approached us from the direction of the buildings. When it stopped by us two smart dressed men got out and walked towards us. They asked us who we were and why we were on this beach.

Imagine this, five people in combat uniforms with a landrover, sunbathing on a beach with a herd of cows, must of seemed quite odd to them. I told them we were doing an exercise in Pinarhisar and we had a day off. We certainly didn't look like pathfinders for an invasion force, though the Turkish military are not well known for trusting people. They seemed to accept our explanation and invited us to follow them to have a drink. It would not be wise to refuse. We ended up at the unoccupied buildings where the man with the binos was spotted.

They asked us a few questions, they obviously believed us as they got more friendly and jovial. One of the men took off my beret and gave me a slap across the head, I wasn't too pleased with this but everyone had a good laugh. We were with them for about half an hour had a few drinks and a few jokes. Heather told them that we had to be leaving soon as we had to be back at a certain time. They were fine with this and said we were free to go. There were handshakes all round but I didn't shake hands with the idiot that slapped me across the head. The two men got in their car and told us to follow them so they could lead us to the main road west. As it happened it was not far from the beach. The pulled in at a lay-by and beckoned for us to carry on. We waved goodbye to them with a great sense of relief. We got back to Pinarhisar with no problems, I don't think anyone knew where we went anyway. It was now time to pack the rest of our gear and go home. This was one if my greatest three weeks, postavanje guys.

Crazy as it seems after this adventure we were give leave for it as well.
When we got back from leave it would be the usual interview with the Colonel. He told me that I could have another two weeks leave, when I return I will be on standby for Bosnia.

HANGING AROUND

June 1997.

I was now thinking of buying a house. I started looking straight away in Mumbles a village about five miles from Swansea. One house caught my eye and I made enquiries about it and put an offer in for it.

So it was time to go back to Bulford camp. There was talk that some people were going to be laid off, as there was not so much demand for staff in Bosnia. Some staff had to work in the NAAFI warehouse in Amesbury to help out as the staff messing contract made demands high.

Kevin and myself were the lucky ones the boss seemed to like us and kept us on at Bulford. Not that it was going to be an easy life though. In one of the rooms was a straw mannequin and it always would give you a start when you entered the room.

In the Op Grapple days (United Nations) our staff were part of the host supply Sqn, things had now changed as we were deployed to shops in Bosnia. EFI Staff were coming back and fro at different times, if you were duty driver it was your job to pick people up.

People were flying back into Heathrow Airport instead of Brize Norton or Lyneham. We often had to pick up Scottish personnel coming back from leave. We would have to go and pick them up at any time of day or night. Leave times were all different so staff would want picking up at Andover railway station at any time of the day.

Times were good though Kevin and myself liked a few beers and we liked each others company. Sian and Helen were waiting to be deployed and it turned out Sian was going to Bari in Italy, there we had a shop to look after the RAF Detachment. The RAF was on standby for any events that happened in Bosnia and there were a few over the years. Helen was told later that she would be going to Bosnia. Kev at least had a date for his next deployment. He was going to Saudi Arabia in June this was still a few months away. We took it in turns to go home on the weekends. There was always a need for a duty driver.

There was always a horrible atmosphere in Double hedges; there was always a lot of shouting going on. Sitting down doing nothing was not an option. We were allowed to have some fun now and then. Heather the SNCO in Turkey was still in Bulford but she was also going to Bari very soon. I decided to play a trick on her. I knew she was going into the storeroom to get some uniform, I moved the mannequin into a room where she would have to go. I put a jacket and a beret on it then switched the light out and went back into the classroom. Sure enough after a few minutes there was a loud scream.

Every morning the duty driver had to pick up the staff from Ward Barracks and stop off at the post office, which was on the way, to pick up the mail. Then anything could be detailed for us.

One day Colonel Smith told Kev to go down to the warehouse in Amesbury to pick up three tri-walls, these being large boxes we used often to pack things in, of course the new ones would be flat packed quite heavy and large. I went down with him to give him a hand.

Now I did advise Kev to tie them down on the back of the Landrover but he shrugged his shoulders and didn't bother. After the three-mile journey back to Double Hedges it became clear that the law of nature had taken over and the tri-walls were no longer in the back of the Landrover. Luckily the Colonel wasn't around, we rushed back to find the massive cardboard boxes. After a few hundred yards we came across the first one, which was on top of a hedge, and not too far from there was another in a field, the last one was a bit more difficult to locate as it was still in the yard we had got it from. Lucky it was a sunny day and even luckier is that we didn't kill anyone; yet still luckier the Colonel would never know, but then again he had a gift of knowing when something had gone wrong.

We decided one weekend to go to Salisbury for some shopping. Sian had a problem with a tape recorder and player as it was not working, Kev had a look at it and couldn't find a fault pressing buttons, checking the fuse etc. we went into a repair shop and Sian told the owner that her tape recorder didn't work, he looked at It and pressed the pause button lo and behold it worked, Sian was so embarrassed. I felt sorry for her. We went into a few pubs and had a laugh about it.

Kev and myself had a whole room to ourselves. The trouble in the ablutions was that the water supply wasn't working properly so I decided that when I went home next I would bring my plumbing tools back with me and fix the problem.

Back in Mumbles I had started talking to a local TA Soldier, he was quite a tidy person. There was a TA centre for a Transport Squadron and a medic platoon. I found out that I could use the TA centre to send boxes back.

Kev was excited about going to KSA saying how fit he was going to get and the weight he was going to lose. Well it was to be four months of no beer and no bacon for him.

It seemed every day was a sunny day then, time was slowly passing. Sian and Heather had both gone to Italy, Kev had gone to KSA (Kingdom of Saudi Arabia) and I was finally told I would be going to Bosnia along with Helen. There was a good chance that I would be replacing Kev in KSA in four months time.

There were some new recruits awaiting basic training, I didn't know why this would happen all of a sudden.

The colonel was recruiting from all walks of life. I was given the task of teaching them a bit of drill. So there was a bit of shouting going on now, this time by me. There was a half-wit Corporal who had just finished his basic training and was waiting to go on tour. He decided that he would join in training the poor recruits, although he had never been in the regular Army.

I was given a long weekend to go home to Swansea, then on the Tuesday I was going to be taken to BZZ to fly out on the Wednesday. I never looked forward to going on deployment, but I knew there were some exciting things going to happen and I would see my friends again.

FRIENDS WILL BE FRIENDS

Things had changed a lot since I was last in Croatia. First of all a driver greeted me when I got out of the airport terminal. I picked up my luggage and followed the driver to a Land Rover, which was for the sole use of EFI. Of course some things can never change the road from the airport followed the sea and the city of Split got larger, reminding me that this was the old Yugoslavia (correctly Jugoslavia) as the high rise flats all painted white seemed

Getting past Split the roads to the warehouse were just two-way lanes and the road always seemed to be dirty. It was easy to find the Warehouse because there was a clear sign, with an arrow, pointing to the left and the letters TTTS. Trgovacko Transportni Terminal Split.

There was no mistaking the familiar sight of DWC with the gate and the guardroom to the right of it. One thing however was different, there were lines of containers stacked two high, it was quite obvious that this was the new accommodation. The actual containers were CO, RI, MEC. Italiana S.P.A. a world leader in design and construction of prefabricated building of living camps. To be referred to as Corimec from now

on.

I entered the warehouse, Neil was sitting in his office and came out to greet me. I asked him where I was going and he told me that he hadn't decided yet, I would have to stay in the warehouse for a while. I told him that I was hoping to go to Bosnia but he didn't reply to me. Neil told me that I had to be in the warehouse in the morning for eight o'clock. There were always a lot of forms to fill in and a rifle would be issued to me, basically it was a military type of induction.

I was taken to the Corimec accommodation, which was four man rooms, and they were all fully occupied so there would not be much room. Our room was the usual EFI state i.e. a mess.

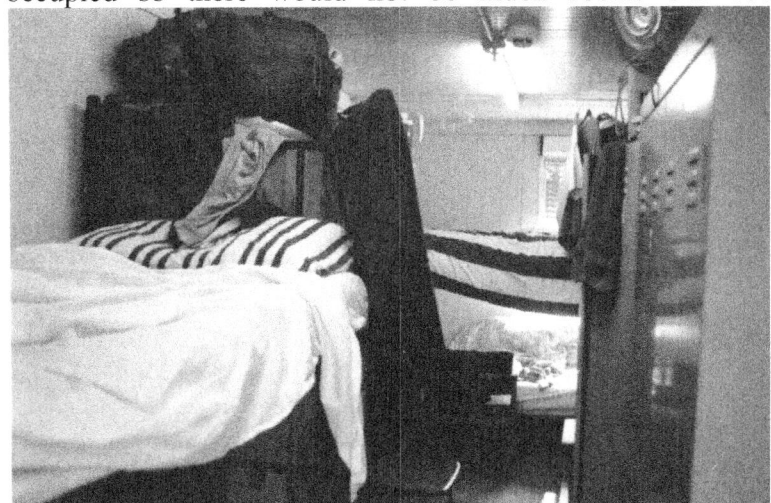

We each had a locker and an overhead cupboard I was shown which one was mine and when I opened it an iron fell out onto my head luckily not the sharp end, my fellow room mates found it amusing.

I could tell that since Nato had taken over in Bosnia discipline was a bit tighter. A strict two can rule had now been put in place not that anyone took any notice of it, or policed it; however there was fundamental reason for it though, for if anyone committed an offence while drinking they would also be charged with breaking a standing order, which could result in the person being sent home, so what. you might think; the unit back home would not take it lightly, their life would be unpleasant and their wife would not be happy.

I had a few beers in the evening and in the morning it was breakfast in the cookhouse nothing had changed there; still the paper plates and plastic cutlery, the food was still good though.

Something critical had changed though, instead of the parade with the supply Sqn it was now a Regimental parade, not now in a room in the warehouse but in the courtyard at the back of the warehouse grounds. Cpls and below were on parade in front of the senior ranks. Of course our uniforms had to be ironed, boots polished and we were to be shaved, of course the males that is.

The routine in the warehouse was still the same picking orders and stacking them. They had to be checked off by someone else; look out if your order was wrong. My routine that I had in op Grapple of putting out the rubbish with the forklift didn't fit in with the crew we had now. It was just made awkward for me so I stopped doing it. After a few days I really didn't want to stay in Dalma and I made it plain to Neil. He asked me why I wanted to go to Bosnia; I told him that I hadn't been there before.

Well eventually he relented and told me that I would be going to a place called Banja Luka. I was quite pleased about this at least I could now see the real Bosnia. I would be going with Helen who I was with in Norway and also Turkey. A few days later our flight had been booked and we were to be taken to DV barracks to fly up in a Helicopter.

We had to get a rifle from the Sqn armoury and also be issued with morphine and rounds of ammunition. Everybody had to carry morphine in case of a serious injury and if you didn't have morphine you were out of luck because no one could give you their supply, even if they wanted to, they were not allowed. So early one morning we were taken to DJ barracks (Squadies called it Divulje or Divulgee barracks but in reality it was DV barracks) Divulje if you can see the difference the J is pronounced Y. the Croatians pronounced it Divulyea. The squaddies seem to have their own version of a foreign language they

say it as they see it, and it is never correct.

There were two Chinook helicopters waiting for us to fill them up with our luggage and ourselves. There is a very clear rule while travelling, if you can't carry it; don't take it. That is because there will be nobody to help you on the other end.

I had already flown in a Chinook while I was in the TA, that flight was going to take some beating. We had got picked up in a place called Castelmartin and dropped off in a battle zone. One of our guys clearly didn't like flying, one of the aircrew noticed him and all of a sudden the aircraft was being thrown about like a toy.

That pilot could handle that aircraft and this flight to Banja Luka wasn't any different; this flight was

for real though, we followed the road up through the valleys

zigzagging all the way, as in those early days it wasn't deemed to be safe to go by road.

The adrenalin was in full flow by the time we landed at Banja Luka. We took our luggage off and then watched the Chinooks take off again and slowly flying into the distance, then leaving an eerie silence, as Chinooks always do. We were met by one of our guys and were told to follow him, it was quite a walk and the ground was rough, here is the law of carrying minimal gear, as here there was nobody that was going to help you.

Arriving at Banja Luka

We arrived at the Det commander's office, where we received no welcome to Banja Luka and no smiles. It was clear this was not going to be a fun place. Helen and myself were told that we would be working in the main shop to begin with. There was a bar on camp but locals were hired to work there. I was told to go to the shop, which was not far away, and ask one of the guys to take me to the accommodation.

I was taken to a massive building with a lot of metal to metal hammering and the smell of industrial smoke; of course this was where the accommodation was. Just like in Split the accommodation was in a Corimec.

Bearing in mind that this was the beginning of summer and inside a factory it would be quite stuffy. Later in the day the two other lads in the Det came into the Corimec I had never met them before Steve and Pete. I noticed that although the place was stuffy there was not a fan to circulate the air around. I asked the boys why there was no fan, Steve told me that they had asked Sandra (the Det Commander) for a fan but she wouldn't give them one. I asked the lads what the building was for and they told me that it was an old metal factory. This factory was right in the centre of the camp.  There seemed to be a pungent smell hanging in the air. I asked about that and was told that there was a fire outside the camp which had been burning for years, for some reason they couldn't put it out. Jokingly I remarked that I would put a claim in for this in a couple of year's time, saying I had been suffering because of it.

Fire at Banja Luka

Fire at Banja Luka

The next day Helen and myself started work in the shop, it was a bit difficult at first as basically we were given a till and float and told to get on with it. We soon got in a routine and it was quite easy because it wasn't very busy. Sandra didn't bother us much, in fact we hardly saw her. On one of the rare occasions I asked her why we couldn't have a fan in the accommodation, she told me the boys didn't ask her for one, this made sense to me. Sandra told me that if I wanted a fan to go into our locker cage and see if there were any spare ones there. That is what I did and found one that was working and took it to our Corimec and great we had a bit of air circulating. It was clear to me that they hadn't asked Sandra for a fan, it seemed they were afraid of her.

After a couple of weeks Helen had a dental appointment. The only trouble was there was no dentist in Banja Luka so she had to travel to another army camp, which was some distance away by road. She had to leave at 08.00. So she would have to sign out her rifle, from the Armoury, this in itself was not much of a problem. There however was a bigger problem, as she had to sign out her morphine, there was no way she was going to be able to get it until the morning. The reason being was that Sandra had these morphine vials and the ammunition locked away in her office. Sandra had told Helen that she would be met in the morning and issued with them.

I went to work in the shop in the morning and I was surprised to see Helen, it was now 07.45

The time came and Sandra hadn't turned up, Helen got in such a flap, she asked me "What am I going to do Taff". I told Her to go regardless, it wasn't her fault that Sandra hadn't turned up. So off she went innocently breaking a strict military law.

I saw Sandra a couple of hours later and told her that Helen had gone to the other camp, without her morphine and ammunition because she hadn't turn up to meet her; she didn't like this at all and told me to shut up. So I did shut up.

Very rare would something happen though and later in the evening Helen returned safely.

Now!! We have to face a harsh reality; If Helen had to use her rifle it would have been because everybody else had been killed, if she had to use her morphine the enemy would have given it to her to shut her up.

The two other lads that were working with me were quite good lads, Pete Ball a Scottish guy and Steve Burgess a nice quiet harmless person but was soon to earn a relic for the war trophy wall in Double Hedges.

Banja Luka was the capital of the newly formed republic of Srbska. This was a Serbian held territory, which was allowed in the Dayton agreement. Contrary to popular belief the Serbs weren't the nasty horrible people that they were made out to be. The locals that worked in the camp were very nice people. Now unfortunately for us we were not allowed to go into Banja Luka itself at night. Now this was a great pity as apparently there were seven women to every man.

One thing I invested in Banja Luka was a camcorder there was so much going on I didn't want to miss a thing. I was in the storeroom (cage more like) with Pete, I felt the need to go to the toilet and left my camcorder on a shelf, I asked him to look after it. When I got back Pete said that it had fallen on the floor, now I was quite livid; the conversation goes thus- Pete "Your camcorder fell on the floor" me "'why didn't you watch it" Pete "well I did, that is why I am telling you it fell on the floor" if he was lying I don't know but I knew I was dealing with a half-wit. It seemed undamaged anyway.

One morning I was told that I was to work in the bar after I finished my day shift in the shop. I was not very happy about this but I didn't have much choice.

As it happened it was ok because local Serbs worked the bar, so I didn't have a lot of work to do, per se. It was quite busy with loud music and the troops were enjoying themselves; basically I had to make sure there were no problems, and then all I had to do was to cash up (count the takings and refloat the till).

In the little time that I had off work I would go to the Heli-pad to take photos of the helicopters coming and going, there were some interesting events. All sorts were coming and going. Apache's, Lynx,

Puma's, Chinooks, Sea Kings and Flying Landrovers.

Anyway I did see a good side in our boss Sandra, she had arranged for a trip to the American PX in Zagreb. Although we did supply most needs for our troops the PX was a different matter.

I couldn't believe that we were actually leaving the camp by road. There was the usual signs of war damage nothing different, roofless houses, glassless, woodless windows and doors and the occasional car with bullet

holes   in   them.

We reached the Croatian border checkpoint and had no drama there, a quick check of our id cards and we were good to go.

What was dramatic after the crossing was the roads changed from single carriageway to a motorway, this was the best road I had seen in time so far in F.R.Y.

After a few hours we reached the American PX that was in the middle of nowhere. There were the usual American goods that were all bigger than anywhere else. There was nothing special or out of the ordinary to be seen here. **Well** that is what I thought. I was walking down an aisle and someone was walking towards me. I couldn't believe my eyes; this person was one of my friends that I used to socialise with, when I was in the T.A. in Swansea. He was a Major in one of the companies of 4RRW. (4th Battalion Royal Regiment of Wales.) After our shock of meeting in some obscure part of the world we had a chat. I asked him what he was doing in out here. He told me he was working for some government agency in Zagreb.

It was time to make our way back, we shook hands and that was it.

After a month of Banja Luka I had enough of the place and I asked Sandra if I could go back to Split and funnily enough she agreed, a week later I was good to go. So another Chinook flight and I was ready with my camcorder to film an exciting flight just like the one I came up on. This however never happened as the Chinook climbed to a steady height and that was about it. I did expect the Chinook to dive suddenly but as time went on I could see this city below me and realized that we were flying over Split. I had hardly taken any footage.

I never thought that I would be glad to get back to DWC. There had been a few changes since the Grapple days, there now was a proper shop by the accommodation. A Tommy Tucker had been installed. Tommy Tucker was a basic a burger bar and it was popular in the evenings as there were no other EFI facilities open, no EFI staff worked this facility, local Croatian staff were employed to work there. The main purpose for Tommy Tuckers was for the soldiers to have something local so there was no need to go to the local pizza shops. A few bars had opened up just outside of the camp; run by local Croatians (somehow, Croats sound too rude to me). Also there was a chilled canned drinks dispenser installed outside the warehouse steel doors, this was a great idea as it was a great way to deal with damaged cases. Previously we would have to repair cases and put soiled cans back in, this didn't look good. Of course someone would have to wash the dirty sticky cans, there was no shortage of volunteers.

We still had to do PT in the mornings, as we were still expected to pass a BFT at some time. Work patterns hadn't changed much; it was just a different unit running the show. The EFI staffs weren't a bad bunch and we generally got on well. Now that we had EFI shops up country in Bosnia we were much busier filling containers. Some would have to be replenished weekly and some not so often. The majority of stock we would put in containers was of course beer pop crisps sweets and chocolates; there would be an occasional Television or stereo system.

I was told that I was going to be put on standby to go to KSA (Saudi) I was much pleased about this and wouldn't have to do a full tour. Surprisingly though I had been given a date for my RnR though I wasn't going to do a full tour but this was kept quiet from the Squadron. Well it wasn't confirmed that I would be going to KSA so they were obliged to give me leave. So of course I was not going to argue with it.
RnR was usually an anti climax but it was a great feeling to know that you were going home. The routine of going home on RnR hadn't changed at all, the same old banter when seeing the returning troops.

When I got home to Mumbles my first aim was to further pursue in buying a house. I never heard anything about the house I put in for recently but when I went to the estate agents there was a fisherman's cottage for sale and at a good price, I immediately put an offer in for it and a couple of days later it had been accepted. All I had to do now was to get a mortgage. So I went to the Nationwide Building Society; I met all their criteria. It was now a waiting game.

I returned back to Dalma and got on with the work. In those days there was no email; all correspondence was by fax. In my Corimec there was a spare pit space, one of the lesser liked persons asked if he could move into our room as he wasn't getting on with Someone in his existing room. I said that he could, this turned out to be a bad mistake, he turned out to not only ungrateful but also a childlike nuisance, particularly inviting a member of the Squadron in to play video games.

The playstation and Nintendo 64 had come a long way since I had my Playstation in Germany. These guys were playing a football game, which was driving me mad. The scenes were getting repetitive with a commentator saying " What an opportunity" over and over. Then there was " A valiant attempt but thwarted" and another skiing game with the lines " Good-good-good" "cool-cool-cool" I felt like smashing up their consoles. Apart from that there was one game that I did like; where you could fly helicopters and hangliders etc and shoot at ships and buildings.

This invited squaddie tried to block me from entering my room one day, I said " excuse me " and he let me pass, lucky for him because I would of hit him out of my way.
I seemed to fit well in the warehouse and was given a task of taking Major Lafferty the OC to Kupres in Bosnia. We had to take all the kit with us, like rifles, ammunition and webbing (webbing is a system that is used for a person to carry equipment for battle conditions, different pouches for rifle magazines, first aid, rations and morphine etc).

I never really understood why us EFI were issued with and made to carry webbing as all everybody did was to pack it away in a bit of luggage, in reality not knowing what it was they were packing away.

Neil who made sure that I had a map and first paraded the vehicle that was the EFI Landrover accompanied us.

We had to make our way to the border with Bosnia, this at the time was to take a long trek uphill, leaving Split behind us and heading for a place called Klis, here there was a fantastic fortress built upon the summit and a breathtaking view of Split, Brac, and the other nearby islands on the Adriatic. To make things simple for drivers Nato had renamed the main traffic routes, for instance our journey on this day was from Split to Kupres and we would follow road Gull on the Nato map. Along the way there would be yellow signs with the name Gull on them. This was basically the road from Split to Banja Luka, though at the time I didn't have any knowledge about this. On this day I was basically the driver and Neil was the navigator. It was an uphill struggle most of the way to Klis and then it evened out, there were not a lot of signs of war activity yet. On the Gull road there were signs for a town called Sinj but we turned off at Brnaze onto Trilj towards Kamensko which was (is) the border of B+H (Bosnia and Herzegovina) There were a lot of lorries waiting to cross the border; for us though no problem Major Lafferty told me to drive past them all, and so I did passing the Croatian checkpoint and not having to stop, we had free passage.

We were now in Bosnia. There were some beautiful sights to be seen when we passed Busko Jezero, a massive Reservoir. Road Gull took us to the east side of Tomislavgrad. Straight away things were changing, as there were definite signs of warlike activities. There was an odd looking armoured car, obviously it was home made but it looked like it didn't get far.

This is when things started to look a bit different. There were occasional house with bullet holes in them but as we got onto the plains approaching Kupres things had changed dramatically for now for the first time I saw signs of real war.

There were many villages along the main road but there was no life there. Just shells of houses and no roof no windows no doors and an occasional car, that had made its last journey then a pile of cars, shot to bits. As we passed the village the ground got more open with massive fields on both sides and in the distance was a solitary tank, now you could not just get out of a car and have a closer look as there was a good chance that you would stumble upon a mine which would change your life. There was no way to know what had happened there, but one day I was to find out, and it wasn't what I thought. One thing is for sure Bosnia is such a beautiful country with mountains always to be seen in the distance. One thing that was outstanding was the sight of a massive ski slope obviously out of use at the time. Another thing that struck me was the graveyards, which were more unusual than any other country I had seen before. Every grave had a picture of the poor soul that had passed, of course mostly before the civil war started. Sadly, some of

them had bullet holes in them, it seems hate has no barriers.

We eventually got to the army camp at Kupres, Major Lafferty and Neil went off to do business and I had a chat with the person who was running the shop. Nothing spectacular but it served its purpose well, the troops were happy with it and that is what we were there for.

I suppose this run to Kupres might have been a test of my driving abilities. It must of been ok as a week later I was given the task of taking a member of staff to Kupres to replace one who had finished his tour. I had no problem with this, as I knew the way now, it was quite straightforward. I didn't even take a map with me. The person that I took up was quite savvy with the new technology of digital cameras; he took a photograph of me on the plains before Kupres. When we got to the camp he managed to print off the photo, that was my first ever-digital photograph, prehistoric by today's standards. A photograph on a mobile phone was still a long way off at the time.

I was about to learn a lesson on this day. As I hadn't bothered to take a map with me I assumed I knew my way back to Split. I headed back feeling confident that I would see a sign for Split or even Tomislavgrad. I soon began to wonder if I had made a wrong turning. I decided to turn back and eventually to my and my passengers relief I passed Kupres camp on my left. I knew then that I was going in the right direction.

It was pretty silly of me really when I talked to Neil a few days after and told him that I nearly got lost, he looked at me with a stern look and said " you went without taking a map", I replied yes, lesson learnt.

On the 31st of August we had some terrible news. Princess Diana had been killed in a road accident in France. It was very sad news and there was a genuine outpouring of grief. A lot of the girls were openly sobbing.

Now this could only lead to one thing, **parades**, and lots of them. So every morning instead of the normal parades it would be drill practice and inspections. This went on for six days with an hours practice each evening after work. Of course on the 6th September we had the parade at the same time as her funeral. It was still a quite hot day in September, things went well and nobody fainted and nobody had been jailed. It didn't rain on our parade.

I was given a further task in my driving adventures this time I was to take major Lafferty to Banja Luka. Of course this was a different ball game, it was a longer journey and probably with more risk involved.

From there we again went to Kupres, stopping off for short while, then back onto 'Gull' heading for Banja Luka. There were some horrific sights to be seen whole towns were emptied with all the houses full of bullet holes and again the roofs and windows were stripped of their timber. Towns with names I had never heard of before muchkornigrad, Gorni-vakuf, Donni-vakuf, Jajtsi and many more names that I couldn't pronounce it was a learning curve for me. We got to Banja Luka in the evening time then the boss tended to his business. In the morning I was just hanging around and it was great I could sit with the civilian EFI staff and chill out, I couldn't do this the last time I was here.

We set off for Sarajevo at 11.00 and this would be the first time I would see Banja Luka in the daytime on the road. There was a mosque that had been blown up, and all sorts of damage to houses, some blown up completely to others full of rocket and bullet holes. Life was getting back to normal it seemed, now that the war was over. All the way to Sarajevo there were signs of fierce fighting, sometimes, whole villages were ruined, some other villages the houses were full of bullet holes and rocket impacts. The scenery was absolutely beautiful with mountains and rivers at every turn of the road. We weren't actually going into Sarajevo as the main shop was in a Suburb called Ilidza. Ruth was working the shop in Ilidza, she seemed to be having a lovely time. Not far from the shop was natural spa where I was told Tito spent a lot of time. All the water was a greenish colour and the steam smelt of rotten eggs. The boss did what he had to do and he told me that I would be driving to the airport where we had a shop. So we set off and it wasn't long before we entered the city.

Of course Sarajevo had been under siege for many years; and it showed. I doubt very much that there would be a building without a bullet hole, I even doubt there would be a pane of glass undamaged. There was a fair bit of traffic on the roads and the trams were running, well not all of them as some were still damaged. The main road into Sarajevo was nicknamed sniper alley dominating the road was a massive building, which was completely destroyed. Another striking sight was a newly refurbished building, painted a bright yellow, it had signs on it saying Holiday inn. I doubted very much that I would be staying there tonight. It was clear how the siege worked out for the besiegers, as the city was completely surrounded by mountains. We came to a turning and what marked this one out was a cemetery and a Clash song ' Spanish Bombs' came immediately to mind with a line saying 'bullet holes in the cemetery walls' I shudder to think what went on in that cemetery.
A strange place to die is a cemetery.

When we neared the airport there was a road in between the runway and a long row of houses and these had seen better days although these houses were considerably damaged there were still people living in them.

There was a famous landmark on the road as well and it was the tunnel that was used so smuggle things into the besieged city.

There were a lot of aeroplanes that had seen better days as well. All sorts of airliners; these ones had made their last journey. There were not surprisingly any people walking around as the fields were littered with landmines. There was a crazy sight awaiting us. Scores of little shops all selling the same thing i.e. CDs and going for a small price. And then there were the other shops that called themselves Px.
The Italian PX, the German PX, the Dutch PX etc. PX stands for Post Exchange and they are found on American army camps. There is also a BX, which stands for Base Exchange, and these are found on American Air Force Bases. (USAF). Although our shop was called simply EFI the foreigners called it the British PX.
We reached our shop and again the boss got about his business. One of the EFI staff said he would take me out on a tour and this is when I started a good collection of CDs. We were talking about two dollars for a CD. Well to be honest the main currency now in Bosnia was the German Deutch Mark, however the vendors would take any currency.

It was dark when we made our way back to Ilidza and of course the driving conditions were different. Now I could see how many people were living in the war damaged houses and there were a lot of them. After a good nights sleep we set off early back to Split but we were not going back the way we came. We were going to head for the Croatian coast down back in Ploc'e. Back this way we could see that the war was no different and probably worse, one town was remarkable because it was obvious that buildings were levelled just by bullets. We were going to pass Mostar, which was famous for its bridge that had been blown up. Mostar means old bridge (Most is bridge Stara is old) I was hoping to get a glimpse of the damaged bridge but it was low in the valley so I couldn't see it from the road. We could of stopped on the road to look for it but we couldn't know exactly where it was and we didn't have the time. We were following the Neretva valley, which would eventually lead us to the thinnest part of Croatia. Which is where Ploc'e is and of course where I visited before in the Grapple days. There wasn't much problem getting over the border as soldiers who let us manned it straight through. It would be quite easy to find our way back to Split from here but it still could be dangerous because of erratic driving. I realized that in FRY that they were unique in their way of driving, they would often coast downhill and overtake on bends and in tunnels. Sadly along the way there would often be flowers and a little monument with a picture on it where a fatal accident had occurred. The roads on the Dalmation coast were pretty dangerous in a different way, there were not many straight roads and all single carriageways the bends were always uphill or downhill and there was little possibility to overtake a slow lorry, but people didn't mind taking a risk. My heart slowed down a bit when the road flattened out as we approached Stobrec'.

In a way it was nice to be back in DWC and back to working in the warehouse. Well I knew that it was probably the only time that I was going to visit Sarajevo. So the next few days it was back to the routine of the warehouse, working Monday to Friday and half a day on Saturday. Eating in the cookhouse with the paper plates and plastic cutlery and the pesky flies that would land on your food if you left it for a minute. I did ask fellow members of staff to watch my food when I left for some reason but I doubt they would of.

23 sep 97

HERE SHE COMES
Surreal in her crown

We knew that U2 promised that they would do a concert in Sarajevo when the war was over; true to their word they kept the promise. There was to be a meeting in our bar, which was in our old accommodation, which of course now was obsolete.

All EFI staff were gathered together and Neil told us that every department in DWC were allowed to send two people to the concert of course EFI were included. There were eight of us there at the meeting and it was decided to make it fair, that we would have a draw. Each of us had a piece of paper with our name on it and it would be put in a beret and drawn by the boss, unbelievably my name was drawn out along with Dalziel the half wit who wanted to be a drill instructor in Bulford.

A couple of days later we were boarding bus; miraculously taking me back to Sarajevo. Of course there were no weapons to be carried just uniform and body armour. It was getting dark when we got to the stadium in Sarajevo and the place was filling up with soldiers of all nationalities. The concert was started by Bono saying " God bless you peace keepers".

Bono actually didn't sing many songs because he had a sore throat so most of the singing was done by the Edge. Bono actually did say 'the Edge has got a good voice'. We were quite a way back in the stadium however the music was loud enough. There was a massive lemon on the  stage that was quite prominent. I took a few photos of it but didn't expect any good results. To me the highlight of the concert was the song Miss Sarajevo sung by the Edge. I didn't expect Pavarotti to be there but there was a gramophone being played with him doing the tenor part. To hear the line; "Here she comes, surreal in her crown", was surreal in itself. It was a good concert but nothing good ever lasts forever. We were soon on our way back to Split.

I was back in the routine of the warehouse and I was called to the office. " Taff a fax has arrived for you". Neil handed it to me, it was from Nationwide Building Society, my mortgage had been approved.

I went to Major Lafferty and told him. His words were "that is great news Taff" "you are going to be a Sergeant", I thought that was a lovely thing to say, but probably this was not going to happen.

Next bit of good news was that I had a date for my tour of Saudi Arabia and my six-month tour was cut short. I was allowed a couple of weeks leave and went to my friend's house to stay until I got the keys to my fisherman's cottage.

The day came for me to collect my keys. I of course viewed the cottage and knew there was some work to do on it. It was sound though, although it was more than a hundred years old. The walls were stone the roof was good and the windows were double-glazed. It was off the main road and no parking but I didn't mind, as I didn't need a car then. I soon started filling it with junk that I had started collecting over the years from Split and other places I had been to. Needless to say I spent some time in the local pubs. I told a friend of mine named Winnie that I was going to Saudi Arabia, she must of thought I was going on holiday when she sarcastically said "you poor dab you".

I was looking forward to going to KSA, I was wondering if I would be able to see Kevin in transit. He told me that he was going to lose weight and get fit. Before I went on leave I was told that I needed to get white t-shirts, as that was part of the uniform worn out there. I also heard that one of our guys had been arrested for taking photos of a military camp.

Next thing I knew I was back in Bulford. I had to prepare for KSA. There wasn't any training to be done for the tour and I didn't have to take a weapon. What I did have to take was a respirator and a NBC suit. I got issued those things but I wasn't too confident in the canisters that were supplied. NBC stands for Nuclear Biological and Chemical warfare. If we did come under a chemical attack I wouldn't like to rely on the canisters that were issued at Bulford to save my life. It was a good time to go to KSA as it was wintertime in the UK and in KSA it was going to be hot.

DIAMONDS ARE FOREVER

On the 16 Oct 97 at 09.00 I was picked up at the Billet in Bulford to be taken to RAF Lyneham at 11.30 I booked in for my flight to PSAB, KSA. Prince Sultan Air Base, Kingdom of Saudi Arabia. My flight was at 13.30, a two-hour wait. I stood out like a sore thumb as I was wearing my Combat 95 uniform. All the RAF guys were wearing Desert Combats. Nobody spoke to me as they probably thought I was some kind of Special Forces.

Of course your entire luggage goes with you but it is put on a pallet and rolled into the middle of the aircraft. Along with any other supplies meant for the destination. The seats are all canvas and not very comfortable, you don't want to be sat in one of these for the twelve-hour flight to KSA. The aircrew came around and dished out ear protectors, as it can get noisy and is constantly above normal decibels. It was time to buckle up and I was thinking this is going to be a long flight. The C130 doesn't need a long runway to take off as by the time it reaches 80mph it is airborne. When we got to cruising height we were told we could unbuckle the seatbelts and walk around the aircraft to find somewhere comfortable to have a bit of sleep. Some people were lucky to find a nice spot and some weren't so lucky. We were given a slap up meal, which consisted of an egg sandwich, two apples, two chocolate bars, a chicken leg and some sweets. I was on top of a packed pallet and I could see out of the window but alas it was too cloudy. The route was taking us passed Germany over Bulgaria and Yugoslavia. After several hours we were leaving the med and I thought to myself this flight is not going to take twelve hours; I realized that I had been a bit naïve. We made a stop at Adana on the coast of Turkey to refuel. We had to get off the plane as it was going to take a while. I thought that it was a busy airport as there was a plane taking off every ten minutes and they were all the same model. After a while I realised that it was the same plane, it must have been practicing taking off and landing. About two hours later we were airborne again and were given more food. When the plane reached its cruising altitude we could unbuckle again. Unfortunately we flew straight into a storm and we had to buckle up again. It didn't bother me too much as I was trying to make a cheese sandwich. In their wisdom the RAF gave us a pork pie. Nothing unusual about that but if someone put the pie into their luggage and got searched they could find themselves being arrested. It was getting dark when we flew over Jordan and Syria. Once you get into Saudi airspace, below you the terrain changes. It is very hard to pinpoint a road but you can just make them out connecting villages and towns together. There is not much greenery to be seen just white sand. There were a lot of circular green parts however I couldn't understand how this was working out. Of course as a C130 is not pressurised it can't fly as high as an airliner but I found this to be more interesting.

Eventually we were told that we were approaching Prince Sultan Air Base, which was more affectionately known as PSAB. When we got quite low I noticed that we had flown over a fence, which must have been the perimeter. Twenty minutes later we hit the runway. We taxied for a while and the doors were opened leaving in some fresh air mixed with Avtur. We were told that we could leave the aircraft and go into the big hanger where we will go through customs. All that was there were trestle tables and you would have to put your luggage on them so the officials could go through your baggage.

This was no bluff as they did a hundred percent search. I do often wonder what would happen if they did find something illegal i.e. a pork pie and even newspapers could be considered illegal as they might have women's faces inside. Books can be taboo from people like Salman Rushdie and T.E. Lawrence, even The Jungle Book, as the animals talk. Babe is out of the question.

Then there was a quick body search and we were free to go. I thought that I might of bumped into Kev but there was no sign of him. When I got out of the hanger the Det commander Dylan was there to meet me. I asked him where Kevin was and he told me that he had left yesterday and he was not sorry to see him go. It was nice to see Dylan, as he was the Det cdr in Norway. It was a good welcome and he asked me how my flight was. Dylan had arrived in a truck to meet me, he told me to put my luggage in the back then he would take me to my accommodation, which was in tent city (Harvest Falcon).

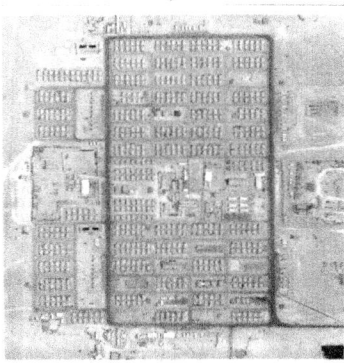

It seemed quite a drive away but most times when you  are in a strange place it appears to be that way. Of course I knew I was going to live in a tent but when I actually saw the layout I was quite impressed.

There were campcots but they had a proper mattress on top, a table and a wardrobe. There was also air conditioning. Dylan told me to settle in and when I am ready to go to the shop that was not far away. I hung up my uniform and put all my possessions away, made up my bed with the clean sheets that were on top of it. When I got outside the tent I noticed something straight away and that was each tent had a name to it.

Now our tent was called Camel lot and the next tent was called Beaver Watch and you can make what you want of this but the pretty American girls walking past were completely oblivious to what it 'might' of

meant.

The shop was a mere ten minutes walk away. The shop was actually a wooden building and next door there was a Chinese restaurant.

Dylan was serving some American customers and when they left he told me that 90% of our customers were Americans. Actually he called them SPAMS, which is what the British referred them as. He told me that we dealt in Saudi Riyals, which at the time were 7 to the pound. Of course being an American base we also dealt in US Dollars. We got most of our stock from a supermarket in Riyadh and sometimes flown in from the UK. Dylan told me that we would go up to Riyadh with the postie some time in the week.

The shop was open twice a day for four hours and we would take it in turns to run it. It was now early in the evening and Dylan told me that he would shut up the shop, and then take me to the Airmen's mess for dinner; Dylan told me that the airmen's mess was the RAFs ace card. If the RAF wanted anything from the Americans it would be conducted over a dinner. This is how good the food was.

It was a short walk from the shop; there was no mistaking it as it had a sign outside with the words, Roundel Restaurant. Next to the mess was the bar, which only served alcohol free beer. It was still busy at times. It was called the Cock and Pullet.

Now I am a great lover of curry and this place was not going to disappoint me. Not only were there RAF cooks but they also had Sri Lankan chefs. When we finished our meals Dylan took me to the ablution tent, which was a good walk away he also pointed out the laundries, which were on the way. There were massive washing machines and tumble driers; this might sound odd that they would have driers in the middle of the desert but the logic was they didn't want people hanging up their laundry, here everything was supplied free of charge, this included the washing powder and Laundry drier sheets.

I was free to go back to my tent and sort my belongings out. I didn't have much to put away, the pit space still looked bare.

In the morning I was to be at the shop at 0900 where Dylan would show me the ropes. First though was breakfast; I wondered what it would be like without any pork. To my surprise it was not bad, there were sausages and bacon, however the sausages were chicken and the bacon was beef. One thing for sure was it was going to take a lot of willpower to lose weight.

My first morning in the shop was a learning curve but it was no problem as I soon worked out the system. Of course Dylan was there to show me the ropes. We were going to open at 1000 so this gave me time to know where things were and work out the till and exchange rates. The Spams of course would only have dollars.

It was a simple shop we sold mostly drinks sweets chocolates and cigarettes. We also sold ornaments and clothing. Dylan explained that all the stock came from shops in Riyadh and Hussan stores.

We opened at 10.00hrs and a couple of spams came in. the first thing I noticed was that I was going to be lucky to get a please or a thank you. More customers came in and again you would be lucky to get any eye contact. Dylan told me that as they were Air Force they thought they were above everyone else.

As said earlier all our stock came from Riyadh. The chocolate bars came in boxes of 48 and the thing about them was their size. They were about half the size we would get in the UK. The cans of pop were normal size but were as cheap as chips, probably equivalent to about 10 pence in the UK. The Americans came to our shop as we sold things that their BX couldn't sell. This is where we had the advantage as all the things in the BX were flown in from the States; all the things we sold were from Riyadh.

Also the Americans were not allowed off the base. One of our best sellers were Cuban cigars as the Americans couldn't buy them from anywhere but us; it was a sort of rebellion thing i.e. something that was banned in the US they could buy here. Diamonds were another bestseller for us, I mean desert diamonds that is. We would go into the desert part of the camp and pick up certain stones and take them to a jeweller in Riyadh go back the next week and they were cut into shiny diamonds. They were even given a carat. They were only semi precious diamonds though but they could be added to a gold ring and it would look like the real thing. They certainly weren't going to make us millionaires.

Dylan told me that he would take me to Riyadh on the weekend to show me the procedures on buying things to resell in our shop. He also told me that the postie would drive us up and that was going to be the way it worked. Except it were just the Postie and myself in the future.

Another perk we had with the RAF was LOA, which was a local overseas allowance. This was an allowance that we could get because the cost of living in a foreign country would be higher. All I had to do was to go to the admin office weekly and get paid cash. KSA was a rich country but the shops were hardly expensive. We shut up shop so we could get some food in the mess. I started to learn a bit more how it worked. There would be a chef who was a Sergeant and two Corporals; there were also two Sri Lankan chefs and a group of bottle washers, these were referred to be TCNs (Third Country Nationals)

We went back to the shop for a couple of hours and it didn't take long for me to get in the swing of things. Another line of merchandise was clothing which also came from Riyadh. Dylan asked me if I wanted any, well I didn't have many clothes so I look a liking to a Nike top and I could have it for the price we paid for it and this was a pittance.

After the shop shut we went to the big American shop, which was called a BX. A BX is short for Base Exchange as we were on an American air force base. Now if we were on an army camp it would be called a PX, which is Post Exchange. It was run by EFES the American equivalent of the NAAFI. The shop was massive and they sold everything you could possibly need, even a Harley Davidson that is if you were an American serviceman or like us worked for the company. I think it worked that you would buy the bike in the BX but not physically, it would be available for when the airman got home to his base in the states. There were the basic things like shaving foam, talcum powder, boot polish, clothing toothpaste etc they were very cheap and they were twice as big as normal. The same went for the sweets and chocolate it was going to take some more discipline to keep the weight down. There was a good selection of bedding so I bought a few blankets and pillows. Not far from the BX a Burger King and a Baskin Robbins, I thought to myself Kev had no chance to lose weight.

The time came when I was to have my first visit to Riyadh. Dylan decided that the shop would not open in the evening the postie had gone to MT to book out a vehicle. Dylan told me that we would only be going to Riyadh on this occasion; it was early in the week and normally we would go on a Friday. Naturally this was all new to me, I found it interesting and intriguing. We had to book out of the camp by telephoning the RAF Police.

It was quite late in the afternoon and by the time we got to Riyadh it was dark. We arrived at the main shopping area and parked the pick up truck. The place was bustling with people but I noticed these were not Saudis but Third Country Nationals (TCNs) a lot of them were just sitting around doing nothing in particular.

Dylan obviously knew the best shops to go in, in this area it was mainly clothing shops selling top of the range designer goods, well to be honest copies of top of the range designer goods. Not that I was a connoisseur of designer clothing. Dylan bought about thirty tops and obviously got a good price for them. We went back to the pickup truck and put away the recently bought goods; he told me that we were going to the Gold Souks, whatever that was.

After a few miles drive we again parked up the truck, after a short walk we were in a different shopping centre, a lot of the stalls were selling ornaments, a few would be selling marble goods and others would be selling metal ornaments like the Aladdin lamps we used to win in the fairground when I was young. We could buy anything we wanted from these shops and sell them in our shop. This was a process we called goods purchased for resale. Then we got to the serious shops, the gold shops and there were many of them.

Dylan seemed to like a certain couple of shops where he would get a good deal. The postie and myself walked around some of the shops; well really he showed me where the good shops were, it was a wonderland really.

We went back to the gold Souk where Dylan was waiting for us, and then back to the truck to put away some more recently bought goods.

It was nearly time to make our way back home but there was another shop to visit, it was a 7 Riyal shop, if it was a coincidence or not I didn't know, but there were 7 Riyals to the pound at the time; basically these were pound shops; it was amazing what could be bought with 7 Riyals. We made our way back to PSAB, there was not much to be seen in the dark and the roads were very quiet. The postie had already been in KSA for about a month so he knew the ropes.

The Friday visit to Riyadh soon came around. I finished my morning shift in the shop and waited for the postie; Dylan told me that the postie knew where Hussan stores was and he would also going to take me to the shopping centre; he then gave me a couple of envelopes one for Hussan stores this contained money and a list of things that we needed to buy from them. The other envelope contained just cash to pay for goods ordered in the Gold Souk and other shops. Soon the postie arrived in a pick up truck and came out to meet me.

Dylan this time formally introduced us; the posties name was Craig but better known as Goose. So we were soon on our way, first we had to fill up with fuel and then book out with the RAF police. We had to tell them what time we were expected back just in case something happened to us.

We made our way out of tent city onto the main road, which was a dual carriage; very prominent was a massive water tower.  This was visible from miles away. There was no traffic to be seen on this road on our side or the other side. There was a checkpoint just before we reached the main road to Riyadh and the Saudi army who manned it would check our ID cards and car registration number. When we got onto the main road towards Riyadh I noticed on the right was a road leading to a dairy farm, the first thing I noticed was a plume of smoke in the distance: I presumed it was a train waiting to leave the station. Upon passing the road I noticed a sign saying 'welcome to the worlds biggest dairy farm'. Further down the road on the left was an entrance to a Saudi army camp, where there was an impressive building. Goose warned me not to take any photos of the camp. One of my predecessors got caught taking a photograph and had a gun pointed at his head until the RAF Police got him out of the Sheisser. As we were now on the main highway signs were coning up with distances for cities. The first sign was for a place called Al Kharg and I later learned this is where the Bin Laden family owned some businesses. You are soon to realize that you are in a country, which is very different to what we are used to. There were camels grazing on the little amount of grass that they could find. Then camels crossing the roads, I even saw a Camel on the back of a pick-up truck.

The distance from PSAB to Riyadh was near enough 100 kilometres. Before we could enter Riyadh we had to book into a place called Eskan village.
Here is where the BFPO (British Forces Postal Service) housed most of their posties, and this is where all the mail would be collected for PSAB, and Goose would also see his boss for any instructions.
Upon leaving Eskan we would get on the main highway for Riyadh. This is where all rational driving ends. There are three lanes on each side of the highway and there are no rules except go fast. Apart from the three lanes there was an escape lane with a thick red line. This was an emergency lane in case god forbid you had to stop. We called this Allah's lane because some drivers would get frustrated at not going fast enough, they would then use the fourth lane as another fast lane. They are now in the hands of Allah i.e. God.
Then you get to the traffic lights, like death and taxes there is no way of avoiding them. If you are the first one at a traffic light you had better have your wits about you and be quick off the mark, because when the light changes to amber you have one millionth of a second to move, or else the horns start blaring and there is no time for hesitation. The odd thing about this is that we started doing it ourselves.
On one bridge over the highway there was a lorry with its cab hanging over the side. When you get off the main highway normality seems to come back, though that's an illusion for what you now see is boys driving cars but they cant even see over the bonnet; but you will not see any girls driving, in fact you will not see any girls at all.
One welcomed sight though was a Burger King, not because of hunger but because it had a porcelain toilet. One thing again though you wouldn't see is any female, as they were segregated to their own area.
We arrived at Hassam stores and the first thing me had to do is ask to see the manager. A member of staff came up to us, Goose knew who he was and asked if we could see the manager. The man got on the internal telephone and spoke to I presume was the manager. A couple of minutes later the manager came down to see us, he then invited us upstairs and it all seemed a formal occasion. He offered us tea, which was a custom we could not refuse. We sat around the table and engaged in polite conversation drinking the plain tea, which was quite refreshing. I gave the manager the envelope that Dylan told me to pass on. The manager looked at it and said ok the order will be prepared for you. The usual thing to do then was to go into the centre of Riyadh for some shopping.
It was not far from the store and goose pointed out a fish and chips shop, I presumed it would be popular with ex-pats.

Goose explained the first stop would be was where the souks were. Now this place was a massive market where there were hundreds of little shops called souks. There were souks that sold brass ornaments we would buy things that we could sell on (goods purchased for resale).

These things were meant for the Americans as the Brits could go to Riyadh when they wanted. The main souks that we were interested were the Gold souks. Goose explained to me this is where we could bring our stones that we found in the desert and give them to the trader and a week later they would be shiny diamonds. How they did this I did not know. They would even give them a carat value. We would pick up orders that we had left a previous week and pay for them and get receipts. All these transactions were legal and had to be put through the books.

After my first experience of the souks we went into the town where the clothes shops were. There were also many 7 Riyal shops in effect these were pound shops as it happened there were 7 Riyal to the pound at the time. Then there were to clothes shops where you could buy authentic clothes like Polo Levis (some spelt as Lives) and all sorts of names. These clothes were cheap but if you bought in bulk, which we would do you would get discount and even free clothes. The quality of some of these clothes was amazing and sometimes was superior to the real thing.

I was amazed the first time I went into a 7 Riyal shop. Here you could buy clocks watches and all sorts of wonderful merchandise. All of these shops sold a special clock in the shape of a mosque it was called an Assam clock. It was a nice looking clock but it had a dark secret behind it. When the alarm actually went off it could give you a heart attack it was so loud it fitted its purpose because it certainly would wake you up.

One thing that struck me about Riyadh is the place was crowded but mostly by TCNs, there were very few Arabs to be seen.

It was late in the afternoon when we arrived back at Hassam stores. We had to park at the back of the shop so our stock could be put into our pick up truck. I had been given an envelope to give back to Declan. Our supply of cigarettes chocolates and drinks had been brought out to us and we made our way back to Eskan village but not before another luxury in Riyadh; Subways, now I had never had a Subway before but that was going to change. I always like spicy food so it had to be Salami and pepperoni with onions and jalapenos. There were TCNs serving here but the concept of hygiene was escaping them; fair enough they wore rubber gloves but they were handling filthy money and then handling food without washing their hands and without changing gloves but hey, ignorance is bliss, best not to look. Well that was my first experience of Riyadh. We got back onto the mayhem of the ring road calling in at Eskan village. Goose disappeared for a while and came back with a handful of letters. Once we got off the ring road and on the way back to PSAB the roads got quieter. There is one more thing you will not see in KSA and that is a stray dog; as they were considered filthy animals by the Arabs they would get run over on sight. What you would see a lot of are camels. It is hard to imagine that every one of these has an owner as they had collars on.

The dairy farm was visible from miles away and still' there seemed to be a train waiting at the station. When we passed the entrance of the farm we knew that we didn't have far to go. We had to go through the Saudi checkpoint where we would show out pass and were allowed into the camp. We had to head for a massive water tower that was a few miles away and we were then back to tent city. We went to the shop where Dylan was waiting for us and put the new stock into the shop. I was free to go to the bar and have a few alcohol free beers.

Of course we had to take our uniform to KSA but it was informal all we had to wear was DPM trousers and a white t-shirt. The only other item of uniform was our NBC suit. In the first week I had to go to the RAF Regiment and be trained in the use of the respirator and suit. I had to get my respirator fitted. The respirator was fine but more importantly was to make sure I had new filters; it is the filter that saves your life not the respirator. There is no point in having a gas mask if the filters don't work. This is what happens; the person being trained is taken into an airtight room, then told to put the respirator on, the instructor then lights a CS tablet, if you haven't got your respirator fitted properly you will know all about it, you will start choking and run for the door to get out, sometimes it will be locked and it is up to the instructor if he will let you out or not. Even if you fit the respirator properly you will be told to remove it and breath in the CS gas and you will still run for the exit.

Now the funny thing is; when there is a threat of a war people go to army surplus stores and buy gas masks, little do they know that they will not work if you haven't got a filter fitted.

I had to perform drills in case we came under attack but I knew all this anyway. Mask in nine i.e. you have nine seconds to put on your respirator, if not and it is nerve gas you will die. This makes me wonder how someone managed to put Novichoc on someone's doorknob without being seen wearing a gas mask.

There was a threat of a gas attack from Iraq; I don't think anyone really took it seriously though.

Propaganda

Talking of propaganda, there was a radio station on PSAB that was playing music on the loudspeakers. Ninety percent of the songs were Supertramp, in between every record was a constant story about how heroic deeds were performed by the American military; like how a single marine help off an entire Army of Japanese on an island or how a soldier on horseback charged a machine gun post and killed all the defenders. Different acts of bravery and heroism this was so Orwelian. This was hammered out constantly day in day out. You would try to ignore it to no avail. Only a staunch patriot would believe the pathetic stories were being spewed out and there were plenty of them. The announcer seemed to be nearly crying by the end of some stories. I got so sick of listening to Supertramp. Like eating eggs it took me five years to listen to Supertramp again.

After a few days this massive base seems to get smaller when you start to know where everything is.

It was decided that goose and myself would go to Riyadh every Friday. We could stay at Eskan village overnight. I noticed then that these posties had a great life. They had a proper brick building en suite bathrooms. A kitchen fitted with all the amenities. And for all this they got extra LOA. The detachment consisted of one Sergeant one Corporal one Lance Corporal and a private. Being as Goose was the LCPL he got to have PSAB. They had their own 4x4 as they had to go to the civilian airport to collect mail and maybe meet a courier. The RAF didn't have anything to do with handling mail it all passed through Riyadh. When you drive through Riyadh it is very impressive there are massive building and the roads are immaculate. Again there is another thing you will not see and that is a statue of anything as these were taboo in KSA. There are massive compounds most of them began with a sign beginning with Ministry of something. When you get near the centre of the city you will see a yellow stoned fort. This fort was immaculate and it looked very nice not if you were a guest here though. This place was known as chop-Chop Square. On a Friday, goose explained is when they chopped off people hands and maybe a head. If you were that way inclined you could go in and watch. I had no interest in this as I thought you would have to be sick to want to see what was going on. There were plenty of takers though, some people are naïve and believe what they are told.

On the first Friday that we went into Riyadh we had to visit to Hassam store gave the envelope. We were having the usual chat and a cup of tea, all of a sudden there was this loud wailing sound and then the manager told us that we had to leave the shop and go outside. Of course Friday is the holy day of the week and four times a day the call to pray happens. Every shop has to close and everyone has to go out into the street or go to a mosque to pray. A half hour later the wailing starts again and the shop reopens. The manager took us into the storeroom, which was typically out of sight and out of mind dingy and unpainted. I was talking to the manager and a TCNs who was working in the storeroom wanted to pass us Ahmed just ignored him and I stepped back to let him through, as he passed in between us he bent as low as he could as a sign of humbleness. I understood the routine now there is no point in hanging around the store so it makes sense to go to Riyadh and get some more supplies for our shop.

We got to the gold souk and collected some desert diamonds and gave the jeweller some more stones. There were all sorts of souks, like gold, fashion, tailors ornaments etc. I decided that I now needed a suit and went to the tailor got measured up and told to come back the next week. Goose and myself then went into the clothes shop to get some more tops. I was rummaging through the clothes when the wailing started again. Immediately the shop deployed the shutters and we were told to leave.

Now this was not like Hassams store where we had to wait in the car park now we were in the middle of town and there were thousands of TCNs where they come from baffled me. Most of them seemed to be Indian or SriLankan. There was nothing to do or nowhere to go; you could certainly hear the megaphones playing the prayers. It seemed like an eternity waiting for the shops to open again. I wondered if anyone took their goods without paying for them. Somehow I doubt it.

Apart from buying the cheap designer copies I went into some tailor shops and bought some expensive looking shirts that were far from expensive. We went back to Hassam stores got our goods and headed back to Al Kharj. Well that was the routine that was to go on for the next few months.

In the meantime some funny things happened. Now in a place like KSA you would not likely to see a pink Cadillac but that is exactly what zoomed past us one day, goose shouted out 'did you see that' we raced after it and even caught up with it but soon lost it our 4x4 was no match for it.

Going past Al Kharj a herd of camels were running riot on the motorway. We had to stop in case we hit one and that would have been big trouble. They were sniffing around the car then one came zooming past us out of nowhere. Then another trotted past us. Some people don't like camels, I think they are lovely animals; they have their own personalities. Another time we stopped off to take photos of some camels that were grazing but their owner did not seem pleased about it and started shouting and waving his stick at us. I was tempted to shout some obscenities at him but thought better of it. We would probably get arrested at the PSAB gate.

On one of the days when we got kicked out of a shop for prayers I was in desperate need for a pee. There are public toilets in the centre if you are brave enough to go in them. I was so desperate I had to go, the place was stinking; all of a sudden my urge for a pee disappeared when I got in there. On a hot summers day in Riyadh, that is one place to avoid.

A problem started; it was called clutter! Things were so cheap I was buying more and more. To be fair a beard trimmer was only 7 Riyals but it would probably take half of your face off though; Clocks; I convinced myself I needed clocks, sewing sets, cups it all became an obsession.

Back in the Cock and Pullet one night I was talking to my RAF friends. They were mostly senior ranks and about my age so we got on well. I mentioned chop-chop square. I was told that if a westerner wanted to see an execution he would be a allowed to; in fact he would be able to have a front seat, this would bring shame upon the poor soul. As for amputating hands they would drug the person and drain a lot of blood out of him so there would be less gore. Then take him to the hospital. What they would do with the severed hand is smash it with a hammer so it couldn't be sewed back on again. That was decent of them to smash it up after it was chopped off rather than before (not always I bet).

I was told when they stoned women for adultery it wasn't like you would think. They didn't actually throw stones at them instead they would dig a big pit and put the poor woman in it, then get a lorry full of stones and tip them over her. Well that is what I was told anyway.

One day back home in Swansea I told one of my friends about this and she said, " Bloody hell Miles, they could kill a woman doing that"

The Roundel restaurant was quite interesting. One of the TCNs was getting mouthier and disobedient, it was quite obvious that he didn't like us; another TCN told me that he was a Tamal tiger, he looked quite proud of the fact as well.

The Corporal cook was getting a bit unfriendly to me for some reason. I suppose he didn't like the fact that I was a Corporal in EFI. We were having a bit of an argument one day and he said to me ' you are just a civvy' I promptly replied' "well what ever rank I am, it is higher rank than what you are then". I don't think he appreciated the day when he called himself a Chef; I put him right and stated that you can't be called a Chef until you are a Sergeant. He knew it was true and he didn't like it. One evening I was eating a curry when I looked up and he was smiling at me, I don't know if he had put something in my curry to make it hot or he had done something else to it.

A couple of days later when the Tamal tiger was not in the mess I asked the same TCNs where he was, he replied 'oh he has been sent home'. I doubt if the Americans would have taken the trouble to send him home. They were most likely to take him to the front gate and tell him to make his own way home. After a few visits to Riyadh I noticed a problem was developing and it was called clutter. Things were so cheap I was buying more and more to be fair a hair trimmer cost about 7 riyal though it could potentially take half of your face off. Clocks I needed more clocks sewing sets cups and more clothes.

One day Dylan arranged for me to visit the RAF Tornado detachment to take a close look at their aircraft. Badger from the RAF police took me there. When we arrived at the site I was just expecting to take a close look. The pilot asked me if I wanted to have a sit down in the pilots seat. Well of course I did. I climbed up the ladder and the navigator helped me get into the seat, he also showed me the dials etc and warned me not to touch anything at all as the aircraft was armed and the engines were running. The aircraft didn't actually take off but it did a bit of taxiing. It was a surreal experience and I dare say there are not many people out of the RAF that have had the privilege that I had that day. Dylan and myself often had a good chat; he was a good person to get on with. He told me about how Kev was behaving. Every time Dylan told or asked him to do something he would tell him to eff off, no wonder he was glad to see him go. I don't think Dylan deserved such disrespect.

Into three months of my tour in KSA there was a change of management Dylan went home and was replaced by another Sergeant Chris Black replaced him. Before Dylan left he told me that he would ask the Colonel if he could have me in Italy as his assistant when he went out to run the Det there. I was sad to see Dylan go he turned out to be a fair boss and a good friend.

Things were now decidedly different, work wise at least, it seemed Dylan was here for work but Chris was here for a holiday. I had a fortnight with Chris before my trip to Bahrain and he wasn't bothered about being on his own for a week. One morning I had to go to Hassam stores to get a truck full of cases of pop. There was no need for anyone to go along with me. When I arrived back in the afternoon Chris opened the shop so we could transfer it into the storeroom, the next thing I knew I was on my own, I had to lug the lot without any help, I was furious to say the least.

Although our tour of duty in KSA was only four months we were entitled to a weeks RnR you had a choice of how you would take this. You could spend two weekends in Bahrain or have a week in the holiday inn in Riyadh. The preferred choice for most people was to have the two weekends Bahrain where alcohol could be consumed. If you chose the whole week it would have to be spent near the end of your tour.

A couple of days before our trip to Bahrain we had a briefing. We were told that we were going to stay in the Diplomat hotel. A RAF policeman and myself were going to drive to Bahrain another couple of cars were going up but on different days. We were given even more LOA. And of course the petrol would be paid for; well it was free anyway.

On the morning of our departure it was decided that I would drive up and Badger would drive back. So I went to the MT flight and got our car, which was full of petrol so at least I didn't have to worry about refuelling for a while. The way to Bahrain was quite straightforward just head for Riyadh and we would see a sign showing us the highway to Bahrain.

The journey was long, all to be seen was the road and the desert. The desert is not what you would imagine in the films like yellow sand dunes, in fact nothing like it. What you would see however were camels, thousands of them. It must of taken eight hours before we got near the coast at Al kubal. Where there was a stinking looking dockyard and an equally stinking looking city.

Eventually we saw the sign for the causeway going to Bahrain. There was nothing to say that KSA and Bahrain were separate states until you reached the middle where there was a solitary building, which was the customs.

We had to get out here and show our passports. This was the easy part going into Bahrain coming back would be a different story. On the way to Bahrain we didn't get searched. This is where badger took over the driving and a great sense of relief and freedom took over me. Badger told me that we had to head for the capital Manama. This is where the hotel was at and it took us about an hour from the customs compound. After a bit of map reading Badger found our hotel and the car park. Soon we were checking in and shown our rooms.

Dylan had told me that he didn't bother with his RnR because he didn't want to go out drinking with the RAF guys; I was about to find out the reason why.

After a shower and change of clothing we went to the main bar to meet up with the rest of the RAF group. I immediately understood what Declan meant. These people instantly changed into anusols.

There was one Chief Technician who was strict and by the books with his guys; he was now acting Jack the lad. All these guys wanted to do was to get peed and stay peed for the rest of the remaining few days.

Myself I just wanted to take my time after not having a drink for three months. Well after a few beers it was decided that we would get a taxi to a place called Burnaby Joes, which was a nightclub. In Bahrain of course there were no pubs as such. You could drink in the hotel but they were expensive and no fun.

In Barnaby's there were a few ladies around but I didn't stand a chance with the younger lads around, not that I didn't try though.

The next day I decided to go out for a walk and hopefully find a few shops but with little success, however on the way back, not far from the hotel I found a little supermarket and they even sold cans of beer. I decided that as there was entertainment in the hotel every night I would have a better time there. There was a Philippine band that played good music and also had dancers, that was entertainment enough.

Christmas day came along and of course the hotel provided a dinner and entertainment for us in the evening. I took my camcorder with me and filmed a few close ups of the dancers.

It soon came around for us to make our way back to PSAB. I was feeling a bit shaky and rough but as it was agreed Badger was going to drive back. I couldn't even remember where the car was parked but Badger soon went off to find it, coming back a few minutes later.

We were soon off leaving Manama behind us and heading for the causeway knowing full well that we were going to be searched at the customs. I hoped that the Saudis didn't want to look at my camera, because the tape in it was a bit naughty but the Saudis wouldn't look at it that way, they would consider it as pornography. We stopped at the checkpoint and the officers looked into the car and took a few books off Badger. They went into their building and a few minutes later they came back out, they told Badger that they wanted to talk to him. They took him into the building and it was quite a while before he reappeared. I asked him why he had been so long and he told me that he had a photocopy of a hundred Riyal note and was using it as a bookmark.

The custom officers then went through our entire luggage; they got hold of my camcorder took the film out and told me to accompany them to their office. They put the tape into a machine and played the tape skipping through parts of it, I thought that if they see the pictures of the dancing girls I am in big trouble. Luckily they skipped past the dancing girls didn't see anything wrong and gave the tape back to me. They let us go back on our way. I don't think I stopped shaking till I got to Riyadh.

It was such a long way back to PSAB I thought to myself if I ever go to Bahrain again I will fly. However this was only the first part of my RnR.

It was a long journey back to PSAB; I never thought that I would be so happy to get back.

It was breakfast in the morning and then back to the routine. I went for a walk in the afternoon and claimed my second t-shirt at 100 miles.

On New Years eve 1997 of course there were to be no fireworks and no parties, it was quite quiet in the Cock and Pullet and I had a few alcohol free beers with the RAF Sqn. After the festivities were over I decided to have some sort of celebration and I lit up a Cuban cigar. It tasted awful and nearly knocked me out, I was soon fast asleep in my pit.

I worked in the evening and accepted the fact that you were not going to get a please or thank from the spams. But one thing I wasn't going to put up with was people throwing money at me. A group of spams came in and just wanted cigarettes ok fine but one of theme pointed at the cigarette display and just threw a ten dollar note at me. I took the note and got the pack of cigs and got as much small change as I could and threw it onto the counter and a fair bit of it fell on the floor. He got quite angry but I wasn't going to back off, I told him not to come back again. That was a bit of an empty gesture though because I doubt I would have recognised him again.

Another US airman kept asking me to get a wedding ring made for him in Riyadh and even said that he would invite me to his wedding in the states, I thought that would be nice. He gave me a drawing of the ring he wanted inlaid with a desert diamond. I said the next time I went to Riyadh I would get the ring made for him. To cut this story short I got the ring for him and gave him a fair price and he was happy with it but that was the last I saw of him. I never did get the invite from him, it was all hot air, I just couldn't understand why all the pretence.

Everything around out tent Camel-lot was in short walking distance with the exception of the ablutions. Going to the showers could be quite of an ordeal. It was at least a ten-minute walk across barren land. On one occasion I was heading for the showers and a Spam was walking along and it became quite clear that our paths were going to meet. The arrogant little grunt didn't even acknowledge that I was there. I was so furious that I felt like smacking him in the face, but I knew if I did, I would suffer the same fate as the Tamal tiger.

Another incident occurred over a few days. I went for a shower and noticed that someone had put up a note. It said ' when you have finished with your razor please don't leave it on the floor as I just stepped on one'. On my next visit a day later there was a reply to the note. ' If I want to leave my razor on the floor I will, don't tell me what to do.' Next day ' I was politely asking you to stop leaving razors on the floor. Please leave your name and where I can contact so we can have an adult conversation.' That was the end of that. It was obvious this was an argument with a Spam and a Brit.

The ablutions were always littered with rubbish and obviously some TCN would have to clean the place up, to these Spams everyone was below them. On another occasion I walked into a shower cubicle and there was sxxxn on the floor, someone didn't have the decency to clean it up after himself.

PRIVATE DANCER

The Americans did care about their troop's welfare. One evening there was a rock group and after them a show with dancers. The girls looked absolutely stunning. In between a performance for some reason a microphone was given to a Spam who was making a fuss. He tried to convey his message but was stuttering ' 'I' 'I''I' ' l love you' and made quite a fool of himself because everything went quiet, and in this lull I felt like shouting out ' shut the eff up you idiot', but of course I didn't though if I did I am sure it would of gone down with uproar. After the show we could meet up with the girls to get their autographs, it was a bit of a disappointment really, as they were pretty enough but not as beautiful, they seemed when they were dancing.

I was getting near to the end of my tour in KSA and there were only a few Fridays left. On one of these weekends I was allowed to stay in Eskan village. Compared to what we had in PSAB this place was a luxury but saying that I would not have changed anything, there was something about tent city that was unique. There was a kitchen there showers, a bath a television but it lacked people, not saying that the posties here weren't a good bunch. Goose had to do a courier run this weekend and he took me with him. He didn't know what he was going to collect the posties never did. Instead of going into Riyadh city this Friday we went to Riyadh airport. It's amazing what privileges we in Efi had at times. No airmen from PSAB would ever be able to go into the part of the airport we did that evening. A civilian flight had come in from the UK and Goose had to meet the courier personally. When the aircraft stopped goose drove to the aircraft and left me in the 4x4; he was only gone five minutes and came back with a package, what was in it I didn't know. We had to go straight back to Eskan village. The posties even got deliveries from Burger King and that was our supper this night. One thing they did not have however was real beer.

On the Saturday we went into Riyadh shopping but I didn't need to get much stuff. I don't suppose many people would go shopping in Riyadh for a weekend. So here is an insight. There was a massive shopping mall but it not a normal day out in Harrods. Of course you would not see many ladies in downtown Riyadh. In this shopping centre it was different there were plenty of women shopping but they were covered up and all you could see was their eyes. In these places you were not even allowed to look at the ladies but I got this feeling that they wanted to be looked at and given a bit of attention. Just by looking at their eyes you could see underneath these were very attractive looking women. Ironically these ladies were mainly shopping for clothes that they could never wear.

When we left this shopping centre we went to get a subway. We parked the car and goose went to get the food. I noticed that there was a commotion going on so I went a bit closer to have a look. Now we have heard of the Mufti, which are the religious police. These policemen were questioning some people and one noticed I was looking on, he gestured me to look the other way and of course that is what I did. I knew not to mess with these people. Later I was looking in a shop window and dropped some money I bent down to pick it up as I was doing this an Arab did an obscene gesture behind me. A bit later I was walking in a crowded area and there was this Arab gesturing for people to get out of his way as if they were low life; the sort of thing you would see in an historical movie, however this was real. In the meantime Chris had been upsetting the RAF guys. It was soon time for Goose to end his tour and his replacement arrived. Goose had to show him the ropes so I didn't see much of him.

The second part of my RnR came up and I was off to Bahrain again on the 14th of January to the 17th, as it happens Goose was at the end of his tour, and unbelievably he had been booked on a flight from Bahrain to the UK. Things were a bit different this time. Goose drove to Eskan village, he was going to stay the night there, and was going to be taken to Bahrain the next day. I was now going to drive to Bahrain with Stu, another RAF guy who was going on RnR with me. I had a pretty good idea of the way. We had to get past Riyadh, which was quite a busy road, and from there on it was quite straightforward; just motorway to Bahrain which would take five hours.

We arrived in Manama at around 2pm. I realized something there was something simple; after all that sand we get to see something simple but taken for granted; Shite Hawks i.e. Seagulls.

I drove to the hotel without a problem. At reception we were told which room we were in. With all this expense we were put in a five star hotel in one of the richest countries in the world, to be given a twin room and only one key. We went down to lunch and met some lads from PSAB, we were then invited to their room to have a few beers, I really didn't want to start drinking early in the day but were given a hard time and joined in. After a few hours we went back down for dinner then onto the Lute bar, this is where I filmed the dancing girls at Christmas. The food was amazing, a starter, main meal, sweet and cheese and biscuits, this sobered me up a bit but felt drained after. I didn't eat an enormous amount but enough. After the Lute bar we went onto Henrys pub for more beer. Goose caught up with us in Henrys, of course this would be the one and only time we would have a drink together. Goose went back to his hotel about midnight; we went onto BJs and because it was Ramadan there was no dancing allowed; strange to believe. The beer was getting the better of me, but that was not the end of it. We went onto the rugby club in Manama where I found it hard to stay upright. At 4 am we got a Taxi back to the hotel and went straight to bed, the rest of the guys went to the conference room where the girls were staying for more partying.

In the morning I felt ok and went to breakfast. I met up with goose and accompanied him to the airport. Strangely when goose went into the departure lounge he went off without saying a word and that was the last I saw of him. The same old routine happened again when I got back to the hotel. I wasn't feeling too good but after a few beers in the evening I felt ok again. We went onto a pub called Warblers, I felt the atmosphere there was not too good, it was an American type of place and quite dirty, I was drinking pints until I saw how they cleaned the glasses, just a dip in the sink. I started drinking bottled beer then. We went onto BJs again, it was a bit of a blank after that.

The next morning amazingly I didn't feel too bad; I decided that I would go down to the near market. I found an old shop, how the building stood up amazed me. There was a massive doorway and shelving as old as the shop itself, which must have been three hundred years old. The man at the front couldn't of been much younger; his two sons were working inside. On the wooded shelves there were hundreds of brass ornaments, they looked like they had been there for years; they all had character though. Here I rescued an unpolished Heron with one leg welded back on. Things started falling from the shelves, I tried to barter with the boys but they couldn't speak English so they used the father as an interpreter, he was a was obviously a wise old man; in the meantime there was mobile phone which was ringing on and off. It was the type of shop (if it was a shop) where you couldn't leave without buying something.

I then went to a cheap clothes shop where they were selling fake goods like Tommy Polo etc but they were good quality. I bought a Rolex and a Levis belt and a few tops. I thought I would be biggest fraud walking in Swansea when I got home.

What I did find out about the Bahrain people is they liked the British because we built up their Country. However they did not like the Americans. They were also bracing themselves because there was an American battleship arriving; apparently they cause hell ashore.

We had news that Pat the Postie that took over from Goose had an accident on the way to Eskan village; this was after less than a week in the country. We didn't go back to PSAB on the day we were supposed to because the SNCO clerk had a bit of business to sort out, and Stu and myself had to go back with him.

It was quiet in the evening because the other group had finished their RnR. I was prepared for a quiet evening but two more lads had arrived from PSAB. Stu said he would drive in the morning; so I decided to go out with them to BJs, at about midnight I got a taxi back to the hotel, spending my last three Dina for the fare. I had a good chat to the driver and spoke to him in a bit of Arabic from my cheap phrase book. Back at the hotel I had a few beers and a smoke but Stu started moaning because he had a sore throat.

Next morning we went down for breakfast, then booked out of the hotel, we waited for the clerk to book out of his room; we all should of booked out by 11.00, by the time he booked out it was 11.30, I was glad to leave that hotel behind. I took the back seat of the car so that I could take photos of Camels and sand dunes. At about halfway I took over the driving, as I knew the way through Riyadh. Stu started to get on my nerves again as he was pointing at the signs for Al Kharj; I suppose he is one of natures worriers, I snapped at him all the same.

Normally when we arrive at the Saudi gate it takes a while to get through, as we get searched; the Americans got bombed in Dammam in the previous year. So of course security was stepped up. I had never actually been inside the Saudi guardroom before. This time I had to because of a routine search. The place inside was stinking and the guards looked as if they were high, maybe they had to do long hours and needed something to keep them awake. All things were ok and I was free to go.

Though this time was one of the quickest times that it took to get through. At one time I waited two hours; Goose told me on one occasion he had waited six hours. At the end of the day it was a good time, it depends on the company you are with. At least I might have had a shitty time in Bahrain; I could have had a shitty time in some dump.

Beautiful South - Cause Rotterdam is anywhere when you are alone; comes to mind.

After my first shift back in the shop I went to visit Pat the postie. Judging by the look of him he was lucky to be alive. There was a big graze where the seat belt burned him, he told me that an oil barrel blew into his path, this caused him to swerve into a lamppost, his escort was also injured and hit his head but is now back at work. If I had not gone on RnR I probably would have been in the car with him, but saying that, the incident probably wouldn't of happened if I had been there.

Pat is being sent back home and is being replaced by someone called " Precious".

When I used to go to Riyadh with Goose we used to be able to claim for a missed meal (around £10). This has now changed because we have to leave in the morning. That was fine by me; at least it got me off camp and away from Chris.

Chris didn't have a clue how the military is run or much else for that matter. He upset a few people and this made life harder for me, though most of them knew me and I get on well with them. One day he was supposed to go on an official shopping trip but came back with nothing, he said that all the shops were shut because of Ramadan, the truth however was that he went to Toys-R-Us then onto a hotel in Riyadh where we were allowed to use the amenities like the swimming pool.

I had been in KSA for four months and still had no notification of when I was to get replaced. One of the clerks asked me if I knew when my end of tour date was, as he needed to know, so I told him that I would ring my boss to ask him.

One evening in the cock and pullet I was talking to the Tornado Technicians and mentioned that I knew Bonnie Tyler. If they left me their address I would get her to send them a postcard. They were a bit sceptical about this but did give me their address.

I was interested to know why so many aircraft took off at once and they told me why. When you see the aircraft going straight up into the sky until you could see them no more. I was told that a bomber needs fighter escorts and in turn so does the refuelling aircraft; so some nights there were a fantastic display. I didn't know hostilities were still going on.

One day I thought I needed to ring the Colonel to find out if a replacement was to take over from me. When he answered the phone I did not expect his response to my enquiry. 'How dare you ring me up' ' who the hell do you think you are' ' I will let you know when I am good and ready' I told him that the chief clerk had asked me to find out.

Well if the Colonel expected a postcard from me he was out of luck. Of course a few days later I was told that my flight had been booked.

In the meantime Pat the Postie that took over from Goose, had been sent home.

I later realised that there was no train at the dairy farm; it was more likely a facility for cremating the cattle that had outlived their milk producing days, as for the circles that could be seen from above they were used for cultivating crops. There was a long pipe with holes in it attached to a wheel in the centre and when this was turned it could cover quite a large area.

Going back home on the C130 I was much wiser about the world below me.

Feb 1998

I got picked up at RAF Lyneham and taken back to Bulford. The Colonel didn't say anything about the telephone conversation but I give him my notice as I had enough of being away from home so much. Colonel told me to go home and have some leave and talk about it when I got back.

As soon as I got home I started filling my house up with the junk I had brought back from KSA.

My quest had now started to seek out Bonnie Tyler, the first place would be the White Rose Hotel in Mumbles, here Sue, Bonnie's friend ran the pub.

I often saw Bonnie in Mumbles, for a famous person she is so humble. I saw her one day kick out a few people from the White Rose in no uncertain manner with a few expletives, you can take a Welsh lady out of Skewen but you cant take Skewen out of a Welsh lady.

One day I walked into the White Rose, Bonnie was behind the bar for some reason, I said to her " do us a favour and pour me a pint" and that is exactly what she did, what a lovely down to earth person.

I had already bought a postcard of Mumbles and even put a stamp on it, I couldn't expect her to pay for the stamp as well. Unfortunately she was not here on this day; as it happened I was walking along the front when I noticed her husband; Robert (Bobby) Sullivan, who was walking towards me. I stopped him and asked if he knew where Bonnie was and he told me that she was abroad. I showed him the postcard and asked him if he would ask Bonnie to write a message on it and send it off. 'Of course I will' he said.

I saw Bobby a couple of weeks later and asked him if she had sent it. He told me that she had sent it and she was chuffed to bits that you had asked her.

Robert Sullivan was a Judoka (Black Belt Judo) who took part in the Munich summer Olympics in 1972. So obviously Bonnie Tyler is not her real name, and that's all I am saying.

A couple of weeks later I got a letter from RAF Bulmer. It was from the Tech Sergeant saying that they had the postcard from Bonnie Tyler (if that was really from her). Well chaps if you are reading this, yes that postcard was from Bonnie Tyler.

In those days Mumbles was buzzing. All the pubs would be full especially on the weekends. It was a destination for Stag and Hen parties and the lads from the valleys would come down looking for women and if they couldn't find one they would look for a fight, mostly they would end up in a fight. There was a good social life and the thought of going back to Bosnia for another six months was a bit disheartening.

DOWN DOWN

I went back to Bulford not deciding what to do. The Colonel called me into his office and asked me if I was staying or not. My better judgement got the better of me; So I said I would stay, the Colonel then pulled out the scrap of paper I had written my notice on and said' I can rip this up now then' of course, I said yes.

Now there was more hanging around Double Hedges waiting for deployment so was Kev. I knew I would be going to Bosnia but not when. I asked Kev how he got on in PSAB. He told me that he didn't get on with Dylan and told him to eff off each time he told him to do something. It was clear that he hadn't lost the weight he was determined to lose; he told me that he was in Burger King and Basking Robbins most of the time. Though Kev was a lovely person he was definitely lazy, as I found out in Turkey with the duty-free debacle and the last day we were told the showers would be closed down. I was going for the last shower and asked Kev if he was coming, " I can't be arsed" was the reply.

We didn't know when we were going but the Colonel told us that he would keep us busy until we left. By this time Dawn had been promoted to Sergeant; the shouting coming from her office was getting more intense; but I do admit that she was always all right with me. These were busy days for EFI and the NAAFI. We were deployed in Bosnia, Italy, KSA and other tasks. People were now being deployed at random in Bosnia and Croatia, as we were not attached to any particular Regiment anymore. The warehouse in Amesbury was busy, as NAAFI had won the latest contract to supply food to all the military caterers, despite the debacle with what happened in 1994. I do believe this was to be the Achilles heel for the NAAFI. We were back and fro to the warehouse, no end. Very often we would have to pick someone up at Andover Rail station or take someone to Brize Norton or Lyneham. This would normally be in normal daytime hours. After these hours someone would have to be the duty driver, now this task could involve driving to Heathrow airport at any time of the night. This is one thing I didn't understand about the Colonel. Whatever the time of night or when we got back we would still have to report to Double Hedges for 08.00; no exceptions. I suppose he would have his reasons for this, maybe some person in the past decided he would take the day off or he didn't want someone lying in bed all day, no doubt he had his reasons.

One benefit of being at Bulford was that if you weren't on duty on the weekend you could go home. I did this a few times if I could get a lift home. I had a good friend who would pass Bulford on the Sunday evening.

A great bit of news had arrived at Double hedges that Steve Burgess had taken part in an operation In Banja Luka to seize some illegal arms.

To thank him for his courage he had been awarded an AK47, of course not for himself personally to keep but for our Squadron at Double hedges. Good old Steve a nice quiet chap and now something to be proud of.

The Colonel must have been in his element at the time. There was no better man to run the show than him. If he was under pressure, he never showed it.

Double Hedges could get miserable at times. It would be great to get your name called out to go and pick someone up at Andover or even better BZZ. This was a welcome break from the shouting going on.

So the routine had started again, start at 08.00 of course as we were away from the main camp it wasn't practical to drive down to the camp for lunch, so we had packed meals made for us. Not the most wholesome of sandwiches but they kept us alive. We were never short of tea though as the NAAFI gave us a steady supply. We had plenty of sugar and milk supplied by the army. Our main form of transport was a big blue mini bus; there was a smaller white transit van for Carrying goods. On any one-day there could be about eight people in Double hedges waiting to be deployed or going on leave at the end of a tour. There was not a lot to do except, again tidy the storerooms.

There was always the anticipated shout from Dawn, hoping she would call your name out for a job. It was all a matter of luck.

I do not know if I was unique but I had some fantastic journeys while I was at Double hedges. To me the best task was to go to RAF Lyneham. The countryside was absolutely beautiful. There were a few ways to go and there was no designated route. I could go up through Tidworth, up to the beautiful town Marlborough, along the A4 Bath road west Kennet passing Cherhill white horse onto Calne passing through New Zealand arriving at **LYE** (RAF Lyneham) I would never take the same route back to Bulford as there was so much to be seen. 35046. I could head back through Devises, passing an old RAF base of Upavon then passing Netheravon airfield down to Stonehenge or even Woodhenge. The different routes were endless and I was guaranteed to see something awesome; Like the battlefield at Roundway Down and many Barrows and White Horses.

I had many trips to **BZZ** (Brize Norton) again there were many ways to go. To start with I suppose it depended on how much fuel the van had. If it were low I would have to go to Durrington to fill up, as we had a fuel card for the garage there. There would be no sense in going back the Tidworth way, so the best way was up to Marlborough passing through Pewsey. I had to pass through the Marlborough Downs it was ok in the daytime but at night that is one place you do not want to break down, there was something very creepy about the place.

In fact Ruth who was also at Bulford at the time said she would refuse to go through there at night. Then again one day I was driving the white van and filled up at Durrington when I saw Ruth driving along the road at a pathetically slow speed and an irritated driver sounded his horn as he passed her. Yes the blue van was a mini bus but no wider than any other vehicle.

The most obvious way to go to BZZ was passing Tidworth up to Marlborough crossing the M4 and heading to the beautiful Letchlade on Thames. From here there were still a few different ways to go, signs for Carterton would come up then the red military signs for BZZ. Upon arrival at the RAF base I would have to book in at the guardroom to get a pass to go to the terminal or Gateway house and pick the person up, to take them back to Bulford.

As there were sometimes a good four or five drivers waiting for a job Dawn would use us in rotation, if you were unlucky it could be your turn next and the task would be to pick someone up at Andover railway station. Although it was a break from Double hedges it was a short one and you would be back in the queue within the hour.

On one particular sunny day in Double hedges the Colonel was going to drive to Heathrow. I was instructed to give his car a valet, a nice little task for me. I spent most of the morning cleaning inside and out and had it gleaming about an hour before he was ready to leave. I was quite happy that I had done a good job and it was ready for the boss. All the doors were open most of the time I cleaned inside the car; I closed the passenger door and then the driver's door. I went cold when I realized that the keys were still in the ignition, I tried to open the driver's door but it was locked and I was staring at the keys inside. I thought this was the end of me, the Colonel was going to wreck me; I wouldn't be writing this story now if the passenger door was locked too. I went to the passenger door and tried opening it and thank god it was unlocked. The Colonel went on his way to Heathrow oblivious to the fact that I nearly ruined his day, and I kept my job.

On job better than going to BZZ or LYE was actually going to both of them. There would be a few reasons for going to both places. I could be dropping a person off at Lyneham and then having to go to BZZ to pick someone up to take them to Bulford or even the other way round.

It was a day away from Double hedges whichever. Of course if I were leaving Lyneham I would have to head to BZZ via Wootton Basset (as it was then) and then get onto the M4 to the junction just after Swindon. There was always a Hercules aircraft in the sky leaving or going to Lyneham. There were always different sights and White Horses to be seen.

After much partying and laying about doing nothing it was time to go back to Bosnia. We were never told exactly where we were going until we arrived in Split. For me this time I was to stay in DWC. I was a bit peeved by this as I was told that I would be a 2ic in some det. There were no more parades at all. There were no more Guard duties or canteen cowboys (watching the bar). However there was one of the girls on guard duty because she had been reported for drinking on the Sunday, apparently by one of our own. We didn't have to work in the shop anymore as locals had been hired. I had to have an interview with the boss, a Major Drummond, I told him that I had been promised by the Colonel that I would be 2 ic somewhere, he said the Colonel must of thought I was going to Banja Luka but it was decided that I would stay in Split. I was soon happy about staying in Split as in Banja Luka you have to be in uniform 24 hours a day. At least here in Split we can go out everynight. On Sunday 31st of may my first first day off I decided to do a bit of admin and intennded to go to the beach in the afternoon but I couldn't as we were not allowed to go out on our own.

There was a new character on the block and his name was Kevin. Why anyone would name a dog Kevin was beyond me. Needless to say he was a lucky dog that had been adopted by the soldiers.

The first couple of days I worked in the warehouse and did a few driving jobs to the airport or DJB. (Divilje Barracks} (pronounced devulyea). On the way to these places we would see some interesting things. In the harbour there was a submarine which never moved over the times I had passed it; there was a reason for this, it was not really a submarine but a concrete replica of a sub. Apparently it was built in the war to make out that there was always a submarine in the bay. By the way I don't know which war.

Another interesting sight was that there were caves dug into the rocks not far from Divulje where Mig fighter jets were hidden. I didn't really believe it until the day I did see one.

Things were decidedly different in the warehouse from past tours.

The SNCO in charge was Glynis a good looking lady. Another addition was there was also a Captain Goodwin who was the admin officer with a broad Gordie accent and a very nice person along with him was a Second luitenant, I never knew what his role was. He seemed to think he was a disciplinarian .The rest of the staff were a good bunch of people and we had a good laugh in the warehouse while working.

We even now had Dustie a mechanic to fix slot machines that had come from camps in Germany that had recently shut down. They were a great source of extra income for EFI unfortunatly they had a tendancy to break down. The Det commanders 'up country' could not be expected to fix them; although a few of them did have a go with a bit of help on the telephone. Sometimes they were sent back to the warehouse to be fixed but this was time consuming and not cost effective. On the first couple of days she had to work in the warehouse putting goods together on the pallets that were to be sent up country. It seemed that she didn't understand the rules of distribution. Ie she put boxes of crisps on the pallet first, then cases of beer on top of them. I said to her ' are you trying to do my fucking head in' I then showed her how to do it properly.

we got on great and we started drinking together in the bar in the evenings; although she was a bit fiesty I took a bit of a fancy to her but I soon realised she would be a better friend than anything else. We did however develop a good bond and we became close friends. One evening however she got a bit drunk and started to get a bit nasty. The next day I didn't say a word to her.

The first few months of this tour I was mostly working in the warehouse. I still had a valid forklift licence and I was given a few lessons on the reach and tier so unofficialy I could stack up deliveries in high places. The best part of being the warehouse was that we would work Monday to Friday and have a half day on Saturday and the whole of Sunday off.

The staff had made friends with some Croatians who had a lovely villa on the Makarske Riviera.

 We drove down there on the Sunday morning and spent the day in the swimming pool.

Sandra the Det commander in Banja Luka would also make her way down for the weekend. Although we didn't seem to get on in Banja Luka I found that she was a lovely woman, there was only friendly words to be said. We would all be in the swimming pool and drinking a few pivo's (beer) or glasses of wine, our Croatian hosts were lovely people. We did the same a week later. The following weekend we decided to make a trip to Sibenik which was north of Split towards a City called Rijeka, (Rijeka is river in Serbo/Croat).

The place was amazing, a wonderland of waterfalls, people enjoying themselves in the waters by these huge waterfalls. I dont think that I had ever been in such good company on those days with EFI.

I did a few driving jobs in the week after and was looking forward to another trip to Makaskar.

I worked the next few days in DWC and actually enjoyed it as the staff were quite nice people and there were no snide goings on.

As it happened a member of staff from up country was passing through at the end of his tour. He was asked if he enjoyed his tour, he replied that it was good, unlike working in the warehouse where there was so much backstabbing going on. Our warehouse staff were shocked by his remarks, someone commented that there was no backstabbing and everyone got on fine. This was the same person that was doing the stirring on op Grapple six.

Now some members of the Squadron didn't particularly like the EFI and one of them tried to be a bit of a bully. Unfortunatly for him he picked on the wrong guy, Mick Masonry an ex regular who promply head butted him.

There was a new member of staff who was a disgusting person; an ex regular. All he wanted to do was drink, he didn't have any interest in working. I will call him Jacko for the purpose of this story. In the evenings in the bar he wouldn't bother with the EFI staff, he would prefer to drink with the regulars and I dare say they didn't like him much. He shared a room with some transport drivers who were away most of the time. At the time it was in the summer and it was very warm. I had just come from having breakfast when I heard the sound of a window opening, I then saw Jacko lift up a bottle and empty out into the courtyard; it was of course urine. I did tell one of the seniors about it but nothing was done about it. It seems that the Colonel was recruiting ex regulars because there was another that had just joined us. He was apparently a sergeant in his regiment and he had been kicked out because of bullying. He seemed to be in the opinion EFI was a back door back into the regular army, he was wrong however as this was impossible. I heard that he was trying to instill a bit of discipline into the EFI staff; this too was impossible. He was sent to work in a shop in North Port which was part of a Maritime (there was no presence of the Royal Navy) base in Split harbour.

.

Dustie was a bit unhappy about having to work in the warehouse,I suppose she was told that he would be trained to fix the machines and that was all. I was doing more and more driving now and basicaly Gucci was all mine. Mostly in the local area like North Port, the airport and Divulje. On some days there was no driving and I would be in the warehouse. One day I decided to fill a container on my own. There was one for Banja Luka, it was a big load and would fill the whole container. Using the forklift and a pallet truck I did it in about 4 hours, being quite confident that I had done a good job.
On another occasion in a team event we filled a container for a det up country. No problems with this, so we sealed and locked the container. While filling the container I would use a sharp knife which was quite expensive. Later I couldn't find my knife, I looked everywhere and came to the conclusion that I must of left it in the container. As the container was sealed that was the last I was going to see of it. Along came a 'drops' which was a lorry that could pull the container on and lock it into place, then be taken to its location and ' dropped off' .

A couple of days later we heard that the lorry was involved in an accident and the container had rolled down a mountain. A week later the container was returned to the warehouse and we had to salvage any stock that we could. My suspicions were correct as I found the knife amongs the damaged stock. As it happened I lost the knife anyway later, I probably left it in some other container.
Things were about to change in the Warehouse. Dustie was going to take over the shop in North port and Karl a new arrival in Dalma was going to take over repairing the fruit machines.

There was no accomodation for her at the time so I had to take her every morning and pick her up in the evening. On one of the mornings when we got to the port I saw a soldier running around with full webbing on, in fact he looked me straight in the eyes, I said to Dustie " look at that twat" I later realised that it was the ex regular Sergeant who was running the EFI shop. I don't know what was going through his head. On a training camp there would be people running around with webbing filled with stones, of course there would be a purpose for this.In an infantry camp yes but not on Maritime base. I felt sorry for Dustie as North Port was a miserable place and apparantly the RSM hated the EFI and he probably didn't like much else either.

In the end of June I was asked if I would take on the task of taking the boss to Kupres which was the second EFI shop in Bosnia in terms of distance , of course I was not going to refuse this offer. It was great to get away from the warehouse although I liked most of the people there. We would have to start off early in the morning as we had to get back to the warehouse for the evening. Of course I had driven up to Kupres before but this time we were going via the first shop in Bosnia which was called Lipa. It used to be a bit of a drag going up the road to a place called Klis, upon which stands a beautiful fortress, looking back is a lovely view of Split and its harbour, no doubt athere was a fantastic view all around from the fortress and more than likely the plains towards Bosnia.

It was always quite a long drive to Kamensko which is the border crossing into Bosnia but the scenery was stunning. Upon arrival at the border there was always a line of lorries waiting to cross the boundary.

We were spared the misery of waiting in the long queue as we were allowed to go straight through. Onto a beautiful Lake called the Busko Jezero or Busko Blato depending on which map you are reading. There were signs literally that a war had gone on, as traffic signs had been used as target practice by whichever

force was passing the way.

here we had a choice of two ways to go either up to Livno or Tomislavgrad which was road Gull the official NATO route. However today we were going to take a little detour onto a different NATO road called Pigeon and onto Kite where Lipa camp was situated. It was only a brief visit, I didn't even get out of Gucci, the boss did his business and we were soon back onto road Gull. There was not much sign of the war to start with; then as we got to the city of Tomislavgrad it changed.

There was still the armoured car or whatever you want to call it, it looked like a lorry that had been converted, it never moved and apparantly it never could of, as the lorry couldn't take the weight.

From here on signs of the war became more frequent. Passing the village of Suica, Bogdasic, Donji Malovan and finally reaching the town of Kupres all to be seen were destroyed houses, a lot of houses riddled with bullet holes some with glass windows and some without, some with roofs and some without. Some houses seemed to have been repaired and had cars in the drive, if these were the original occupiers who knows. There was an abandoned tank in the middle of some field, this had been stopped in its tracks as one would say. In the distance were large white buildings that looked like some kind of warehouses. In another direction in the distance was a Ski resort which had seen better days and was about to see better days.

Not much seemed to go on there. Upon entering Kupres it seemed some houses were spared being blown up. There was a metal container which had a sign saying ' SFOR SHOP' I don't think I ever saw the place open.

The entrance for the army camp was on the right. I parked Gucci outside the EFI shop and the boss went in while I didn't do much. In about

an hour we were on our way back to Split, on that road where people used to live. We all seemed to assume it was the rotten Serbs that did all the damage to these villages. Maybe Just maybe we were wrong.

the next day it was back to the routine of the warehouse.

Now Dustie told me that she had a boyfriend who was a sergeant at a camp in Sipovo, which was north of Kupres. She said that she would like to go there to see him. I told her that I would take her if she got permission.

Amazingly she was granted a weekend leave and I drove her up there on a Saturday morning in an army landrover which was loaned to us. This meant I had to first parade it and keep the logbook up to date with mileages and times. I had heard a lot about Sipovo but I never thought I would go there as we didn't have a shop there. The area had seen some heavy fighting and there was still a lot of tension in the area. It was a strange camp to be in compared to what we were used to in the EFI. It was not a great evening, I had a few beers and had an early night as we were going to have to leave quite early in the morning..

I filled up with fuel and filled in the logbook, picked up Dustie and we made our way back to Split via Kupres. There was a chance that I could be stopped by the Regimental police (RMPs) on the way back. Before I reached Kupres I stopped to check to see I had the logbook and to my despair it wasn't where it should have been. I remembered that I had put it on a fuel pump when I filled up and must of left it there. I had no choice to go back to Sipove because I had got stopped by the RMPs and didn't have a logbook I would have been charged with a serious offence. In Gucci there was little chance that we would get stopped as it was a civilian vehicle. When we got back to Sipovo the first place I looked was the fuel pump but there would be little chance it would be still there. Dustie went to the MT building and luckily came back with the logbook. Now this had added hours to our journey and would be late getting back to Split. There was nothing said to us on our return, so I had a lucky escape. In the next week I again took Dustie to North Port in the mornings and picked her up in the evenings, she had changed from being happy go lucky into a sad go lucky person.

19 jul 98

By now I had been appointed to be the Ocs driver and I was now starting to do some long haul trips up country. I had a trip to Sarajevo passing Mostar(most-bridge Star-old). However the City wasn't named after the bridge it was named after the bridge keepers who were called the Mostari. There were some beautiful sights to be seen in the Balkans (A turkish name for mountains). Every turning could spring a surprise there were rivers, mountains, lakes, reservoirs, railways tunnels and lovely villages and cities and a lot of bullet holes and RPG impacts,

cars in all sorts of places some with wheels some without, some with windows and some without, some with roofs and some without…

From Split I had to head down the coast using the Nato road called Gannet , passing the Makarska Riviera down to Ploc'e then go up the Nato route called Pacman passing the beautiful city of Mostar which is in a valley which of course the Neretva river flows through upon which the bridge stands, although at this time it was in two pieces, so it was not technically a bridge. Up to Jablanica (Yablanitsa) onto Konjic and then into Ilidza, a district of Sarajevo. We stayed at Ilidza for the night and the next day we went to Butmir and the airport. After breakfast we met up and made our way to Butmir, the cemetery under the bridge and on the roundabout was a clear sign we were in the right direction. This was probably the first time that I had been in Butmir in the daylight. In a way it was quite crazy there were all nationalities visiting the German Dutch French American Italian and British PXs the list goes on. There were numerous sheds selling CDs, you could make up a good collection for next to nothing. But who was running these shops? I heard they were run by gangsters.

Another sight to see was the mine clearing tanks that were very busy. There would not be an explosion when the tank reached a mine as you would think. In front of the tanks were a steel flail which would smash the mines to pieces. Easy to do on those sunny summer days when the ground was dry. I can't imagine what the place looked like a few years ago during the siege.

July 1998.

18 aug 98

Well, my RnR came around with the usual hope of meeting someone new came to nothing. I, however, went to Bristol to see my lovely sister Linda. My brother Nigel from Swansea also came with me. I went to BTM to travel back to Oxford along with my siblings. I was feeling sick and almost threw up. Nigel said" he is feeling nervous about going back to Bosnia" in fact he was quite right. Another thing I missed while I was in Bosnia was my best friend's wedding and the birth of his daughter Ruby; I was, however, designated as her Godfather.

You could never get used to the early morning flights from Brize Norton. the flight could be at 09.00 but you still had to get up at stupid o'clock to check in. one thing that didn't help was the bar in the transit hotel was tax free.; the price of a pint was less than half of normal.

There were still telephone boxes in Gateway house, mobile phones hadn't caught on much at the time. Another thing which was peculiar at the time was that there were separate toilets for Officers and other ranks. There was also a separate bar for officers. They had RAF cooks making breakfast which always went down well. Our flight was meant to be at 08.30 but we were told that the flight was delayed, and we didn't have to get up until 08.00 as the flight was not now to leave at 10.30. We boarded the Tri-Star at 11.30 at 12.00 and we were hurtling down the runway when the pilot slammed on the brakes and put the engines in reverse and catching us up slowly was a fire engine which added to the wellbeing of the passengers. We had to get off and return to the passenger terminal while the engineers repaired one of the engines. Two hours later we boarded the plane again, it was harrowing again taking off again knowing already something had gone wrong. It was a smooth flight after that over the Alps and the Adriatic approaching Split airport expecting the slap on the runway that the Tri-stars made instead of a smooth landing. I saw a picture a couple of days later in the papers of a jet that had twice tried to take off the third time it crashed and made a right mess of it, it looked like a Tri-Star as well. It would have been the same old banter on arrival at the airport lounge but this time it was 18.00 hrs. And we could only feel sorry for the ones waiting to go home. Unfortunately, some things happen, and it puts a spanner in the works.

You soon get back into the routine of work, once you start RnR soon disappears into the past. Well, if it wasn't for the fact that there were only three of us in the warehouse when there should have been six. We had there lorries making a delivery, I had to borrow the Hyster (fork lift truck) we had a bit of help from the army guys and it took me all morning to get the job done, I was thinking I shouldn't have to borrow equipment and need any help, as after all we were meant to supply the whole of Bosnia and beyond. We had taken a cut in wages as the NAAFI had stopped our end of tour bonus, and we had to work unpaid overtime.

As the song says "Aint no use in complaining, when you've got a job to do".

I had some devastating news that the Colonel was coming out for a visit, I of course would have to drive him around the country.

I was starting to run the 2nd LT around as he was the bad cop and had to go round giving people "tongue lashings" in his words. Many a time we had to go to Banja Luka, Sarajevo, Kupres and other places. We got on quite well. I still had a problem with the webbing we had to carry, 2lt couldn't understand why I was in such a flap about it, and he even said" for an ex regular you are a bit messy". I couldn't understand why we had to carry it and 2lt never understood what use it had. We were up and down in Bosnia nearly every day. When we leave Sarajevo and go up to Banja Luka, we would see some devastation, especially in Vitez and Zenica.

The Colonel arrived in Split, and I had to pick him up at the airport. I had great respect for him, but I knew it was going to be hard work driving him around. He himself was an aggressive driver. I took him to the warehouse. He was in Theatre for only a couple of days. Of course I didn't know what his business was. I had to take him to Kupres and then onto Banja Luka. I knew what was coming up "you have got to watch the speed limit, or you will get in trouble" or words to that effect. I had to stop in Mrkonjic' Grad as he had some business to do there, after a few hours we made our way to Banja Luka, where we stayed the night. In the morning, he was going to fly somewhere by Helicopter, I had to take him to an Army camp by Kotor Varos. He advised me not to go back to Banja Luka but to carry on down to кнежево which would take me back inland to Road Gull. We waited a while for the chopper (Helicopter) to pick up the Colonel. We soon heard the familiar sound of the Lynx; it landed, and the Colonel said, "see you soon Taff" "cheers sir" and he was soon airborne and off into the distance. I found the place called Кнежево. (Knezzevo) easily enough, yes the scenery was stunning but the villages were blown to bits, there were a few farmers tending their sheep and an elderly lady passing me, I said to her 'Dobar Dan' and she replied 'Dobar Dan' and walked on by, she seemed to be carrying a shopping bag but I hadn't seen any shops and where she was going there didn't seem to be any inhabitable houses. Further on up the road was a lone schoolgirl; I presume walking to school.

To me it was very surreal, there had been a lot of work going on judging by the amount of hay around, but where were the people living? This must have been a thriving community at one time, but it looked to me that it had turned into hell. I was alone driving down roads that probably had minefields around them. Valley roads that went on for miles. Me myself my rifle and Gucci in a place in the middle of nowhere in the aftermath of a brutal war. A lot of the villages had Serbian Cyrilic names to them. It was well worth the visit though.

. I was in the warehouse on a Saturday morning wondering what I would be doing this weekend; I was soon to learn.

I was told that I might have to drive down to the border with Bosnia near Ploc'e as one of the Senior staff running the Det had been involved in a near fatal accident, and she might need to be given the last rights. It seemed that she might have broken her neck.

Communications in those days weren't too good. We had mobile phones, but they were not very reliable, and the landlines were not too clever either.

The weather this weekend was atrocious and I knew the roads on the Makarska riviera were dangerous enough in good conditions. I was not looking forward to a drive down there in those conditions.

I had to get Gucci ready for the journey and was waiting all day to be ready to move.

In the meantime, a Padre had entered the scene. As I was responsible for the safety of everyone in my vehicle, I had to write down the names of all passengers, for the logbook and to book out with the Guardroom.

Of course, I knew the names of our staff, but I didn't know the Padres name, as it happened though he had the name 'Christian' on his name badge; So naturally I thought that was his denomination, so I asked him his surname, he replied "Christian".

As it was getting dark the consensus was that we would not be going this evening. Things changed again hours later, unfortunately we had lost comms with the army camp, so it was decided that we had to go regardless.

In the evening the weather had got even worse but to add to the danger it was dark. I knew the roads would be like mirrors when the lights were shining on them, as they were always greasy.

So off we went onto the main road and then turned left towards Dubrovnik. The Major did the navigating, and we eventually reached the hospital.

When we arrived at the hospital we found the halfwit in the casualty department; for someone with a broken neck she seemed fine. As it happened, she only had whiplash.

What really happened was that she went to an illegal party and made up the story to cover her tracks.

The boss signed her out of the hospital, and we took her back to the army camp. I thought that she would have a telling off, but she didn't; in fact, all she got was praise for how hard she was working, and she was even told she was a workaholic.

We spent most of the morning in her shop, here the boss looked through the paperwork and gave the Det Commander some training; it wasn't a very interesting day, and I was glad to leave the place.

On the way back to Split the boss was chatting to the Padre, in this conversation he invited him to come with us on a trip to Banja Luka that was coming up in the near future.

19 sep 98 Northport

On the 19th of September Dustie moved to Northport. Now Northport was not a pleasant place, for one thing the RSM hated EFI and probably everything else. It felt like a miserable place. I don't think I ever saw anyone smile. I felt sorry for Dustie, but I knew she would get her job done.

The ex-Sergeant had obviously been sent home. She wasn't very happy to be leaving Dalma, and I didn't blame her, a Military Dock is not a nice place to work.

We were told once that if anyone falls into the water here they will instantly be hospitalized because the water was filthy with Hepatitis etc. I don't think anyone would be that desperate to go home as to jump in the water.

There was news that the disgusting ex regular in Split had been caught drink driving in Bosnia and had been Court Martialed and sent to Colchester, which is the forces jail, however the military called it a rehabilitation Centre.

BON VOYAGE

The time came for us to take a round trip to Banja Luka and Sarajevo of course taking Padre Christian with us. This time around we would be going to Banja Luka first. The Padre had not seen the real Bosnia yet. Also with us was Captain Goodwin, who was the admin officer in DWC and my co driver. I told him that there were some bad sights to be seen on the way, where some towns that had been levelled. We heard of battles that had gone on, and fighting from one side of the street to another, what we saw was proof that this did happen. By this stage I didn't need a map of Bosnia because I had been up this way many times. I drove all the way up to Banja Luka to let my passengers see the beautiful sights, literally, because Bosnia was a truly lovely place to visit before the civil war; well, it still was beautiful in its silence. My passengers were mainly silent on the way up, passing Komensko at the border passing east of the Busko Jezero, passing through the town (Grad) of Tomislavgrad with its still not moved armoured car, the wrecked houses on the way to Kupres, here we stopped off for the boss to do some admin while the Padre went to talk to the troops. After refreshments we passed through the ravaged city of Bugojno, up to Gorni (upper) Vakuf, where there was a contingent of the Royal Green Jackets then up to the stunning city of Jajce where stands a beautiful Fortress and further up from there, in Podmilacje was a blown up church (crkva s v Ivana Krstitelja) with a few crosses and a few statues still standing, here there was a shrine of St John the Baptist. Apparently, this was blown up by the Bosnian Serbs. A bloody terrible crime. We had a shop in Mrkonjic' Grad and the Boss wanted to have a stop off there. So, we had to leave road Gull and get on the Nato Road called Bluebird. While the boss talked to the manager in the shop I had a chat with the sales assistant. He seemed to like the place and was quite fond of the Civilian sales assistant, he told me her name was Slavitsa and she was very pretty, unfortunately I never met her that day. .

from now on there was not much more signs of war but some more stunning scenery after every tunnel would be something different, rivers lakes more tunnels sometimes there would be a sign with a camera on

it, this was not a speed camera but a sign letting tourists know  that coming up was a scene that was worth taking a picture of. We were not going further than Banja Luka this evening, so it was an overnight stay.

29 Sep 98
Early in the morning we set off on our way to Sarajevo and went on the NATO route called Clog down to Travnik onto road Diamond passing Vitez and onto road Pacman towards Sarajevo If the Padre thought he had seen some sights on the way up to Banja Luka, he was in for a big surprise. Upon entering Travnik and Vitez there was carnage; there was not a single house that had not been damaged. Captain Goodwin said " I see what you mean Taff about this place being bad" it was silent for quite a while as my passengers were taking in the scenery.

There were bullet holes everywhere and occasionally a massive hole where an RPG hit a building. Some of the houses had been raised to the ground by small arms fire. Obviously there had been battles from one side of the road to the other. Padre Christian was aghast and all he could say was "Oh My goodness, look at this" then a bit further down the line Major Drummond said, "this is" then a little pause, and then with surprise in his voice "there are people still living in these houses". For some reason instead of going straight into Sarajevo we made a detour down towards Jablanica probably for the Padre's benefit.

There were two different parallels from now on, there was stunning scenery passing a river and on the other side a railway tunnel carved into the mountain.  Then a Hydroelectric dam with another tunnel above it. Not far down the road there was a viaduct for the train,  here the water was like glass, then another tunnel passing through a bit of rock,  suddenly a taxi passed us and beyond that a bridge connecting our side to the opposite side,

this bridge looked a bit damaged in the middle, indeed it had been blown in half but it had a temporary fix to it. A bit further down another unusual sight was awaiting us "Russians Hooray" shouted Major Drummond.

There was an APC and a temporary shelter where a stern looking Russian Sentry was positioned, bless him.

Over a temporary bridge and around the corner were more Russians, with SFOR written on their vehicle. People can be forgiven for not knowing Russia were part of the peacekeeping force.

 Around the corner from here was a different scene of Lake Jablanica with its Swing bridge that could only handle one way traffic.

 Soon another bridge was under

repair. We then entered Konjic and its own carnage. We could see school children just like our schoolchildren off to their classes just like our schoolchildren hundreds of miles to our west.

Wrecked buildings and amongst them a Billiard bar where people used to play Billiards or Pool just like we did back home, but their bars were now shuttered and boarded with a few bullet holes added for effect. unlike our bars back home.

our destinaion on this day was going to be Butmir airport where we were going to stay the night. There was more carnage to be seen on the way into the city and onto Butmir.  once onto Butmir camp there were more interesting goings on, there was a fighter jet worth millions of Dollars on top of a scrapyard now worth next to nothing.

 We found our EFI shop and parked Gucci, from here the managers went their own way and I found my friends who were going to show me around some of the bars owned by different Nations. A couple of years previous the local people could not imagine the difference to come. It was still light, and the Mine clearance tanks were plowing their fields, all the shops seemed to be selling the same goods, the German PX seemed to be the best in my eyes. I stocked up on more CDs from the local huts. At 19.00 hrs the bars opened, and it was time for a few cheap beers. There was a party atmosphere and there were no restrictions on the amount of beer to be consumed. Those days were surreal, and I don't think anything like this would happen again. The next morning, we headed back to Dalma again going via Jablanica.

Something happened this morning that I will never forget. We had just left the outskirts of Sarajevo and got back onto the main road to Jablanica. All we could see in front of us was a bail of straw and a farmer laying down enjoying his journey. I said aloud "Oh there be farmer Giles" everyone in Gucci was taking photographs and the farmer was in his element. We overtook him, and he blew us a kiss. I said I bet that made his day. He certainly made our day. God bless him he etched a fond memory in my heart.

a few miles down the road we were approaching a bridge and in the distance, we could see a mosque with its minaret blown off. Below us was the river Neretva we were now leaving the city of Konjic.

We were soon back on the Jablanica Lake now looking in a different direction to yesterday's journey. There was a railway bridge over lake Jablanica which was not very special looking.

Luckily on the way back, my camcorder wasn't recording everything in blue. Then a quick glance at the single carriage swing bridge. The lake seemed quiet and beautiful on this day, I couldn't imagine what it was like a few years ago. I could tell though that there had been a lot of repairs going on lately. At Donje Paprasko we left what was now a river and joined E73 towards the town of Jablanica and stopped off to look at the beautiful scenery. We then got onto the R419 and started on the rough road of which I called Death Valley at the time, later I found out

the place was called Sovici. Here there were scenes of devastation  and the road got very rough. I can't imagine the horror of what must have happened here. There would be no lighting and nowhere to run to and then watching your house burn down. There was a house that makes me think of minecraft, I don't know why.
We started going uphill reaching the summit and here was a beautiful sight of Sovici, just over the hedge though were not so beautiful sights depending on the way you look at it.

we were now entering yet another different world. At the summit we could see the beautiful view down the valley towards Jablanica. We were now entering the beautiful nature park of Blidinje, though at the time I didn't know this . It was not a proper road, more like a dirt track. There were mountains on both sides, and we were on a big plain. Further down the road there was a sort of church strangely in the middle of
nowhere.

I thought at the time it was a church and a graveyard. There were a few other buildings around that seemed to have been spared war damage, we came across a sign reading Tomislavgrad to the front and Posusje to the left. The road was getting rougher after we passed the sign and we were going downhill. Captain Goodwin was on his mobile phone trying to arrange something with Georgia, a Croatian civilian working for us in Dalma. As we leveled off, I could see green fuel tankers on the right of us. We were now passing Lipa Camp. In the sky appeared a chinnook helicopter right above us, then a minute later it

was right in front of us coming our way. one idiot from our shop on the camp said "I wanna go in a woka-woka", a woka-woka is military slang for a Chinook helicopter. The main road had now been shut for the aircraft to land and drop off something I presume. Chinooks are always, an awesome sight, but this one has got to be no1.

there was an armed Ghurka guarding the barrier who saw me filming but he didn't say anything or shoot me. It seemed the chopper (Helicopter) was struggling to get off the ground, somebody who was next to Gucci said "he must have had a few beers last night" we were soon on our way and passing the armoured car that never moved in Tomislavgrad. It was a

stunning view of the Jezero and the panorama around it from our elevated position on the road. it was like a plain with a river going towards the Jezero but apparently the river has always been there but not the Jezero which used to be a bog, but they turned it into a reservoir. It was always a pleasant sight to see Split from the distance as we knew we would be back home soon. We arrived in Dalma late afternoon Padre Christian thanked us for the journey and he was soon off on his way, courtesy of his driver who had been waiting for a few hours. I went to the armoury to hand in my weapon and had to give my morphine and 30 rounds (bullets) to Glynis to put in her safe. I was ready for a few beers in the evening, but I was told to take it steady as I was going to Banja Luka again in the morning to take Karl the fruit machine mechanic to fix a lot of machines.

HIGHWAY TO HELL

The morning came and I put Gucci through her first parade. I was told that there would be two drivers, as Fitzy was going to Banja Luka with us as well. So, the three of us went to the armoury to take out our weapons. We had a good breakfast and were ready for the takeoff but of course first we had to get our morphine and ammunition.

This journey turned out to be one of the best ones I had with EFI in Bosnia. I had my camcorder recording most of the time. Fitzy, my co-driver was filming everything and commenting and calling Karl (the slot machine fixer) Brigadier Thrower; that was if he wasn't sleeping and most of the time he was. I knew from the start that this was not going to be an ordinary journey. Fitzy was a classic Scouser. I didn't know Karl too well, but he was a nice bloke but a bit dry. On this day we would be taking the NATO road, named Gull which takes us up to Banja Luka and there would be different road signs all the way up but underneath them it would say Gull. I drove the first part of the journey up to Komensko the border town and past and the Jezero and through Tomislavgrad, my two passengers were amazed by the armoured car that never moved, further up country before Kupres we could have been on the Yorkshire Moors, except that there were loads of houses with no inhabitants in them anymore. Most of them didn't have windows or doors but oddly they still had roofs on them, this might sound odd to say but there is a reason for it.

There was a brick square with a cross on it, this was in the middle of nowhere I didn't know what it was about it could have been a mass grave but who knows.

 A little further up a beautiful building which must have been a hotel for a ski resort obviously not being used but waiting for better days.

 So the first part of the journey was not so exciting until we got to the villages approaching Kupres, Suica, Bogadasic, Donji Malovan, Malovan, Gornji Malovan and on the right Brda, Vrila and large barn like buildings it was clear that there was nobody living in these places anymore.

 It was quite quiet in Gucci as my  two passengers had not seen the wrecked villages before

and the piles of cars which had been ruined, today was going to be an eye opener for them. After passing Kupres and going through the Kupreska Vrata (Gates of Kupres) tunnel I gave Fitzy my camcorder to film our journey, I tried to instruct how to work it, as we were going, I said "don't record any crap). I told the boys that we were approaching Bugojno I said there are a lot of buildings that had been shot to bits. However, one of the first buildings we came across was being repaired, it had a caravan which was the main living quarters at the time.

. Fitzy was now doing comments as he was filming, " So Corporal Rees what are the main problems you encounter out here while you are driving" " Flipping idiots" was the reply Karl then said "yes and camcorders in your face".

For a few miles it was mostly forested, there were a lot of corners so the place must of mountainous. There was the occasional sign saying Gull, so we knew we were going in the right direction. The roads were quite rough at the time with potholes everywhere and the middle of the road seemed as if it was tearing apart.

The comments kept coming, "last time I was going this fast, I just robbed a bank" "in a getaway car" with a scouse accent. "so Brigadier Thrower are you enjoying your trip" "oh its great "was the reply "he always enjoys his trip" I said. The scenery was not the best at the time as we seemed to be going in a forested area, indeed there was a sign with a leaping deer for 4 Km. I said something to Fitzy, and he replied, "I have switched of the camcorder, and why do you think Capt Goodwin is a grunt". Finaly, we reached Bugognja, amazingly the first thing to be seen was a Mosque and undamaged by the looks of it. We stopped here and Fitzy took over the driving, as we were passing Bugojno I said "as long as you don't say anything about Capt Goodwin" he replied "He's allright its only that he is a Geordie"

It would be a while before we would see any war activity, it changed as we were passing through Bugojno, again village after village with houses with no roofs and this went on for miles though some houses were left intact. It looked like the local bus service was running again, with many bays but not so many buses and not many customers.  There was a petrol station, well technically it used to be a petrol station, before it caught fire. We passed a village that had newly renovated buildings, I suppose these were the victors in the town. A sign soon came up for Sarajevo and Gorni Vakuf (Centar). There seemed to be an odd thing about these destroyed buildings in some places like Kupres, the roofs were still on them but here in Bogojna there was not a building with a roof. Someone told me that the wood was taken and used as firewood There was an occasional house that looked like it had been renovated and we passed a timber yard that seemed to be doing quite well.  The next town on the way was Gornji Vakuf and it was not much different to the previous town but what I did notice was that some men were walking around aimlessly, they seemed to be lost souls, seemed dejected and robbed of something. it might have something to do with  the fact the Hvo and the Bosniacs who were allies, here had turned on each other leaving the place severely damaged. There was no help with them to cope with PTSD. A strange sight was a gentleman taking his Krava (cow) to the river. Karl shouted out "Daisy don't do it" I don't know why. He had a strange sense of

humour.

we were now leaving D.V. and we came across a sign, Fitzy asked "which way now" well it was not rocket science , we were not heading for Sarajevo, I just said "left"

leaving the town we passed a Soviet time monument and yet another Moslem graveyard.

There were british Warriors (Infantry armoured vehicle) coming our way, and they were stopping for

nothing.

We had obviously been following a river all the way so far. Further up the road Fitzy said "you sure now, I said left or right" meantime there was a bus heading in our direction. I said, "never hit a bus" and by God it was close, all I could say was "oh cuff" more tank transporters were coming our way, they were quite close as well. Then school kids are waiting for a bus, just like back home, waiting for a bus. I thought to myself that there is no difference to these kids and our kids, they act the same and dress the same.

The road conditions were atrocious and so was the driving by the locals.

To be honest, the roads were built for tourism, but the war had put an end to that. Nearly every signpost had bullet holes in them, as they were used for target practice, by whichever force was going that way on that particular day.

There were cars coming towards us on bends then cars overtaking us on blind bends. I could tell that most cars going downhill were cruising, i.e. out of gear I am sure that there were many fatal accidents as there were bunches of flowers on the road marking the spots. We also had the threat of the RMPs stopping us for

speeding or routine checks. Like examining the logbook.
12.41 1 oct 98. Although the roads were quite rough, at least some authorities were trying to fix them. It looked like caravan sales were on the up as well, we passed more houses being repaired with a caravan outside.

It was now tunnel time and Karl was fast asleep. We had left the forested areas behind, and it was obvious now that we were following the Vrbas River. 12.58. The road we were on was only two-way traffic and it was getting busier; there were a lot of slow-moving lorries and chancers overtaking them. The tunnels were getting more frequent, and Karl was still fasters (sleeping)

13.05 we were now approaching the mysterious city of Jajce, I never stopped off at the city, but it was a steppingstone for Banja Luka or Sarajevo. In Jajce (yayayatsee) there is a fort high on the hill, like many other towns; today with the web it is easy to find its history but at this time there was not much information on hand. There was a big bridge over the Vrbas River. Leaving the city behind us I could see a cemetery in the distance that seemed quite new. Minutes later when we left the city behind there was another business that seemed to be thriving, a scrap yard. A few miles later we approached a large wooden cross which was a sign that something horrible had happened in this place. I had passed this many times but never stopped to look, I told Fitzy to stop here, and I will take over driving. I had my camcorder handy at the time and decided to take a closer look; there was a slight hill while I approached the cross. The place was quite tidy because all the rubble had been put aside, I could see two statues above some old steps

and I walked on a marble floor to get a better look. Of course, at the time I didn't know anything about what I was witnessing. I learned later that this place was called, Podmilacje (crkva s v Ivana Krstitelja), here there was a shrine of St John the Baptist. Apparently, this was blown up by the Bosnian Serbs. A bloody terrible crime. What makes me wonder though, why would a Christian faith blow up another Christians faith Church? that doesn't make sense to me.

All the while, driving up to B.L. on the E661 we followed the river Vrbas, that is why the roads were twisting so much. There were some beautiful sights to see and plenty of tunnels to get through. On the river were Dams to produce hydroelectric energy. When getting up to the higher ground, there are massive lakes with stunning scenery. Karl was lost for words he sais " Now that's" a pause "wow" When we got to Banja Luka I didn't have much time to spare as I had to take one of the girls, Anna back to the warehouse as she was flying back home the next day: leaving Karl to fix the machines and Fitzy was going to work in the shop at Banja Luka.

I was now back in Jajace, only difference now is, the girl filming me. It was just around 18.00 and it was starting to get dark. I had the beautiful city behind me. She said "this is Taff doing his catalogue pose. Just admiring the sights, unfortunately this time there is no woman in the picture with him, but there would normally be"

It is something to see the wrecked villages in the daytime but at night, it is something else, very eerie. Some of the Towns that had been wrecked of course had no lighting in them at all. Some villages around Gorni-

Vacuf were just shells. With the headlight all I could see was the road and white shadows that were some people's homes not long ago. These places were not somewhere to stop and look around and certainly not a place to break down; especially if you were alone. I said to my companion that if I don't see a ghost here, I was never going to see one. Of course, I never saw a ghost, but I did have a feeling of despair that was overwhelming.

I was well into my fourth month of this tour when I was given the news that I would spend my last month in Sarajevo. The reason being was that I told my boss that I was interested in furthering my career with EFI and would like to be taught the books and records needed to run a Det (Detachment) the EFI management thought that the manager in Sarajevo would be my ideal tutor. There had been a flight booked for me the next day; this was a first, as we normally went by road then again, I was the O.C.s driver a few days before.

21 Oct 98

This was a surreal time; I booked in and had to wait for my flight, but I was amongst civilians who were going to different places. There was a little boy that kept looking at my rifle. It's a strange thing; there had been a horrible war going on, but a weapon was a special thing to look at. . I didn't have any rounds or magazines so I could have handed the little boy the rifle to look at; it's a pity I didn't though. A sign came on the notice board saying to book in on the flight to Sarajevo. I checked in my luggage and went into the departure lounge. I could see the Turkish Hercules through the window being refueled. It was a short walk to the aircraft. Inside the aircraft there were no windows. When I was at DWC I was told that I would be flying with the Turkish air force, here I was taxiing on the runway. I was a bit wary of flying with a foreign air force, but it was a great experience all the same. There were not many passengers on this flight, I was wondering how Admin managed to get me on this flight, I suppose it was just available at the time. I was the Boss's driver a few days ago, who was going to take me to Sarajevo. It was about a six-hour drive to Sarajevo, but this flight took less than an hour. There were no windows in the aircraft, so I missed out on the beautiful scenery that no doubt was below me. To my relief the aircraft landed safely on the runway that had seen some extreme landings. When Sarajevo was under siege it was a very dangerous place to land at. The aircraft were forced to nosedive to the runway and pull up at the last second. I don't know it there were any serious accidents with this manoeuvre.

I have seen Sarajevo from all angles now, when I left Split the weather was still quite warm but here in Sarajevo it was definitely colder. I was taken to terminal building and Dylan (who was my Det commander in Saudi Arabia) was there to greet me. I was not actually going to work in Sarajevo but in a place Called Ilidza, a spa town and a municipality of Sarajevo. I had been there many times as it was the first Det we would come to when arriving in Sarajevo. It was clear that Dylan was glad to see me. I had got on well with him in Saudi, and I knew he was a fair boss. First, we went to his office in Ilidza where I had to fill a few forms in. he told me that I would be working in the shop with Irma and Denis, who I knew already. First thing to do was to hand my rifle into the armoury along with my rounds; I would keep my magazines in my webbing. I was then taken to my accommodation. It was not far from the shop and office. The accommodation was in a tatty hotel, which to be honest was probably not a tatty hotel before the war. (Now it is called wellness Terme health spa) I had to share a room with three other people but that was ok as the room was quite spacious. There must have been a few repairs done to the place, as there were bullet holes everywhere, also RPG (Rocket Propelled Grenades) damage.

There were no lifts working so we had to walk upstairs to the room, that was ok though as there was a ramp to walk up to, or we could use the stairs. I don't think this was the preferred way previously as it was badly damaged by bullets and missiles. Whatever the state of the hotel was in, it was comfortable. Dylan told me that it would be dinnertime soon. At around 17.00 we went to the restaurant. This was different to what I had been used to; all the staff were civilians. The choice of foods was amazing with plenty of choice. A beautiful pea soup, to start with then a beef dinner and to finish a sweet; was my first meal in my new home. There were a few bars in the hotel, on my first night we had a couple of beers and Dylan told me the next day would be more of an admin day.

On my first day of work in Ilidza as Dylan said would be mostly admin. After all the form filling in Dylan told me that we would go for a walk around the camp. Of all the military camps I had ever be in, this was the most bizarre or most beautiful. There was a complex of four Hotels in Park Banjska.

Srbija (now called Austria),

Hungaria (now called Crystal)

Herzegovina (still called Herzegovina),

Austria.

Hungary Austria these were in a circle and in the middle a round garden. Today the Hotels are not the same Srbia doesn't exist anymore and is now called Hotel Austria, with a smell political correctness.

A little bit further down was and alley of trees; so beautiful, it is called the 'great lane'; somehow that doesn't give it justice, Velika Aleja (Velika Alley) sounds more romantic to me. If we wanted to, we could walk along the beautiful riverbank of the Zeljeznica, with a few submerged cars with bullet holes in them, and flooded engines.

After this tour we went back to the shop that I was going to work in. I had been there many times before but never imagined I would actually be a member of staff there. The most amazing thing about the shop is that just outside is a beautiful natural Spa. Someone once told me that Josip Broz Tito liked to visit this place, and it would not surprise me, in its heyday it would have been outstanding. Unfortunately, even this place didn't escape the horrors of the war. The place had obviously been cleaned of lethal munitions but there were clear signs that something had gone on there. There was an RPG round stuck in the wall and a few bullet holes around the place, I suspect some poor soul used this place as a firing position. One thing for

sure the place stunk of rotten eggs.

There was a beautiful building not far from our hotel; I could see it from my room, I doubt there was anyone living in there as there were a few slates missing from the roof and all the windows and doors were sandbagged. The chimney was struggling for its existence. It was still a beautiful building all the same; it's

a pity I never asked anything about it at the time.

I suppose our hotel had not fared much better. The entrance had red walls on both sides, and they were full of bullet holes and shrapnel, I thought at first people might have been lined up and shot but it seems it was more shrapnel, hopefully anyway. Inside the door was an entrance to a room and it had a sign saying 'Do not enter' but someone had scratched the painted window so, I was able to have a look inside, it looked very macabre, probably a makeshift morgue.

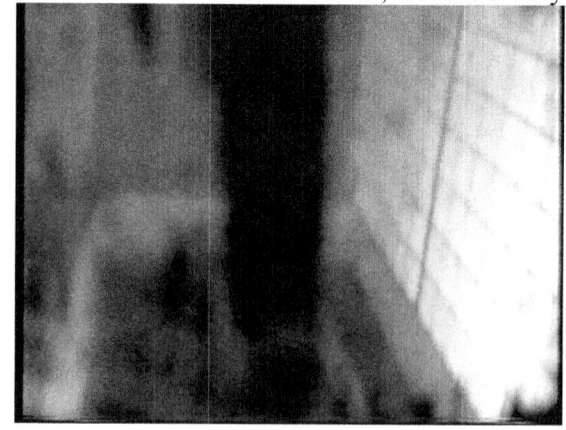

It is strange though that Park Banjska had suffered no damage at all. If there was a lift in the hotel it was not working. There was a ramp leading up to every floor in the hotel, on the first floor where the restaurant was, it wasn't a struggle to walk up it as it didn't have a sharp

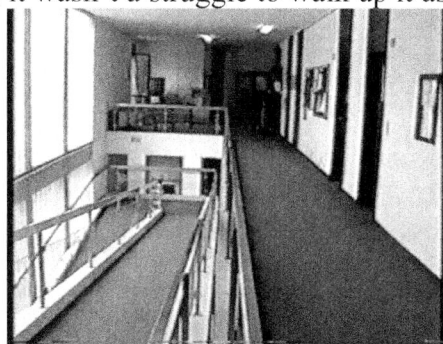

inline and a wheelchair could get up it with ease.

At the side of the building inside was a staircase, now this place had seen some action there were bullet holes galore and RPG impacts that if it didn't kill you, it would certainly make you deaf.

Looking out from the hotel it seemed the other buildings had not faired too well. There was a strange one, there was a spiral staircase outside a building, and it looked like someone had run up the steps and had a

machine gun firing behind him, following him up the stairs. A pylon that had been bent in half, maybe it had a radio antenna on top of it, if it was a television Ariel it

would have ruined the latest news broadcasts.

A house with a crack, down it's middle ready to split in half, like a broken tooth waiting to be fixed.

This hotel must have been great in its heyday, especially my room, the river in front of me, a fantastic view of the city in the distance and then Mount Igman overlooking us. I was to spend many a night sitting on the

chair on the balcony.

Dylan told me that I was going to work in the shop but only to cover the locals staff days off and occasional evening shift. I mentioned to him that I had been sent to Sarajevo to learn the books and records. He told me he was a bit peeved off as he was in the Cadre and was always on hand to go wherever the boss told him to go, he seemed to be a bit bitter and that was it really.

It was not a very busy shop by the standards of Split and Banja Luka, but it was steady enough to make some money.

A funny thing happened one day while I was working. A German officer came in and was looking at the perfumes and aftershaves, he took a look at a few and pointed to an EDT called Escape, I handed it to him, and he seemed to be interested. I was going to say to him "you Vill be shot" but I thought better of it, pity though.

Denis and Irma were the two local civilians that worked in the shop full time, they were good people, and we trusted them because they were Muslims and of course they would never steal anything. So basically, we left them to run the shop on their own. I would help Dylan in the storeroom when needed, it was an easy life really and we got on great.

SLIP IN THE DITCH.

It was the birthday of one of Dylan's friends coming up. Dylan told me that we were allowed out of camp and go to a restaurant; the only rule was that one person had to be armed, of course with a pistol.

Though there were many differences between the fighting factions there was one thing that they were proud of and that was Slivodic' (Slivoditch to us mortals). (Slivovitz) It was (is) a plum brandy; every Eastern European country produces it. We used to drink it in Split occasionally, it was a spirit that was very strong and one of the girls called it slip in the ditch, which was a very apt name for it.

There was a restaurant not far from the camp, it only took us about ten minutes to get there. Although there was nothing wrong with the food on the camp it was nice to go somewhere different. When we arrived at the restaurant Dylan ordered a Slivodic' for each of us, I cannot drink beer with an empty stomach let alone a strong plum Brandy. Of course this went straight to my head. The menus were not so great as I suppose there was not that much money around in those days. Most places would do Pizza or a steak with fried potatoes. We all decided on having a pizza and Dylan ordered a large one for us to share. There was nothing exciting about our evening, but it was a start of a great adventure in a City that was in the news a lot in the last couple of years. I don't think anywhere in Sarajevo had been spared a bit of fighting bullet holes were everywhere.

It was time to do a shift in the shop after a couple of days. It was not busy at all just selling a few packets of cigarettes, some sweets or cans of coke. A German officer came into the shop, and he was interested in the perfumes and after shaves we had on the shelves. He had a look at a few like Eternity, Obsession Davidoff etc, then he noticed a bottle called Escape, he said "Let me try escape" I was very tempted to say "you Vill be shot" unfortunately I thought better of it. The Germans were well known for not having much of a sense of humour.

I was expecting Dylan to show me some paperwork for running a shop, but he seemed reluctant to do so. It was a good day to take some photographs.

There was still a lot of Ordnance left around the place; I doubted that they would be hanging around for

much longer.

It must have been a beautiful place to have a holiday. A river in front of the hotel, the Velika Aleja a beautiful lane of trees, a Roman bridge, a view of Mount Igman and a walk away from the local shops, you could get a bus into central Sarajevo, no doubts then that you could get tours to Mostar, visit the Winter Olympics site and in the winter go skiing. Yet I was being paid to stay here.

Dylan told me that there was a free bus service that took us into the centre of Sarajevo and would take me there soon. We also had use of a Landrover so we could go to Butmir camp for many reasons. I started to make friends with the soldiers in the squadron and with some Americans. Although it was late October the weather was quite placid, we had a few snow showers, but they didn't stick.

One thing about being in Dalma was that we had to do PT with the Regiment there, which was a good thing. I wanted to keep up my fitness levels, so I started running every afternoon. It was lovely to run down the alley of the trees and over the Roman bridge, the air was clean as well.

Early one morning told me that he had been allowed to use the Landrover and we were allowed to go into the centre of Sarajevo. It was about an hour's drive to the centre and Dylan found a place to park, with just a short walk to the City Centre.

A lovely thing happened along the way. I was oblivious to what had just happened. Dylan said "from a Soldier to a Soldier" I didn't know it, but a Bosniac Soldier had saluted me as we were walking past.

A GOOD DAY FOR THE ROSES.

The centre of Sarajevo was amazing with cobble stone roads and beautiful buildings which all had one thing in common; they were all riddled with bullet holes. Some of the shops that had got back into business had their windows reglazed. They couldn't do much about the bullet holes at the time though. Sometimes when walking down a road we would come across damage on the ground. Where a mortar round had exploded on the ground, killing people. This damage on the road had been painted a crimson gloss red to denote blood had been spilt here. These roses were a memorial to the people killed while out walking or shopping.

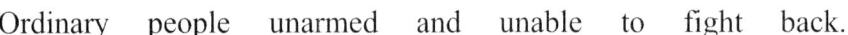

Ordinary people unarmed and unable to fight back.

There are around 200 of these scattered over Sarajevo. Coming closer to the city centre there was an indoor market with a glassed roof; I don't think it was very waterproof judging by the holes.

There was an outdoor market that had been hit by a mortar round and this killed 69 people. Looking at the place where the mortar exploded it was very unlucky for the poor folk shopping on that day. Which

Which was on the 5 Feb 94 at 12.37.

Walking around the centre made me wonder how people could survive such traumatic events, but I suppose they had no choice. I never did see any sad people feeling sorry for their selves; it must have been

a great relief when the bombs and bullets stopped.

At least the Trams

were running again.

That was my first time in the Centre of Sarajevo, and I was sure it was not going to be my last. Five years ago, I would never have dreamt that I would be doing this. Dylan told me that there was a bus service that made a trip into Sarajevo every few hours; I thought that would be interesting. Wherever we went with EFI we would never be short of friends, the Troops really did appreciate us, especially in remote locations. Dylan had been here for a while and had a bunch of friends. I had started get on with the lads in the Mechanised

Infantry Sqn. I even went out running with them in the evenings, along the avenue of trees and over the Roman bridge. One of them said to me "you are quite a big bloke, and I am surprised how fit you are"

Here is a picture of them with their Warriors. Notice the steam coming up from the Roman Spa.

There were a few Americans and one of them called Ray was friendly with Dylan, he seemed a bit crazy to me. Dylan had a local Rep, and she was quite a pretty lady. I happened to be carrying my camcorder one day and she was sat talking to Dylan, so I decided to turn on the camcorder and approach her while she was sat on a chair with its back to me. When I got to her, she turned around startled looking in the camera and looked shocked; I said to her "Do you want to make a film with me" a moment later Dylan was howling with laughter and so was she.

I did a bit more walking around with my camera, to take some holiday pics. After all these things were not going to be here forever, except beautiful Mount Igman (which was showing signs that snow was

on its way) and the beautiful River Miljacka. Across the river there were housing complexes that seemed to have survived some

trauma.

There was a two-sided sign, which has living proof of the Hotel names at the time. It looks like an  RPG round hit this sign and didn't explode; at least it didn't kill anyone.

On the 1st of Nov 98 a strange thing happened. I could hear some music approaching me; it was not normal music. Just flutes and drums, it was very repetitive. Then passing me was a parade of the likes I have never seen before. Every man had a moustache and no beard, each carrying a sword, swaying from one side to the other as if to show 'we are here', my first impression is that they were Turkish. Not surprising as they had a big presence during the Ottoman Empire.

A day after that it was my Birthday, so Dylan said that he would treat me to a meal, knew what was in store, it would be the old Slivodic' again, and again it was a glass of the Plum brandy on an empty stomach, nothing exciting happened we had our meal but what I realised was that Dylan had turned out to be a good friend, he told me that he had asked the Colonel if he could have me as his assistant in Italy, but he couldn't as the Colonel reminded him that only the boys could go to Saudi Arabia, the girls could not go there, so they had Italy.

One day I was invited by the RMP Detachment to accompany them to a visit of the Bobsleigh site, which was on mount Trebevic'. Of course, I gladly accepted the invitation. It was around an hour's drive from Ilidza. On arrival I was aghast of the tremendous sight ahead of me. This place had seen better days, in 1984 when Yugoslavia hosted the winter Olympic games. There must have been a lot of work and money involved in making these structures.

Today these structures have been covered in Graffiti, in my opinion sacrilege to those special days when the games were on and disrespect to the people that suffered around this place.

This is not the only Olympic game's structure that has been left in ruins. At least Bosnia had an explanation, nevertheless. I had wondered why the Olympic games site had been kept as it was, apparently there was so much unexploded ordnance and mines left around that made it impossible to accomplish. Another tragedy in a war that shouldn't of happened. The RMPs then took us further along the mountain there was some beautiful scenery looking over Sarajevo, it would seem this place was an obvious choice for the games. Unfortunately, it was also an obvious choice to place Artillery guns and tanks to bomb the city and snipers to shoot at anyone who moved at the wrong place at the wrong time.

Further along there was a view of the cemetery that had been filled before its time.

I wonder what the attackers thought when they could see the cemetery growing day by day. They certainly  had a commanding view of the City.
 Reporters used the Holiday Inn during the siege. The surrounding area of the hotel was known as sniper's alley. When I first saw the Holiday inn, I thought it had been renovated after the war, really it looks like it was just the spared damage, although it has been claimed it had been hit a hundred times. What seems crazy to me is that nearly every building that has been hit and damaged are dull and dark but the brightest building in Sarajevo was still standing and appeared to be almost untouched.
As I said before there was a bus service that went to the centre of Sarajevo from Ilidza. So, one day at the beginning of November Dylan and myself got aboard. First stop would be the airport at Butmir and then onto the city. There was nothing new really as I had travelled these roads many a time, however this time I was not driving and could sit back and see the wonders of Sarajevo. The end of the line was the Parliament  building, this where we got off.
amazingly I was about to stumble upon history. I found myself on the Latin Bridge. More infamous for being the spot that sparked World War 1. This bridge is also known as Princips Bridge. On the 28$^{th\ of}$ June 1914 Gavrilo Princip a 19-year-old Serb by a quirk of luck had a second attempt at the life of an Austrian

Archduke Franz Ferdinand, this time he was successful.

After visiting this historic site, we went into the centre of Sarajevo. Walking past a shop with pictures outside, one caught my attention, so I bought it. A picture of the Most in Mostar, I had it hanging on my wall for many years but unfortunately lost it when I had to move homes.

There was the SREDNJA TECHNICKA SKOLA amazingly none of the statues has been hit by a bullet.

Looking better these days. I bet the students did a fair bit of repairing to this building.

A bus has been put on a ramp for a repair that it never received.

How much work had been put into this star?

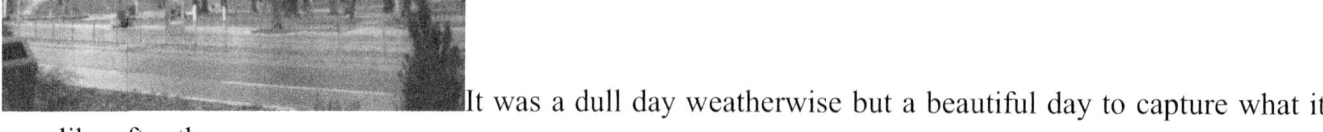

It was a dull day weatherwise but a beautiful day to capture what it was like after the war.

On the 19th of Nov 98 I was in for another special trip. This time I had been booked to take a trip over Sarajevo in a Black Hawk. I had seen much of Sarajevo from the ground now I was to see it from above. The weather had got a lot colder, and snow was appearing in some places. I was told to be at the Heli pad at 11.30, it was only a five-minute walk from my hotel.

Where we took off from in Ilidza there was no snow. The sun was reflecting on the makeshift helipad that we were stood on five minutes earlier. At about 200 ft the chopper turned towards the river and surged  forward then the river was to our left.  Following the river Zeljeznica for a short distance down below was an  industrial area, it looked like a cement factory, the river was to the left of us, 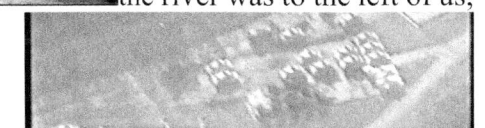 we were then following a main road, then passing over a military base. Over a rural area there seemed to be not much war damage. Coming towards a forested area and snow was making an appearance, all of a sudden as we descended the forested area was covered in snow. There was a road snaking along the valleys and making its way to higher ground. I am pretty sure now that we were over Mount Igman as there seemed to be a lot of ski slopes and maybe a bit further back it is possible the

remains of the Olympic village. 11.58.

Strangely a bit further on the snow was not

there. Maybe we had gone down a bit

lower. Minutes later in the distance there was another ski slope very high up the mountain and below clear signs that vehicle had passed through.

. In this resort it looks like a bus and a minibus have been abandoned. Soon In the distance high rise flats in the sun and no snow.

12.03 looking down there had obviously been warlike activity, as some of the houses had no roofs, maybe the ones with roofs had just been repaired. Shadows our Black Hawk and our fellow Black Hawk were flying over the golden trees below us. We were now in terrain where

only wolves could live.

 Two bridges were side-by-side over the river as we were coming into more populated areas. We seemed to be going over a horizon with a mountaintop with a little bit of snow on it. Then all sudden we were above which looked like 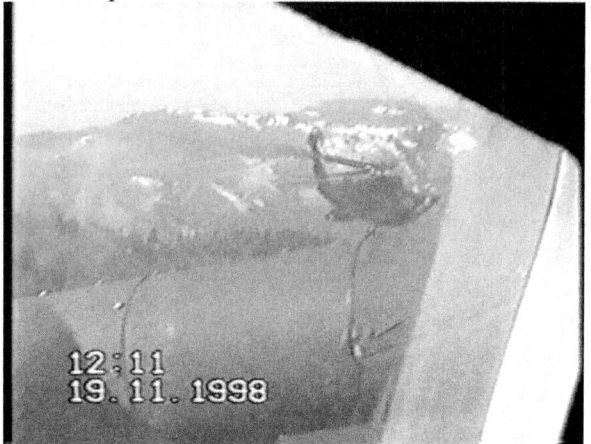 more ski slopes. At 12.14 below was a main road and a winding river, then a main junction that must have been the main route to the city. We must have been headed back to Ilidza, as the villages were getting bigger. The city of Sarajevo was in view as well. 12.19. The houses below had certainly not been under siege. We were now approaching where we had taken off about half an hour ago.

The Black Hawk and its partner stayed on the ground for a while to refuel and were soon off back to their base in Butmir I presume.

I had one more little trip to make. that was a bus ride that took us on a round robin of the bases in Sarajevo. I wasn't going to get off anywhere, just sit back and see Sarajevo at evening time. I didn't have to take a weapon with me, so I took my camcorder instead. It was already dark when the bus arrived. There were already people onboard but there was still plenty of room, I managed to get a seat on the back making filming easier. There was a lot of chattering going on in many different languages. It was a civilian bus but with a military driver.  Then of course we would go through the town of Ilidza which was over a bridge as we were in Banja Ilidza. Ilidza had by now modernised itself after the was days as plenty of shops were open and brightly lit up which a few years ago would not of been possible. Our first destination would be Butmir camp, easily recognized by the CD shops that were doing a thriving business. A solitary figure could be seen picking through the wares on sale.

Then passing the wrecked buildings near the airport that by now had got electricity back it seems some

buildings had been abandoned.

Of course I had seen these building many times but not many times as a passenger. The city roads were now very busy after we left the wrecked buildings. The petrol stations were doing well now I suppose a few years ago they were all out of business.

Out of the doom and gloom of the blown up buildings we crossed the river Miljacka (Milyaska to us mortals) and entered the main city, which was now alive and well. Most of the people who got off in the city were civilians that worked on the military bases. It wasn't an exciting journey but it was a unique experience not many people could take. The city was not going to stay ruined for much longer. Though some places will be scarred forever. What will happen to the Bobsleigh runs?

At the end of November the snow had started to get heavier and Ilidza was covered in snow and my days here were getting few. Walking past the Austria hotel, Ray the US soldier was pelting snowballs at people passing.

At the end of my six-week stay at Banja Ilidza I was sorry to leave. Sitting on my balcony with a few cans of beer, looking at the great view I had of Sarajevo, I got a bit emotional and kept saying to myself. " I love you Sarajevo".

Equally sad was my last day in Sarajevo when Dylan presented me with a certificate saying. A Bloody Good Bloke. What an honour and what great times I had in this short tour of Banja Ilidza (Sarajevo). Although Dylan hadn't shown me the books and records, it didn't matter to me as I had a great time there.

You could say I was at the right place at the right time.

Going back to Split was not as quick as I got here. I had been picked up and we made our way back through road kite. It was truly wintertime here now as everything was covered with snow. Sovici was still as dead as it was before but now covered in snow. Blidinje was absolutely beautiful although there was not much going on here, as the Skiing business wasn't doing too well at the time. In fact the whole of F.R.Y. wasn't doing to well with the tourist industry.

It was nice to be back in the warehouse for my last couple of days. The bosses were really good to me; they weren't too pleased that I hadn't been taught the books. I had a good end of tour report and an indication

that I would be going to Norway again to learn the books.

My flight had been booked for the next day so I had to hand in my rifle, morphine, magazines and rounds; and that was it my tour had ended. In the evening time it was in the bar to violate the two can rule.

I was taken to Split airport the next morning. Going back home was not as stressful as starting a tour leaving from BZZ. It was always and afternoon flight and checking in was a much simpler task, then again when going home nothing matters as long as the flight is not delayed. On Arrival at BZZ things were a lot quicker all you had to do is show your id card and then collect your luggage. Once all that was done the duty EFI driver would be waiting for you. Normally arriving at Bulford it would be evening time and the EFI HQ would be shut. One thing had changed now though our accommodation was in a more modern block and it was much more spacious. There was always someone waiting to go on deployment so we would go to the NAAFI bar on camp.

In the morning it was to the cookhouse for a breakfast with the duty driver, there would always be some staff waiting to go on deployment, having breakfast, we would leave at 07.50 to go to the EFI HQ. Nothing much had changed except for the fact that the chief clerk was now a staff Sergeant. I had to stay in Bulford for a few days, as there were no duty drivers available. On my first day of driving I was given an unusual task, Dawn called me into her office and told me I had a task to do. I was to go to the military prison in Colchester to pick up the disgusting person from Dalma that had been done for drinking and driving. Apparently it had been found that he had been imprisoned illegally, as he was classed as a civilian working for NAAFI and he had to be released. So I had to go to Colchester to pick him up and bring him back to Bulford. It was only a few hours from Bulford. When I got to the prison (it was not classed as a prison but a Military corrective training centre). I know from experience it is worse than a prison, because I know people who have been there.

The person was released to me and we made our way back to Bulford. I had to endure a few hours of self-pity from the bloke. We arrived at Bulford and I took him to a room in the transit block. I told him he would be picked up in the morning. He was shocked by this as he thought I was going to take him home, he said "but cant you take me home", "no" I said, "the colonel wants to see you in the morning" and that is how I left him. Did he really imagine that the Colonel would let me take him home; he really was an idiot. In the morning I had to pick him up and take him to Double hedges, I don't know what happened to him after that as I had a job to take someone to BZZ. Of course the idiot had been sacked and taken to Andover railway station.

It was great to see the Colonel, when I got back; he always had a smile along with a handshake. He told me that I could go home on leave and be back after Christmas as I was going to Norway again.

It was still nice to be back home though going to my new house and the Antelope pub a short walk away. I would see my old friends in the many pubs that were still open then. It was strange as my best friend Durkie had bought a house not far from me and we had the same postcode. Back in the pub I used to work in the bar staff hadn't changed, I was glad that I had got out of that place of work though, but such is the tapestry of life. People didn't know what job I was doing, some would assume I was a cook in the Army, indeed someone once said to me, " you are back in your whites" meaning that I had always been a cook although I had never been one, so I kept them in a kind of mystery. On a weekend I was talking to someone who said he was a friend of my brother, he knew I was in Bosnia. After the pubs shut we went into the nightclub called Bentleys at the time. I didn't realise he was latching onto me to try to chat up the women. He had told one lady that he was with me in Bosnia, I told her he was lying and the stupid cow said " how do I know you are not lying" so I showed her my MOD 90 which is the Army id card. She still didn't believe me. I never had much luck with the ladies in Bentleys, thank God or I wouldn't be writing this book now. In fact I found the younger generation as not very nice.

As usual the leave flew by and I was soon back in Bulford.

As Cold As Ice

Neil who was now a Warrant officer was going to put us through the training. It was more like a health and safety course. Everything was about how we could get injured from Hypothermia, touching metal objects etc, it was not any different to the training I had done a few years earlier. It was mostly doom and gloom and death by PowerPoint. While we were all in a class at the end of the training I said to Neil " what is the chance of coming home alive" all the students found this funny.

Once again it was to the movements centre at South Cerney and the flight to Norway. It was the fifth of January when our little squad arrived at Grotsund Fort; we had arrived there before the main party of the Royal marines who will be doing their Arctic survival courses. We were waiting for our deliveries but they didn't arrive although the beer did. So at least Neil had something to teach me, like counting the bottles and putting them into the computer system. It was dark most of the time but between 11.00 and 13.00 it is like evening with no sun. The temperature was not too cold being at around minus two. There was plenty of crispy snow beneath our feet. It was lovely to see the snow covered mountains and it was so quiet, because there was no pollution in the air.

Until the arrival of the Royals we had to live off Compo rations for two days before the arrival of the fresh food. You can only eat so many biscuits that block you up. The boil in the bag rations was ok but they made everyone excrete gas a lot.

Once again Neil was in charge of our Det, which was in a large room with wooden walls, it looked like a massive Sauna. There were six of in all to work the Det, Yuan who I was with in the big shop in Gutersloh, (it's a small NAAFI world) a Corporal Black who I had worked with in split at some time, Lee a bit of a simpleton and Pete, I was with him in Split he was however a hard worker, a grafter as he would say. Again we were with the royal marines who were going through Arctic Warfare training. Our accommodation was good with lovely warm showers and a sauna next to them.

We had a busy shop in the daytime and in the evening we would go to the Marines bar for a few beers. In the evening time Neil was going through the books and records with me. At the time NAAFI had a system called system 20, developed by their own IT team. It was complicated but Neil was a good teacher. He told me at one time

" Never touch this button", as it would cause havoc. A few days later I was going through things on my own on the computer when Yuan said to me "what's this button" and I pressed it, it locked down the whole system. Luckily Neil was in a good mood at the time and managed to get the system up and running again after some work. I am sure Yuan had heard Neil telling me not to touch this button, that was the devious person he was. I was told that I would soon be going to a different location and would be taking Pete with me; of the bunch he was probably the best choice.

The royals had started their Arctic Warfare training and had asked Neil if we could act as the enemy. This was great news. We would have to be in position in the night. Evening time we had to get our weapons and I was given a GPMG. (General Purpose Machine Gun) commonly known as the Gun. Any unit that has this normally does a test fire to make sure it works. Being as the royals were so professional we didn't think that they would give us anything less. As we were acting as the enemy it didn't really matter what we wore as long as it was Combats. I decided to wear a pair of hiking boots that I had bought on my previous tour in Norway. They were lovely and warm but they weren't the standard combat high boots, in other words they were subsebtical to let in water, which would ice up causing problems, Neil was a bit annoyed by this and told me off, I just hoped nothing would come of it.

It was Yuan and myself sitting in a trench waiting for the assault from the enemy. Sure enough they arrived I was going to give a burst of fire from the gun, I had already cocked the weapon and opened fire; **bang** and that was it, only one round fired. I had to cock the gun every time to fire a round and believe me it is hard work to keep cocking a GPMG. Yuan took over and tried a few times but he was not up to it. Of course the enemy overwhelmed us. To this day I have never understood why the Royals gave us a defective weapon. Luckily I didn't succumb to frost bite.

On the 15th of January Pete, Lee and myself were taken to the military airport and flown down to Tromso by an RAF transporter. It was not actually in the city of Tromso cut across the water at a place called xxxxx Tromso, there was a beautiful view of the city. Our Det Commander was Les, a Staff Sergeant who had been coerced into running a Det. He was the manager of NAAFI bar in Tidworth. At first we were not too keen on him, as he didn't seem to be on par with Neil, so we gave him a bit of a hard time. I realized one day that he had a hard job to do. I said to my colleagues that I think we have been a bit harsh to him. It turned out he was a good bloke and taught me some more paperwork; I spent most of the time helping him in his office. The shop that we ran was not very busy so we had plenty of time to do some skiing. The skiing slopes in Tromso were out of this world. There were long stretches with a slight slope and on the other hand high slopes with short stretches. The weather had improved a lot and there were starting to get more hours of daylight. The low sun was making the scenery so beautiful and the wooden buildings came to life. There were tepees that only had the wooden frames left, maybe they had been used in the colder days and left for the next year. The children were a world of their own with their brightly patterned bobble hats. There were plenty of stretches for cross-country skiing they seemed to go on for miles.

When I was in Norway two years previous we must of left in February; we were still here in March this time. It must be the best time of the year as the sun was highlighting all the beauty of the Arctic. And when the sun had gone down it was the turn of the northern lights to show their part of the spectacular events unfolding. Just like my previous tour in Sarajevo I was reluctant to leave this place Norway had its special beauty and so did Sarajevo and Blidinje, which was still in its slumber. Though Sarajevo was scarred with the war it still had its special beauty even with the damaged caused, in Norway hadn't seen war for a long time. Started collecting rocks.

Bulford 1999

We left Norway and were given a few weeks leave. I wasn't told where I would be going, so it was just a case of waiting again and doing the duty driver thing. There were not so many people waiting to go on tour but many passing through on end of tour and people going on RnR, so I had plenty of jobs on. I was able to go home to Swansea most weekends and get back to the same old routine. One day I was working in the HQ, and we had a visit from Mr Stones who had been the OC in Grapple six. As it was a sunny day the Colonel and Mr Stone went up to the top of the building and were having a good chat, I had a bit of a chat with him, and things were ok. I was in for a surprise one week though. One of the girls from out tour in Bosnia was acting as Dawns assistant, as things were getting quieter in Bosnia. Taking me to one side, she said "Taff you are going to get promoted next week". That was a shock to my system, as I never expected that. Of course, I kept it quiet until I got home. I told my friends and of course they were all glad for me. However, I always had one heckler every time I went home, he was always trying to put me down. I never really took much notice of him, but he always seemed to be part of our company, but I didn't really know him or class him as a friend. It was a good reason to party for this weekend.

On the Monday morning, I got in for work at the usual time. I wasn't quite sure to believe what I had been told. It worked out to be an ordinary day without anything happening. On the Tuesday I was summoned to the Colonels office. Colonel Smith came straight out with it and told me I was being promoted to local Sergeant. I really didn't know what that meant but it was promotion. He kept me in his office for about ten minutes and handed my stripes; I could tell by now that he knew I had already been told, and he looked annoyed; as I hadn't shown much surprise. He told me to hand him my Corporals stripes, which I did, he then handed me the Sergeants stripes shook my hand and told me to carry on.

Even I knew that I was going to be promoted it still hadn't struck me. Dawn called me into her office and congratulated me on promotion. She told me that my first I was going to be the Det Commander in Kupres as it was quite a quiet place to learn to run. I had been booked a place in a learning centre in Amesbury to go on a computer course, which would be over two days.

The Colonel told me that we were getting a visit from high-ranking officer, and I had to delegate work to people. I gave a few jobs to people like tidying rooms and cleaning outside. I told one Corporal to go and clean the gent's toilet, he was in there for about ten minutes, when he came out, I asked him if he had completed his task and he said yes. About half an hour later I went to have pee and to my horror the Colonel was scrubbing the urinals. I immediately went to Dawn and told her; she was aghast and told the Corporal to get in there and take over from the Colonel. When I saw the Colonel a bit later, he gave me a stinking look, he was not too pleased, my first task as a Sergeant had not gone down too well. I now had a new home in the Sgts mess. I had a single room and got waited on at breakfast and evening meal, I had to pay a small figure for this. I went home for the weekend and had great congratulations from my friends.

When I arrived back on Monday morning Dawn told me that I was booked in for computer training, I would have my first lesson on Tuesday. I didn't know what to expect. The whole thing was new to me. My first day was spent on learning Microsoft word. In fact, this is what I am using now. I realised that computers had come on a great deal. The tutor was fantastic and clearly taught us the system. It was amazing to be able to write a document, which helps you along and with the assistant.

It was a long day, but I learned a lot. The tutor showed things like auto correct and how to put in words that wasn't in the computers dictionary. There was a lot I learned in that day. The next day was a lesson in Excel and again I found this fascinating, I learned I could make my own spreadsheets and how to change cells along with columns and rows. It was to make my life a lot easier. The Tutor was excellent and thorough.

It was a marvellous experience for me to be going on my tour as a Sergeant, it was amazing how much respect is shown from the junior ranks that didn't even know who I was. Starting at BZZ. A soldier said to me "Hello Searge" I didn't know him, but I felt the respect.

I had known Kupres of course because I had passed through there many times, but I hadn't met the civilian staff before.

On my first two weeks I knew I had a lot to learn, practically I was starting from scratch.

Anything I was taught in Norway was of no use. Of course, the Sergeant (Mag) I was taking over from was going to show me the ropes. She would often say I didn't have a Scooby, (Scooby Doo) which rhymed with clue. In the first two weeks I had learned enough to take over the Det.

I had plenty of support from the warehouse and could get in touch with any Det commanders as communications had improved significantly. To be honest it was a great day when my predecessor left as now, I could run the place the way I wanted to. I had one Corporal and a Croatian civilian to work the shop. The civilian's name was Maria, and she was fantastic, her English was good, and she was so polite: and what was in the charts at the time? Only: Maria by Blondie. We also had a Tommy Tuckers and there were three Croatian women working there. They only had a small burger hut to work from, but they had plenty  of customers.

Kupres was a main stopping station for troops going further up country. There was a permanent Transport Squadron stationed there, and they were very busy. On the civilian side I could see it was a timber yard and that too was very busy.

To begin with Maria worked in the shop and Lee the Corporal would stand in for her breaks and her day off. She was very good with the customers

and always had a smile on her face.

My office was a bland place, and the walls were a filthy colour, I decided to do something about that. In those days mobile phones were but were not very reliable. The military provided phone booths for the guys to phone home, this is where we came in as we provided the phone cards needed. They cost ten Deutch Mark and would last for about half an hour. When the cards were finished with the customer would normally leave the used phone card on the shelf by the phone or on a table.
The first thing I would need was some silicon. I asked Maria to get me some from the village. I started

sticking the phone cards to the wall in my office. It was a great improvement.

NAAFI had a system at the time. The managers had to file all the weeks' work and send it off to Amesbury. This was called the weekend returns. On the first week I was on my own I was quite worried that I would not do it on time, but I got there. I knew I would cope ok after that. Some clever people in NAAFI had developed a new programme making it easier than the previous system 20. I had now a better understanding of computers thanks to my courses I went on before I came to Kupres. Of course, I was responsible for the takings and storing the money. I had a safe in my office, when the shifts changed in the shop the cashier would 'cash up'. I would have to enter the takings onto the computer and at the end of the week everything should tally ready for banking. Of course there were no banks in the town of Kupres, so we ha to wait for someone from warehouse to collect it on their way through. After a month of running the Det I had everything sorted. Of course I would have Tommy Tuckers to look after as well, so in effect I had two Dets to run. We were not allowed to leave the camp so we couldn't get stock for resale. If I needed anything Maria could get them for me, but I thought, it unfair on her to buy anything for the shop. Saying we were not allowed to leave the camp was not quite true as we were allowed to go out for a run if there were two or more. One thing I asked Maria to buy for me was a pushbike. I gave her the money, and it was delivered soon it was a lovely pink bicycle. Lee my Corporal assistant wanted one as well soon after, so Maria sorted that one out. We were allowed to leave the camp on the bikes for P.T.

It was summertime now and the skies were blue. A sad thing could be seen in the skies, and it was NATO aircraft on their way to bombing Serbia. The ones I could see were probably coming from Italy.

I thought our shop had been a bit boring, so I went out around the camp and picked up things like barbed wire and twigs for our displays in the shop. I could buy stock from a visiting military stockist, who would visit our shop monthly. He sold things like clothing and survival tools. I could use the money from our takings and do a 'goods purchased for resale' of course this would have to go into the system. Another thing did was to freeze the cartons of orange squash, these proved to be very popular with the Drivers early in the morning.

There were three staff in Tommy tuckers and one of them was a very pretty young lady, her name was Nena. She had a friend who was an interpreter and what they had in common was that they were Muslims. When Nena had her dinner break in Tommy Tucker, she would often come to meet me in the shop, then we would go to the cookhouse together. I didn't know she was a Muslim to start with. She told me that she had a lot of trouble with the local Croatian workers because she was a Muslim. I asked her what happened in the war, but she didn't answer me. Nena and the two Croatians got on fine and there were no issues. Lee and I started going out for runs around the local area. We could either go left, right or straight on into Kupres village but there was no point in that. The best option was to turn right, after the camp the road started to get steep, we would end up at a tunnel, it was about a mile up the road and we would have to turn back as there was no path for pedestrians. The tunnel was (is) called Kupreska Vrata (Gates of Kupres) if we turned left out of the camp we would be running on a busy road, however we noticed that there was a road leading to the mysterious white sheds, but it was too far to run there. This would be a job for the pushbikes.

In my second month we had a visit from the new EFI OC from Dalma. We had a good clean up and the place looked good. In the morning of his arrival, I went to meet him at the gate and brought him to the shop. When lee saw him, he put his hand out to shake hands, but the arrogant man totally ignored him. He looked around the shop and went through my paperwork and all was fine. He wanted to look in the freezer container, everything in there had been ordered by my predecessors except for a few things like bread rolls. There was a vast amount of chips stacked in there, I told him that I hadn't ordered any, he snapped back at me and said "get rid of them" he soon left Kupres to carry on with his sorry day. Talking about the freezer the Transport Squadron was going to have a bit of a party and ordered half a pallet of beer. I put the beer together for them for the weekend making sure that it was going to be cold for them, I put the beer in the freezer, I knew that the beer wouldn't freeze up and I told the customer where I had put it. The next day I had heard that the customer asked Lee how long the beer could stay in the container, before it freezes,Lee had told him about four hours, this made the customer panic and told Lee to take the pallet out. He wasn't too clever, our Lee.

From our canteen we could see the white buildings in the distance, I asked Nena what had happened there, she replied, a Serb village. This puzzled me a bit. So, these villages and the ones leading to Kupres were Serb villages, I was wondering how come we have never heard about these villages in the news. To me something was not quite right.

One day Lee and I decided to take our bikes down the road, we found a turning left through a village and we found ourselves at the white barns that were barren. Well certainly something went on there as there were still empty cases of small arms weapons scattered all over the road. We stumbled along a written message to NATO. It seemed that the former inhabitants were not very keen on Bill Clinton. All the fences were broken down so we could go into the buildings, this was probably not a good idea as if no one went in there, there was a good possibility that the buildings were mined. We were within a hundred yards of the broken-down tank was, there was a certainty that this place was heavily mined and that was the reason the tank was still there. So, I told Lee to go and take a close up for me. That's the last I saw of him.

What I saw on that day, I think started to change my view on what really happened in the civil war. Someone had written on the road CLINTON HITLER. I don't think the writer of that message thought the message would get anywhere. It might have been washed off in the rain or scrubbed away but the message is there forever with this photo, I think the towns approaching Kupres are upper and lower Malovan. (Gornji and Donji)

One day while talking to Nena she suddenly came out with "The war was horrible Taff; I lost many of my friends" obviously now she trusted me. The interpreter was also a Muslim, but that never seemed to be bother her.

One of the staff told me some swear words in Croatian, I was talking to the interpreter one day and the staff member came into the room, I said to the staff member Odi Ebi and the interpreter was astounded and she said "where did you learn those words", it meant eff off in Croatian.

Captain Goodwin came to visit me one day and he told me that as Tommy Tuckers is making a lot of money it could do with a bit of an improvement. It was proposed that a roof could be erected over the cabin. Capt Goodwin asked me through the interpreter to arrange for one of the locals to plan and build the roof and to give us a price. Days later a drawing was given to me with a good price, I faxed Capt Goodwin and gave him the details. I had a reply soon after and Capt Goodwin gave me the go ahead. All I had to do was to pay the builder weekly his wages, which was a set amount. As the camp was situated in a timber yard the builder would have had a good deal. He was happy and we were happy. The work was started

without much delay. Another thing that I suggested to Capt Goodwin was to get another civilian member of staff to help Maria; there was not much need for two EFI staff. Capt Goodwin agreed and told me to ask Maria if she knew anyone interested in a job. She told me she knew someone who would be interested. A few days later Maria brought a lady in with her. I arranged with the interpreter to assist me in an interview. All went well and Irma was given a job and could start immediately. However, after a few days I noticed a problem was surfacing. Irma's hygiene was not too good, and she smelled a bit off. I mentioned this to Maria, and she told me that she would have a word with her. I gave her a week, and it didn't seem to change and I told Maria I would have to have an interview with Irma through the interpreter.

About halfway through my tour I went home for my RnR. It was great to see my friends and be in my house. I had great congratulations for my promotion, and the pubs were still busy, it was halfway through the summer, and all the students and Valley people were filling the pubs. Which at the time were many. As usual the time flies when you are having fun, but I was actually looking forward to going back.

I of course had my new friends in the Sergeants bar. There was a strict dress code, no jeans and  shirts had to be tucked in. the RSM was a Ghurkha and a fine chap.

My assistant Lee had a great idea. He was going to assist the Military Police dog handlers. He had got in touch with NAAFI news and told them he was going to send photos. On the day in question a reporter from NAAFI news came to visit Kupres for the event. So, Lee had a sleeve put on his arm, which of course was bite proof. He had to stand there and wait to be told to run, and the dog would be set free. I was asked if I wanted to do the same and of course I did. I had put the sleeve on and told to wait. The vicious dog was behind me, and I was told to run, I didn't get far before I was brought to the ground. I didn't think much more of it until a week later and a copy of NAAFI news had arrived at Kupres. I had a whole section spread over two pages. The start of the news was as such. Sergeant Rees of EFI doesn't just relax on his days off he is busy helping the Military Police in their training. Many photographs of me, but Lee were not to be seen. Lee didn't get a mention. Those dogs were nasty things though; they were trained for a special job. Very often you would see them straining on their leads to get a bit of human flesh, these seemed to hate humans, I wondered why.

One evening a concert had been laid on for troops on the camp. There was nothing special just a bit of music. The concert was being held in a tin clad building not far from the shop. I made my way from the shop and there were quite a few people making their way. There was a spiral staircase leading to the first floor, as I was approaching, I could see all of the local staff and they were waiting for me. They let me climb the stairs and they then followed me; I was humbled by the respect that the staff had shown me. The concert lasted about an hour but that was irrelevant to me, what the ladies did for me I will never forget.

MAKE HAY NOT WAR

When I was in DWC on my last tour I was eating a bar of chocolate a marathon to be exact, one of the nuts broke a filling, it didn't seem to do any harm at the time. While I was here in Kupres it was starting to get painful, so I decided to book a dentist appointment. The only problem being was there was no dental facility in Kupres. The nearest dentist was in Sipovo, no problem there I could drive there myself. I set out early in the morning not bothering to take my camcorder with me. What was so different to this journey was on my way the locals were cutting the hay, and what song was in the charts at the time, only 'Make hay not war' what an opportunity missed, I was thinking I could send a video to Catatonia then they could put it to their song. When I got to Sipovo I found my way to the dentist who happened to be a Lady officer who happened to be a very pleasant person. She gave me the usual injection and after a wait for it to numb my face. The dentist got her equipment together and turned on the drill, but nothing happened, she told me that the drill bit had broken, and I would have to come back tomorrow. Ok fair enough I made my way back to Kupres feeling like I had been punched in the face for nothing, anyway at least tomorrow I would be able to bring my camcorder and get another chance for fame. So, the next morning I am all ready and equipped, to my dismay they were not working the fields. At least this time the drill worked and I got my tooth fixed and I managed to get one photo taken of the farmers working. Catatonia never did get the photo though.

Well, I had my RnR, and I had about six weeks left of my tour. On one Thursday Captain Goodwin gave me a visit. He had a look at the progress with Tommy Tucker, and he was quite impressed with the work done. Capt G came out with a bit of good news that I wasn't expecting; I was entitled to a 48-hour pass. Capt G suggested that I go to Zagreb for a visit and I agreed that was a good idea. He told me the best option was to fly up or alternatively I could go by train, which would take much longer. I decided on the latter as I wasn't going to see much out of an airplane. Capt Goodwin told me that I could go back to the warehouse with him on the Friday and Georgia would sort out my tickets for me. On arrival at DWC Georgia handed me the ticket for the train that would leave at midnight. CG said he would take me to the rail station for the overnight train. I arrived at the train station at eleven forty-five for the midnight train. I thanked CG for the lift, and I entered the lonely ticket office. I presented my ticket and five minutes later I was sat on the train ready to leave. The odd thing about this was that I was the only person in the compartment. It was now dark, and I could see a few people arriving and leaving the station. At 23.59 slowly the train left the dark station, I said to myself this was a train from the sixties. It was uphill for the first part; I could see the lights of Split and probably Brac' Island. The city was all lit up with white lights, there was however a large building that was a bright blue colour; I thought that must be the football stadium.

The first station we stopped off at was Labin Dalmajinski. The only person there was the guard.

Soon after we were approaching Knin where there was a beautiful fortress looking down on our train. The train stopped off at the station but there was no one waiting to get on the train. There was not much to be seen outside, as it was too dark. There was not much to do but go to sleep. I woke up at about six o'clock and it was starting to get light. By now I was a bit hungry. The guard was passing through my carriage, and I stopped him. He could speak a bit of English, he was a bright and cheerful chap. I asked him if I could get something to eat, he told me that the only thing available was a sausage. I followed him to the engine room, and he produced the sausage, I was famished so I said I would like to have one. He put it on a flat surface I don't think it was a cooker, but it started to smoke a bit. The guard told me that he would bring it to me when it was cooked. About a half hour later he arrived at my compartment with the cooked sausage. I bit into the sausage, and it was awful it seemed it was made of all sorts of a pig's body, suddenly I didn't feel hungry anymore. Hopefully some hungry wolf found it at the side of the track.

Saturday 9 Oct 99

When I arrived at Zagreb early in the morning my first task was to find a cheap hotel. I didn't have to look far, before I came across a decent pension not far from the centre, the room was at the top of the building and at a good price. I had a feeling though that I was being watched. Outside my window were many white statues looking at me.

I decided to go out for a walk to see the sights. The place was beautiful and spotless I found myself in a square. Now, I didn't know if this was a special occasion or a regular Saturday thing as the place was bustling. A strange man dressed in black saw me filming and gave me a wave.

I had a feeling this was not going to be the last I would see of him today.

The centre was full of music; there was a man playing the violin and another man selling their wares. This man also gave me a wave, then picked up a CD showing it to me. It would have been rude of me if I didn't buy one.

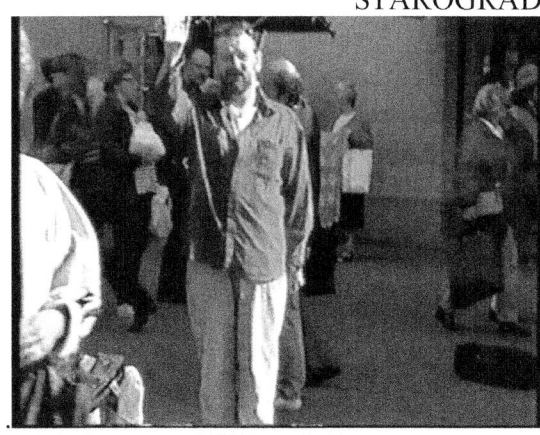

STAROGRADSKI, means Old City and Kraljevi Ulice means Kings Street. . I still play it

to this day; there are some lovely songs on it.
I walked around a bit more and came across a beautiful statue of a man on his horse. Ban Jeric etc. he also waved to me. I decided to leave the centre to explore the town a bit more; there were steps leading uphill,

so I decided to take a look. I found a street that was going uphill, a cat had a home in a home the lucky

thing.
I came across a daunting sight; it was a set of steps that was quite steep. I thought that it

 was bound to lead to some great  scenery. I said to myself 'here goes' and went for it. A bit of huffing and puffing I reached the summit. Not much to be seen

here, until I turned a corner and came across a strange looking church; well, that is what I said to myself at the time. A little bit further on my expectations bore fruit. I was overlooking the city. I didn't know it at the time, but I was at the steps of love. I could see a funicular but wasn't tempted to go on it. I decided to make my

way back down and was passing an alley, I looked up and there were four thugs coming down the steps, they were not stopping for anyone.
I couldn't say what it was about, but it looked like a scene from a film it did look like Paul Weller was in Town though. I found myself back in the square and the mime artist was still at it.

Not far from him now was a group of indigenous tribal people from the Americas.

The local people were looking at them strangely; they had obviously not seen the likes of before. As it happens though I have seen them a few times in different countries. I didn't expect such a fantastic day; I seemed to be at the right place at the right time. The mime artist was still at it when I left.

 In the evening, I had a few beers around the town. My train back to Split was leaving at six in the morning, so it would be an early night.

Sunday 10 Oct 99

At 06.00 the slowly the train left the dark station. This time there were a few people on the train. It was a misty morning but for a Sunday the roads were surprisingly busy.  There were a few stops first thing not unusual for a large city. When we actually left the city, it was getting lighter very quickly. Zagreb like Split had not seen any fighting so was undamaged. After three hours into the journey to Split there was a stark contrast. Suddenly there were war-damaged buildings, and the telephone poles had their wires cut.

 Now looking at the side of the track there were mainly fields, and little signs were to be seen; this picture says it all. , A person walking her cattle didn't seem too worried though.  I hadn't heard of any battles going on in Croatia, but I found this strange. I thought what I was witnessing was that the JNA attacked Croatia and this was the aftermath of it. The train speeded up, as no doubt there were not going to be many people wanting a train at this stage of time. Further down the track miles after miles were villages that had been laid empty, not many had roofs on but there were still fire marks rising above the glassless windows. The fields with 'Mine' signs come to an end and now a road took its place. On the other side of the road were still war-damaged houses, obviously

there was nobody living in them. And behind them were a mountain range with snow still on the summits. An armoured car with an antenna on its top and a machine gun mounted at the front was on its own positioned off the road. I presume there were people inside it, who knows? Shortly afterwards villages appeared all severely damaged. If I said I might have seen a glimpse of an Eagle people probably wouldn't believe me but here it is.

Villages surrounded by trees; it must have been idyllic before whatever happened to them. I saw many small railway stations but their sign was gone. Soon after an expanse of water appeared I think this is part of the Zrmanje river. Then more villages in the woods, again it appeared that the telegraph wires had been cut recently. I am sure I passed something strange, there appeared to be a group of people around a car, and a Croatian police officer was amongst them,

something bizarre was going on there. Further down the track we approached a junction, this place had a lot of damage inflicted on it. The sign said Zermanja. Lets say the

place had seen better days. A car further down

had met its end. I don't think this railway station exists anymore; I don't think these villages names exist anymore either. Some buildings had writing on them; I couldn't work out what they said but they must have been written before they were damaged.

Soon after this further down the track a passenger said

"Krajina" (Krayeena) "what was". After that there seemed to be carnage.

I heard this placed mentioned before in Split in 95. (Page 43) now after this there was not a village in one piece. There were certainly no Railway stations that were spared damage. Looking back, it was possible to see the route that the train had taken, the track had been cut on the sides of the mountains, and obviously it was impossible to cut a tunnel through the mountains. It was not possible to take a photo of the tracks along

the mountains.
Out of my window on the right a viaduct could be seen and soon after the train was on it, there was a beautiful view of the buildings below.

I can't imagine how beautiful it was to live here before the war. The area we passed through after was vast  with villages' surrounded with trees.  A telegraph pole had been cut down with its wires still hanging on.

Soon after we were entering the City of Knin, with its fortress looking down on us.  This is where I thought the Hvo had liberated on Operation Storm. What you imagine and what is real are two different things. There were people on top of houses doing repairs, I very much doubt these were people who had come back to rebuild their houses.  There were still telegraph poles with their wires cut.  Ironically there were pillboxes for some sort of defence.

Actually, I could see these pillboxes all over F.R.Y. (I very much doubt the Jugoslav's would of called them pillboxes) I was surprised how near to Split the war was in 1995; to us it seemed Bosnia was a long way off.
Split came into View as we started to descend from the hills, and it was a beautiful view. Someone mentioned Brac' (Brach) island and it was quite impressive.

When I got to the train station in Split Capt Goodwin was waiting for me. He asked how my trip went and told me that he would take me back to Kupres in the morning. I only had about six weeks left in Kupres, so it was like a sort of draw down. Tommy Tucker was nearly finished, only the roof needed putting on and

Nena was working hard

She was very good with the customers so sweet and polite. I had one problem to sort out though, Irma the shop assistant; her hygiene had not improved so I had to arrange with the interpreter for an interview to take place. It was a very hard thing for me to do. The interview took place in the interpreter's cabin. I told Irma that her hygiene hadn't improved, and we would have to find a replacement for her. She didn't produce a real answer. There could have been all sorts of reasons so I couldn't be harsh on her. I had asked Maria what the problem was, and she couldn't explain. Anyway, I had a short time left so I was not going to recommend getting a replacement.

Winter was arriving and it started getting colder quickly. Luckily the roof was put on Tommy Tuckers so it would be warm inside and free from

rain.

Tommy Tucker looked good when it was finished and at least the ladies had a proper shelter. It was a great honour for me to present Nena with a certificate. She looked really proud and with good reason.

Suddenly the weather changed, and the snow came down, but this didn't change it for the worse. The place looked beautiful with some stunning sights; maybe the Ski slopes will open soon.

Maria struggles.

Kelly is not smiling now.

I didn't have much of a handover as the new manager had been here before but of course I had to hand over money and all the stock. It was a sad time to leave Kupres I had made many good friends. I even said goodbye to Irma; I didn't think I was going to get much reaction from her. I was surprised as she gave me a hug and a kiss, maybe I did something right. Capt Goodwin came and collected me to take me back to DWC. I had a good report obviously the management were pleased with me. I had to hand in my weapon and ammunition along with the morphine. My flight was in the afternoon the next day so I could have a few beers in Stobrec' with my friends from the warehouse.

When I got back to Bulford the Colonel had a good talk with me and he was happy with my performance. He told me I could go home for leave and would have to be back at the beginning of January. Then I would be going back to Saudi Arabia for four months. I thought I would have a great time back home, as it was the millennium. I was wrong about that, Christmas was great but the New Year was such a letdown. It was so over hyped. I was glad to be back in Double hedges as I was looking forward to going back to PSAB, Prince Sultan Air Base, Al Kharj, Saudi Arabia. I dint have much to do now as I was a senior rank and didn't have to do any driving, it was a pity though as it could get a bit boring. I had my own room in the Sgts mess and got waited on by some civilian staff. Colonel Smith was in fine form. He didn't give me much praise for my work in Kupres. To be honest why should he? I was given a task to do and he expected me to fulfil it.

At the end of January 2000, I was again at RAF Lyneham ready for take-off to Saudi Arabia. It was the same as before with all the briefings. Of course, they were cold days but I knew by the time I came back it would be the beginning of summer. On arrival we would have our luggage searched for the hundreds of illegal things we would smuggle into KSA. Stevie was waiting for me when I got out of customs, he was glad to see me because in a week's time he would be going home.

Stevie took me to the accommodation, which was a far cry from what it was like last time. Tent city had now been taken down. The new blocks were stunning; everyone had their own room with all the facilities like showers and a kitchen. There was a lovely view of the road, which circled the little town and the big water tower, which could be seen for miles, so there was no excuse for getting lost.

The new shop was not far away. Anyway Stevie had already sorted things out for me in my new home, my bedding was sorted, and he gave me the keys. Stevie told me he would pick me up in the morning and take me to the shop where we would commence with the handover. The handover would not take long as we had little stock and no other satellite facilities.

I had a good night sleep in my home. The apartment was quite big with en suite bathroom and a kitchen. A far cry from the tents we lived in last time not saying they were that bad. The way the handover worked was Stevie would run the shop for three days and I would take over on the fourth day. Of course there was a Corporal to work the shifts. Lawrence had been here for two months and knew the system. The first day Stevie handed the stock over to me. This took a few hours while the shop was shut in the afternoon. There was a bit of a naughty thing going on as we were selling CDs and play station games, which were not on the books. In other words, the staff were buying them and selling them on at a great profit. This was one of the first things I was going to stop. A part of the stock handed over was laundry tumble dryer sheets. This was a ridiculous thing to have bought from Hussam stores as all the laundry facilities were free and that included the tumble dryer sheets. So, nobody was going to buy them. By the afternoon I signed for all the stock. Stevie told me that he had booked a truck for the next day to go to Hussam stores to get some stock. So early in the morning Stevie went to the MT Section to get the pickup truck. It was arranged that I would wait in the shop for him. At around ten o'clock he arrived at the shop. Before we could leave the camp, we had to telephone the RAF Police to let them know where we were going and when we would be back. If we were gone for too long, they would have to come to look for us. Well as it happened, they might well have had to. After leaving the camp we would have to take the mile long road to the Saudi Guardroom, where we would have to stop and show our credentials. Then leaving the Base and onto the road to Al Kharj which would be the first turn off of course we wouldn't take that road. The road would be quite simple as it was quite clearly marked Riyadh. We were about ten miles away from Eskan village when Stevie stopped in a lay-by, I asked him why he stopped and he told me that the steering had gone funny, in other words we had a puncture. I thought no problem we would have to change the tyre. We found the spare tyre but there was no spanner to take the wheel off. We were now in the proverbial Sheisser. Mobile phones were not so good in those days, so we were in a bit of trouble. I asked Stevie if he had used this truck before and he told me that he had used it often. I asked him if he had ever checked the toolbox and of course he never did. The tyre was not completely flat so I thought the best thing we could do is carry on the road and hopefully make it to a local town. Luck was on our side that day as we managed to see a garage that was off the main road. We left the motorway and found the garage. The mechanic changed our tyre for us and we were soon back on the road to Eskan village; I found these poor people were always the kindest of people.  We got to Eskan village and checked in; next stop would be Subways in Riyadh where I would have a spicy beef submarine. Next stop would be Hussam Stores.

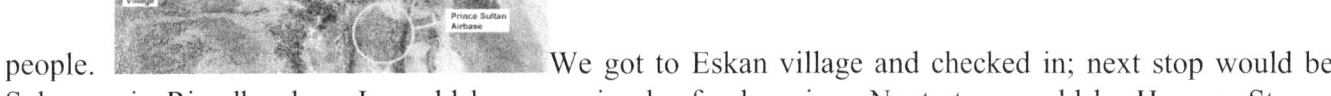

I don't know if anyone was having a laugh with the sign that was outside. Although it looked scruffy outside it was actually quite tidy inside just like any department store back home. This is the place where we got the essential stocks like shower gels, toothpaste, chocolates, sweets, crisps and cigarettes. I of course had met the manager on my previous visit to KSA. I didn't particularly like him; he seemed to be too full of his own importance. What we had to do in this shop was a thing called goods purchased for resale, what we buy from the stores we record on a form and add 20 percent for the resale. As Stevie was still running the shop he paid for the goods. We had given the manager a list of the goods wanted, and we would have to wait for them to be assembled, this wouldn't take long. Once the goods were in the back of the pickup truck we headed for Batha (Bat'ha) Street. Although it sounded like Barter Street this was just a coincidence.

Although in most shops you would barter. Here we would park the vehicle. We could leave the goods in the back as it was quite safe, if someone got caught stealing, they would be in serious trouble. The first thing we did was to go to Subways where I would always get a spicy beef submarine. There were hundreds of clothes shops where we would buy Kelvin Klein or Levis etc again for resale. Then onto the Gold souk where we could buy brass ornaments or Gold if anyone ordered something. We didn't want to stay in Riyadh too long as I had to take over the stock from Stevie when we put our purchases into the computer.

When we got back to PSAB we would have to phone the RAF Police to let them know we were back. Back in the shop I had to count all the stock including what we had just purchased. This took a few hours, and we had to agree all was in order. The second phase of the handover was completed. The third phase was quite simple Stevie was in charge for the day and at the end of the evening shift he handed me the keys to the shop. I could run the shop as I wanted from now.

We were talking and Stevie said that he was a bit peeved that he had to work the millennium. I told him that the real millennium was next New Year, well that was what I had been told and in reality, it was true. It sort of brightened him up a bit.

Stevie was now free to do what he wanted to do, and he was looking forward to going home. His day soon came, and he was on his way home.

Things had changed so much; two years ago, I was just a Corporal with no responsibility and living in a tent. Now I was a Sergeant and living in a palace. I wanted to improve how the place worked and to get rid of the stock that we could never sell. I wasn't quite sure about Hutch, I thought he was a bit dodgy, but he soon convinced me that he was honest enough. I asked him about the things that were going on with the CDs and Play Station games. I told him that it had to stop because it was illegal. One thing hadn't changed, and it was the arrogant American Airmen. I didn't know why they thought they were so special; they spent some money I suppose, and they loved the Cuban cigars we got from Hussam stores; it was like a rebel thing for them as the cigars were banned in the States. Also, our cigarettes were a lot cheaper than the BX. The Americans looked after their forces and they provided entertainment quite regularly, in the first week I was there they had a rock band on. One thing I dint have that I had on the last tour was my Postie friend, Goose. The Posties we had with us were a bit reluctant to escort us to Riyadh. I had to get Hutch to come with me so we didn't have much time to get to Riyadh and back. I had managed to get some Squadron guys to come up with us, they were glad about that, as they never left the base before. I also had a bit of difficulty with the SNCO of the MT Flight as he was making it awkward for us to get truck. Another thing I had a problem with was that Hutch was a wannabe American; he was hanging around with them on his time off. When you drive in Saudi you have to have your wits about you, the Arabs still think they are riding Camels and apparently, they believe if they die in a car crash, they will go straight to Heaven. There are cars alongside the motorway that have been there for months, someone told me that if a person got killed in an accident, they have got to leave the car there for three months so that the soul is not disturbed.

The roads are full of potholes and sometimes a road can just finish without notice. Women are not allowed to drive but the boys can drive when they are fourteen, no lessons just get in and go. The worst things that are on the road are the trucks; things fall off them and the tyres look like they are about to explode and sometimes they do. There are three lanes on the motorway and an escape lane we called it Allah's Lane, the Arabs use it as a fast lane no doubt with fatal results at times.

At one time when I was in Riyadh there was something going on with the Mufti or religious Police, it looked like they were arresting someone. I was looking on and one of the Police made a gesture for me to look the other way and of course I did. A Frenchman got arrested for writing something down on a piece of paper, it was only a shopping list, but the Saudi's thought he was making notes of a building. There are all sorts of restaurants in Riyadh Burger King MacDonald's etc, but you had better be careful if you take your girlfriend.  You might be in for a surprise.

It was time for the mandatory NBC training that had to be done within the first three weeks. The instructor was of course a RAF Regiment Sergeant. The RAF regiment were responsible for the defence of airfields and equipment. They looked at themselves as Special Forces and I am sure some of them were quite capable. There were only three of us on the course on the day. I thought the instructor would have had a bit of a sense of humour, but I suppose he just wanted to get the job done quickly. There is a set procedure that I have explained about already on my first visit to PSAB.

The Americans could not understand why they were not allowed off base, indeed I heard one say, "Why do they hate us so much". Another time when some Americans were let off base, they were in civilian clothes, but their haircuts were a giveaway, and they put their DPM (Disruptive pattern material, i.e. camouflage) rucksacks in-between the back seats and the windows so the whole world could see who they were. Although things were sort of working out Hutch decided to get a haircut, just like the Americans, which was a ridiculous short back and sides. He would stand out like a sore thumb in Riyadh so I told him that he couldn't go there, funny thing is he didn't seem to mind, he could spend more time with his heroes. I thought of a thing to alleviate the stock problem was to make a big order from NAAFI in the UK. We were allowed to do this, but it was quite a Logistical problem. I made an order that would probably take up two pallets, the RAF would send them out to us, if they had the space and time.

In the meantime, I could still go to Riyadh shopping if I could get a vehicle and an escort. Sometimes if the right postie was on shift, I could go up with them. One day when the time was right, I managed to go to Riyadh with a postie. What I had in mind was to take the stock I couldn't sell i.e. the laundry sheets up to Hussam stores and see if he would take them back. When I arrived and had the customary cup of tea, I asked him if he would take back the laundry sheets and reluctantly, he agreed. I had now got enough stock to last me until my order arrived with the RAF.

Around about the same time the Squadron told me that I was told to ring HQ EFI, at a certain time. Of course this is what I did, it was Neil who answered the phone. It was about the order that I had made. Everything was fine but I had ordered a substantial amount of shower gel, the NAAFI had a tight budget and by ordering so much it would take a lot of time to recover the money, Neil asked me if he could cut down the order a bit, of course, I agreed and that was it. Although I was not allowed to go to Riyadh on my home I was able to go to local places alone. I decided to do a few probes into Al Kharj to see if there were any large stores there. I didn't have much luck there but there were a few petrol stations that I could buy some goods from.

I went to a certain garage a few times and tried to speak the little Arabic that I could. One of the assistants was getting a bit funny and his boss told him to shut up. Al Kharj apparently is where Osama Bin Laden was from and indeed there were a few shops with that name (Bin Laden). I found a shop and asked the owner if he could get some cigarettes, he asked how many and I told him about two big boxes. He agreed that he would do this for me. I had to come back in a few days to pick up the stock. I managed to get back to the base alive. Two days later I intended to go back to shop in Al Kharj, but the MT Sergeant told me he didn't have a vehicle available, so that put a spanner in my works. Three days later I managed to get a vehicle for a few hours. I found the shop and had a talk with the manager. He told me that he had the cigarettes, but I didn't turn up. He told me it was tradition to fine me for not meeting our agreement, luckily, he said he would waiver the fine. He no longer had the cigarettes and so I missed that opportunity. It was time for Hutch to go on his RnR, so I would be on my own for a week, I didn't mind at all, and I wasn't going to miss him and his American friends who were becoming pests. That week went quickly, and Hutch only had a month left. Although life was better with the new accommodation things were not much different as before, the food was good, and it was sunny most of the time. Sometimes though you could look into the sky and you would see a yellow cloud coming your way, a sandstorm was on its way.

About a month into my tour there was another night of entertainment. This time it was a dance troupe. They were good and looked attractive with their short skirts. There was a lot of security around, but I doubted that anyone would attempt to jump on stage and be stupid, but you never knew with the

Spams.

The Saudis had a sort of a show on one day. It was cultural exhibition. I decided to take a look. There was

a falconer and his bird. It was a close match but

the Falcon was victorious over the pigeon.

Not far from there was a show of lovely Camels.

Not to be out done this beautiful horse was a bit of a competition. Her name was Poppy.

There was a strange looking man with an equally strange looking lizard.

He asked me if I wanted to pick it up and I said no thanks "scared are you" "no" I replied, he was bloody good judge of character though. The highlight of the day though was a weaver. I could have sat there for hours watching his skills on the

loom.
.

It was soon time for Hutch to go home.

I was starting to look forwards to my RnR. Hutch's's replacement Dave had arrived on the same day although they would not see each other. I would have to go to pick him up though and arrange for his accommodation to be sorted out. This was no problem though because the RAF PSF sorted that all out for me. They would of course show me where his accommodation was and give me the key to his room. His flight had already arrived, and he would have to go through customs and have his luggage searched. I worked out what time he would get through customs and wet to pick him up. He looked a bit lost until he saw me. I could empathise with him as I had been in the same situation a few years ago. It was nice to see him, as I knew him from one of the shops in Bosnia. I took him to his accommodation where he dropped his bags off before I took him to the shop. I showed him around the shop, and I said he would do his first shift tomorrow morning. It was still early in the morning, and the Roundel Restaurant was still open. He already knew there would not be any pork but was surprised to see bacon and sausages, I told him they were beef and chicken. After breakfast I told him he was free to do what he wanted, he was probably tired and needed a rest. When I was working in the evening he came into the shop and had a go on the till. We all got used to dealing with different money, it's all numbers in the end. In the morning the both of us were on duty in the shop. Dave was a scouser and I said to him, I bet you are a bit dodgy or words to that effect, "oh no" he said. He soon proved over the next few days that I could trust him. He took great pride in the way the shop was presented.

STRAWBERRY FIELDS FOREVER

Two months into my tour of PSAB I went on my RnR. Instead of having two periods I decided to take a week and instead of driving I had a flight up, it was a lot quicker and safer. It was the same old thing nightclubs and watching cabarets in the Diplomat Hotel. I booked in for my flight back to PSAB. The flight was not what I expected instead of going straight to Riyadh the plane went into a different direction, and we landed on another base I don't know where it was, but I think it was UAE. We were allowed to get off the aircraft and we were told to walk to a hanger nearby. Getting closer to this hanger I could see a crowd of men all with no tops and quite muscular. On arrival I thought this was strange they looked like wrestlers and indeed they acted like wrestlers as they were slapping each other and pushing each other around.

We were told to get back on the aircraft. The wrestlers started to take photographs of the plane and were told to stop by some officer; they bluntly told him where to get off and carried on.

We got onto the aircraft and sat down. By this time a hangover had kicked in. opposite me was a young woman wearing a blue vest; she was twitching her chest muscles to show off. When we got to a certain height, we were told we could unbuckle our seatbelts and walk around, now these wrestling men were making me nervous as they were pulling the guidance wires that run along the inside of the aircraft and slapping each other. I thought the aircraft was going to spiral out of control any second.

I got talking to the woman opposite me and I asked her what all this was about, and she explained that they were all professional wrestlers, and they were touring the Gulf to entertain the American troops. She told me her name was Strawberry Fields and in a couple of weeks' time she would be appearing on the Oprah show. We finally, against all odds landed in PSAB safely. The wrestlers were greeted by their agent and taken away, still slapping and pushing. I went to work for a few hours and was told the wrestlers were at the sports ground entertaining. They put on quite a good show and I left thinking no more about it.

Two weeks after my RnR the RAF Police asked me if I wanted to go into the desert to see an old Fort. Of course, I did it was nice to get out of the camp. We went for a few miles down the road and then took a dirt track that led into the desert. The scenery around was stunning, as I said before the Desert is not all sand

dunes and without life.

It looked like someone had been doing a bit of target practice. And you had to be careful where you walked.

. We took a hike up a hill and the wow factor hit.

I took a picture overlooking the plains and I don't know if I had taken a photo of something sinister

happening. Back down the road in a different direction was a show of lovely Camels.

One was showing off her magic trick to her baby.

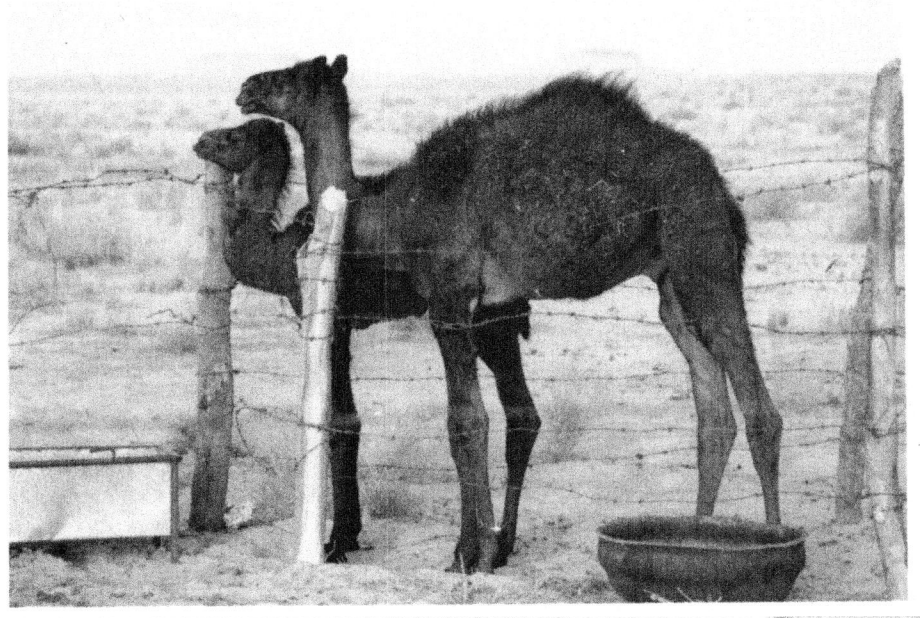

They are truly beautiful animals.
My four months had come to an end, and it was time to hand over to the new Det Cdr, same old routine. At least I had got rid of some stock that would have been there forever. I was sad to leave PSAB; it might have been because I knew my probable next tour would be Kosovo.

2000 Kosovo aug to dec.
When I got back to Bulford it was the same old routine, a bit of a briefing and I was given a couple of weeks' leave. And I was given the news that I would be going to Kosovo. Rather than carrying our luggage home we were allowed to send a big box of belongings through the army system. I could send things to my local TA Centre, they were a Transport Sqn, it would take a few weeks, but it was worth the wait. I had packed in a lot of clothes and ornaments. It was the beginning of the summer, and I had missed most of the winter. I still had a lot of things in my friend's house that I wanted to move, I had an idea that when I got back to Bulford maybe I could borrow the white Transit van. My leave was soon over, and I got picked up

at Newbury station. There was no calling of people by their ranks, it was all first names, except Dawn when she was calling for someone.

Sometimes the Colonel would call you by rank depending on how much trouble you were in; this happened to me. The Colonel called me into his office and was going to give me a grilling. Apparently, an RAF Officer made a complaint that EFI had been illegally selling fake Play Station games, CDs and gold. He asked me if I was selling the Play Station games and CDs, I told him no and that I had stopped it, nothing more was said about that. Concerning the gold, he asked me if I was selling it. I told him yes, I didn't see anything wrong with it. He asked me how I knew it was real gold, I really didn't have an answer to that one, although the shops were real jewelers. He said, "are you an alchemist". Though I did trust the Arabs and never thought they would sell us fakes, and to be honest I don't think they ever did. Anyway, that was the end of that. When I left his office and was talking to my colleagues, I was told that Lawrence had confessed to his crimes and had dragged other people down with him, telling on a few of his accomplices. He had got demoted to Lance Corporal. This would lead to EFI reverting to having Lance Corporals as standard practice. The next day I found the courage and asked the Colonel if I could borrow the white transit van. He said it was fine as long as I put the fuel back in it. So, on Friday I was driving down the M4 in the old faithful. At the weekend I managed to move all my stuff. Time soon flew by, and I was about to go to Kosovo, I wasn't looking forward to it and knew it was not going to be as easy as my last two endeavors.

BLACKBIRD

The flight to Kosovo was a bit longer than the flight to Bosnia as of course it was further East. There were a few EFI girls on the flight who were re-touring, they seemed to be excited to go back there. They knew when they were approaching Pristina airport. It seemed to take forever for the plane to go into its descent into the airport. The girls were pointing out places on the ground including the Apod, whatever that was. When I got through the routine of arriving at Kosovo, I was met by my predecessor who was obviously glad to see me, only because she was going home. It was the same Det Cdr May that I took over from in Kupres. It was going to be a two-week handover as Murphy lines was a much busier shop and bar to run. It was the same old sarcasm as I had in Kupres with the "He hasn't got a Scooby" line. Supposed to rhyme with hasn't got a clue. (Scooby doo).

The OC was none other than the boss, who was the OC in Dalma in Grapple six. He had in tow with him a sergeant who was his assistant. He had great experience of EFI as he was the manager of the chip shop in Rhein Dahlen in Germany. How he became a Sergeant was beyond me.

The people running the show in Murphy lines were X Sqn 45 Cdo Royal Marines. At least I knew I was in good hands with them.

I wasn't going to do much on my first day as it was mostly an admin day. I was taken to my accommodation which was a single room, basically I had a corimec to myself. I had to get issued with a rifle and magazines plus the morphine if I got a leg or an arm blown off. We wouldn't have to carry these around the camp, and I could lock them away in my room, they would be safe there

May then took me to the shop to meet the staff. There were three EFI staff and three Civilian staff two females and a male. The civilian staff were Albanians they also worked in the Junior ranks bar. There is not much to be said about the handover just counting stock and money, basically. On my second evening in ML there was a fancy dress party in the Sgts mess. The topic of this party was headwear, as big and ridiculous (in a nice way) as possible. A lot of thought and imagination went into creating some of these hats. Not all of them though, a cowboy hat was sufficient for one, and a bicycle helmet was good enough for another.

THE FIELD OF BLACKBIRDS

On Murphy lines there was a Helicopter landing pad that was quite busy. There was a large field which was

very busy with black Birds.

I had heard of the field of Blackbirds; this is where a major battle had been fought with the Serbs and Albanians in 1389 and they still hold grudges. I knew it was called Kosovo Polje (Pole yeah) this literally translates to Kosovo Field, though it is known as the field of blackbirds. I asked someone where Kosovo Polje was, and they told me that we were standing in the actual place. To make sense of this "Kosovo" itself

is derived from Kosovo Polje meaning "Blackbirds field".
It's amazing to think these crows have lived in the same field for hundreds of years.

The handover went ok but I was not confident as there was such a lot to learn. I knew I had my work cut out. However, I had some good staff who would help me along. Especially Anna, she was a cheerful girl, and we had some good laughs. Sadly after a few days I had a phone call early in the morning, it was Anna telling me her mother was not well and she had to go home, and this really saddened me. Apart from running the shop and bar I had other accounts to sort out like the Sgts mess. The local girls who worked at the bar and sometimes the shop were ok. They were not so well trained as the EFI staff. Their English was good enough when they wanted to. Mimosa, who I called Mimo, Leerie and Anita. They could be left to run the bar themselves. There was one male Albanian member of staff, Ali who could speak good English and could be handy for interpreting. Every Friday I had to do my accounts for the 'Weekend returns' it wasn't too bad to begin with as it was mostly the shop and the bar. I could deposit our takings to the BFPO (posties) after I balanced my accounts.

After a few weeks things started to change, and I had to bank another dets takings. They would hand their money over to me and of course I would have to count it and put it onto my system. We had a good number of satellite Dets scattered around Pristina and to begin with banked their own money. The Boss Major Steines had a good idea that all the dets would bring their money to me and I would bank all of them in one go. This put more of a burden on me, but I managed to cope as long as the form A2 and money matched.

Apart from that we were dealing in different currencies. Our main currency we worked in was the Deutschmark, there was also the Dollar, but we had to be able to take any currency. Another problem was some of the dets didn't have transport so they would give their money to an agent- so to speak. A lot of these dets would be running their shops in shipping containers but that was their responsibility. There would have to be a lot of trust put into those individuals, but I suspected some were not so honest, and some were not so competent.

We had some civilian visitors from the Apod, and they were not too friendly and were rude to my staff. I saw them going into my shop one day and one of them asked for five sleeves of cigarettes. I told the staff not to sell more than one sleeve to them. So, this is what she did, he said "this is no effin good to me", so told him that is all he is getting. He went off in a huff, shall we say.

Most of my staff were nice people but there was an odd one out. He seemed to have a chip on his shoulder. I will call him Jack.
I was talking to Kerian one day in the storeroom and he came in. we didn't say anything bad to him, when he was leaving, he shouted, "you pair of grunts" and slammed the door. I was going to chase after him, but Keiran told me not to bother. Now I have this terrible habit of calling myself an anusol when I make a mistake. One day I was working in the office, and he came in and asked me for something, of course I gave him what he asked for. A bit later the boss came into the office and said to me that I had called Jack an anusol, I told him that I didn't. Jack had obviously complained to him. We were talking about the civilians from the Apod one day and he said "I am going to nut one of them" I said "no you won't" he did not expect that.

Occasionally I would have to visit the satellite shops to see if things were ok. One of these was a steel Iso container being run by Fatty my co driver to Banja Luka at one time. Someone told me that he was up to no good. I checked through his paperwork and things didn't tally, especially Television sets. When I got back, I told the boss, he said he would look into it. I didn't hear anything for a while. The boss had given him a visit and was going to investigate his books him. Next thing we knew Fatty had booked himself a flight back home, how he did that, I do not know. I think Colonel Smith had probably sacked him after that. Someone else had taken over the Det and received a letter from Fatty asking to send him his Television set, brazen I would say.

THE BOXER

We were told that we were having a visit from someone interesting, none other than Frank Bruno. He was going to use our EFI bar. There he was larger than life entering the bar, he had a tremendous welcome with the troops clapping and cheering "Bruno-Bruno".

It started off with an interview by Gary Richardson, a sports commenter and reporter. This is how it went. "You were working on a building site at the time as a labourer. You wanted to turn professional". Gary asked him how surprised he was when he had a telephone call from Terry Lawless, Frank replied, "I was very surprised as I didn't have a telephone at the time". "you get a crack at Mike Tyson" "you were standing in the ring waiting for Mike Tyson" "what were your feelings, can you describe it?" "I can I was waiting for him to enter the ring, and I was twitching" (I can't write exactly what he said but there is a very common saying when you are scared out of your wits). It was a very scary experience but when he comes in the ring it all disappears, but he keeps you waiting". "What did it feel like when he hit you?" " it was like a baseball bat at the end of a whip, it numbs you and makes you do funny things like a body pop" " the fight went very well and in the second round Frank whacked him, I have got to say this to you Frank, that if you had another one two three or four blokes in the ring with you, you might of won". I think that part was unscripted.

"you're so funny" Frank replied and then did his famous laugh. Soon after he made a Chris Eubank impression. This went down well with the audience.

It was now question-time, and the third one came from one of our own, It was pretty appalling, he referred to something about CDs and DVDs with a Gary Glitter connection. To be honest Frank looked a bit stunned. "These villages do have their Effin idiots," said Gary Richardson.

They then did an autograph and photo session. Telling people to line up. It was my turn, it's amazing to shake the hand that knocked Mike Tyson down.

When this session ended, I got hold of Frank. I had already put a message on my phone, ready to send my sisters my phone. I asked him to press the send button. I didn't expect the response I got. "Eff off" he said, "I bet this phone is going to explode". He then went on a walkabout around the camp shaking hands with people who probably didn't have a clue who he was. Frank was oblivious to that though.

. He then

came towards me, and I shook hands with him again. "Cheers Frank, thanks for that" "you'r allright, no  problem, take care of yourself man".

GONE FISHING

Another CSE show had come to Kosovo, and it was by Fish the former lead singer of Marillion. I had to drive our packed land rover into Pristina. I came upon a tight situation, as the traffic was constant and I wanted to get onto the main road. Nobody was going to stop for me. I saw a small gap and accelerated onto a side road that enabled me to have a chance to get to the concert on time. "Good driving skills Taff" someone commented. The show started off with a dance troupe who didn't wear much. Next was a sort of magic show. There was a person on a blue robe, it was not possible to tell who was underneath to begin with. The person was playing with fire, that's for sure. Then the magician tantalised us with the opening of the hood to reveal a

mask and she was still playing with fire. Eventually she showed her true self.

and started

playing with ribbons throwing them around everywhere. She probably put a lot of work into her show; she has at least gained fame now.

Then there was a comedian, he was funny as I could hear myself laughing in the video I made. I could not repeat the jokes he made. He then made way for the guitarists who were warming up. Fish came on walking back and fore, of course he didn't look like the Fish we knew when he was with Marillion. He gave me a menacing look straight into my face.

Fish then went back offstage and the band started playing the guitars seriously soon he came back on and gave is a Wai. This is an oriental (Thai) greeting consists of a slight bow , with the palms pressed together

I didn't know the first song but the next ones were familiar Kayliegh and Lavender. Of course the group now playing were not Marillion, Fish had left them long ago. Fish stopped singing for a while and pointed to someone in the audience. The person was an Albanian that was helping them. Fish said that the night before they were staying in a hotel and the guy threw a television set out of a window crashing into a building below making a massive hole in the roof. Well Fish found this hilarious. I suppose the albanian thought that all rock bands wrecked their hotels. The band started playing more songs and after a few a military band entered the stage. It probably was the Band of the Royal Marines.  it was a brilliant innovation. The group played a few songs then the band joined in on the drums and flutes, this brought the house down, the crowd

loved it.

COME FLY WITH ME

I got to know an Officer in the AAC. He was quite a short person but this didn't affect his ability to fly high in the Army. One day whilst talking to him I asked what the possibility of getting a flight in Gazelle. The Gazelle was probably the smallest helicopter in the British Forces. He agreed to this and said he would arrange for this to happen. The time eventualy came around and he told me to be at the helipad early one morning. The gazelle was probably from the military airport, so it had a few miles to get here. There were actually four of us in the helicopter, the captain, his co-pilot, me and another lucky passenger. It was a beautiful sunny day which in a way was not perfect as there were a lot of smudges on the window which took up a great part of the helicopter. It has an unbelievable top speed of 193 mph. I don't believe it reached that speed on this flight.

The captain turned the key, and the helicopter started to liven up. It has an amazing engine sound like a high-pitched whistle which gets louder as it reaches its flying status. For a small helicopter I could feel the immense power it had. It took about two minutes for the rotors to reach their flying speed. A couple of minutes later we started ascending slowly and we were then above the large green hangers and from there

a good view of Murphy lines.

Minutes later we were approaching the city, someone told me that I would probably fly over the building that NATO dropped a precision bomb on. That event was in the papers at the time. There were villages that had been attacked as they didn't have any rooves on them. The Captain probably was talking to us on the intercom but obviously my camcorder was not going to pick that up. On the outskirts of the city the chopper banked to the left and that was to show us what probably been a Serb position but all were left were craters. The football stadium and a nearby building were in great shape though. when we left the city the aircraft picked up speed, I could imagine why they called this 'chopper' a Gazelle.

CHANGES.

I was to have a month off from the shop in MLs as the boss asked me if I would prepare a shop on the APOD. Well of course I would like a month in a different place. I asked the boss who would run the shop while I was away and he told me Sergeant Chippy, I doubted he would do it on his own. That was not my problem though. When I arrived at the shop in the Apod it was totally bare. All the shelving had been delivered and was on the floor. I was told that when the shelving was nearly finished, I had to tell the boss, and he would order some stock.

It took about a week to get the shelving in its proper places. Then the boss ordered the stock, it would arrive a week later. There were other things to do meanwhile like getting the office sorted with the bookwork, the safe and the till. All had to be in working order. The social life was good as well. The Apod was staffed mainly by the RAF. There were four of us in our little gang, we would visit various bars.

There were two arrivals at the Apod, they were the ones who would be running the shop. I had a week with them to show them the paperwork and bank their money, of course they had to bring their takings to me. I showed them how to order more stock when they needed it. I told them not to come to me when they got low. When the shop opened, they seemed to be ok so I could go back to ML.

When I got back things were getting harder. The boss was trying out a new system of ordering stock. The AtoO he thought was out of date; all he did was to make it harder for me. On one occasion I said to Keiran, who was my main helper, "I am not doing this, he can send me home. Luckily, she managed to do it and probably saved my job. On one occasion one Det Cdr brought her money to me and left for a while. The money didn't tally so I had to work it out. I corrected it and left a note on her money book. All I put was 'Get it right." She came back and took her book. A while later the boss came to me and said that I was rude to her, I told him what the mistake was, and I corrected it. He replied "oh you fixed it then" so I told him of course I did. After about two weeks back at M.L. the det commander from the Apod came to me asking me for more stock. it was difficult to keep my own stock to a manageable level. I told them not to come to me as I was not the warehouse. If I gave them my stock I could find my self short. I point blank refused to give them anything, they left very dissapointed. By this time I was getting very despondent. Just like in Dalma the boss was putting extra work on me. I mentioned this to Kerian one day and she agreed. "He does'nt like you, does he". I was seriously thinking, this was going to be my last tour.

In North Macedonia we had warehouse and a shop. We had a duty of care to them. Occasionaly we would have to go down for a visit. I welcomed the time I was appointed for a visit. Two of us went down sharing the driving, an MT driver and myself. it would be a good four hours drive.

At least the weather was good on this day. going down towards the border was quite busy and the roads were not very good. I knew there was a large American base on the way and I certainly did'nt want to visit the place. There was a large military convoy coming the opposite way, many fuel tankers and tank transporters. There was plenty of smog in the air. we approached the border crossing not knowing if we had to stop. It soon became clearer as there was a slip road for military vehicles. next we headed for Skopje (Skopeyea) the troops called it Skopeshe, this did my head in.

My co-driver took over from me as he knew where the warehouse was; this was in an industrial estate. I found our shop, Ruth was there at the time not very interesting except for saying "you have changed" a few times. After checking the books went to the animal sanctuary; I mean the warehouse. there were cats and dogs everywhere, they had taken upon themselves to look after them. They were lovely animals though, at least they were being looked after. The girl looking after the warehouse seemed more stressed with the pets rather than work.

All things were well with the paperwork, I took their takings from the shop and we made our way back to Pristina. The caption says, people might be enemies but the cats and dogs were friends.

On the way out of the city there was a little market and my co-driver wanted to have a look, he was interested in buying some perfume. I strongly advised him against it, he bought one any way; he later regretted it. There is something about these countries that is unique, that is when you stop at traffic lights, you will get mobbed with people with buckets of water and sponges and they will start cleaning your windows, and you were expected to pay them for this. This was to find its way to the UK soon. We passed the border and made our way back to Pristina, it was a sunny day but when we got nearer the city, the sky was a sickly yellow colour.

Three lions

Winter had set in over Kosovo, and Christmas was coming. Not deterred, we had a visit from two English heroes. Jackie Charlton and Alan Ball. It was a more serious talk than the Bruno episode, but it did have funny moments. I was six years old when England won the world cup and I can still see my father jumping from his seat when they scored the decisive goal.

Alan Ball was talking about a feller called Gary Whittingham who was in the Army and was playing for Aldershot as an amateur, he was a good footballer. Alan was managing Portsmouth at the time and went to Aldershot in an attempt to nab Gary. On approaching the football ground, he heard a lot of cheering not once but twice. "It must have been a goal" says Alan "I said to this feller, has there been a goal? He said there has been two" "I came to see Gary Whittingham, who scored the goals?" the feller replied "Gary Whittingham" (this was exactly the way Alan described the event. "terrific" "so I walked around the front and one of the Captains or Majors or whatever it had come and shook my hand and said would you present the prize or cup at the end of the game type of thing" This was half time obviously. "I asked the guy, what is the situation with him" referring to Gary. The guy was probably a Colonel, he said " well he wants to be a footballer and you will be able to buy him out of the Army" Alan said "during half time I bought him for 450 quid" "The Officer asked what type of contract are you going to give him., I said

I am going to give him a two year contract, the main man said that's fine." After the game he brought Gary to me and said to Gary, this gentleman wants to sign you for Portsmouth. We agreed on the terms which were £450 quid. The officer said to Gary from the Army's point of view, "your job will still be there in two years time, if you don't make it at football". And I thought that was terrific on the Army's part. He played about 18 months, and we sold him for two and a half million." Then followed a bit of laughter.

    Jack and Alan were having a chat and Alan must of said something that irked Jack. Jack grabbed Alans cup off him, a show of, I am still the big boy here, all in fun though.

Jackie Charlton started talking about tactics in football and how they have changed. He then started talking about a match he had played for England. He said "I took off my jacket and my tie off, took my sweater off

and went downstairs for a pint" this had to be in a hotel. "I went to the bar and ordered a pint, the guy gave me a beer, and I held it up, as you do, I was inspecting my pint and Alf (Sir Alf Ramsey) walked through the door, he said hello Jack still on the pints I see. Well, Alf I have been playing today, and I am not due tomorrow. He came across and we had a conversation, not because he wanted to talk to me, it was just that I was the only one in the hotel, we stood at the bar, and I said to Alf why did you pick me. "Well Jack, I always pick the players that play the way I want them to. It's to make the pattern work, it's not necessarily the best player-pause- JACK," then laughter from the audience. He then started talking about Jimmy Grieves, "he was a strange player to play against, I remember playing against Jimmy in Tottenham, you just take your mind off Jimmy for a split second, and you don't know he is there. Then suddenly he is there on top of you. He had three kicks in the game and had three goals, and I had a rollocking after the game".

In the club we had a table football. Alan and Jack decided it would be a good idea to have a game. Of course they would not be on the same side, this give the soldiers a chance to be able to say that they played football with Jack Charlton and Alan Ball.

It was a special time for me and even more for the Englishmen, who were there on that day. Jack and Alan were such gentlemen and showed much respect to the troops.

Christmas day arrived and there was a dinner laid on for us. Also cans of beer were plentiful. The only trouble was there was a stupid tradition to have a food fight. They made hell of a mess in the dining hall. These people thought that they could just leave it as it was. The head chef was not happy, he made everybody sit down again. He gave everyone a rollocking and told them that nobody leaves until the place is cleaned up.

It was time for me to leave Kosovo and I had made my mind up to leave EFI. I handed over to my replacement after a week. On my last day I would of expected the boss to at least say goodbye, he was not to be seen. The snow had now settled on the ground. My flight was in the evening and I was wondering if the aircraft would be able to fly. Evening time I checked in my luggage onto a Bedford lorry and then had to get on a bus to take me to the airport, I was soon sitting on the aircraft. It was dark when the doors were shut. It was a very surreal time.

The bus moved slowly out of M.L. going past which must of been Serbian barracks, nothing was left standing. All the barbed wire had been broken. It took about a half hour to get to the aircraft, and another half hour for it to take off, then we were soon into the dark clouds. About three hours later we started the descent obiously we had not reached BZZ. I didnt have to get off the aircraft , thirty minutes later we were airborne again, two hours later we were making our descent into BZZ.

n the morning I had to see the Colonel, I told him that I was thinking of leaving, I told him that I had been caused a lot of unnecessary work by the boss. "I know" the Colonel said. I told him my id card was in tatters and it needed changing. The Colonel told me to go and see Dawn. He told me to give her my id card, and she will get a new one for me, also she will give me a train warrant. He said we will see how I feel when I come back in a months time. When I went home I was determined to leave this time. I was not using my logic though. I was doing well and got through the hardest part but I decided to leave anyway.

When I got back to Bulford I told the Colonel that I had decided to leave. He didn't try to talk me out of it. Within half an hour I was out of the army. I told Dawn that I had left, she said "its a pity your new id card has arrived" and that was it, I was soon on my way home.

I soon got a job in a factory, doing MHE (forklifting). I knew I had made a big mistake. the worst thing was I felt like a nobody, at least with EFI I was someone.

To be continued.........

[D1]..126
[2]..126

[D2] 126
[D3] 127
[1] 1

TCN. Third Country National.
NBC Nuclear Biological and chemical

Disruptive pattern material

gas mask

tear gas

AFTERWORD

There is a reason for mentioning this book. Gwladys is my great aunty. When she was six months old, her father got killed in the Somme. If you didn't volunteer to be a brave soldier, you would be sent a few white feathers. His brother, who is my grandad was next to him. Luckily for me, he survived the war. If you can get hold of this book it is worth a read. There are some parts that people don't know about WW2.

Printed in Dunstable, United Kingdom